"No matter how good you are at your job, you have to be good at the office politics too. I spend more time these days protecting my job than thinking about the work."

"Why is it people who are talented think they can treat you like dirt? One prima donna has several high-powered executives shaking in their shoes. They hired the prima donna at great expense, but the prima donna is telling them what to do, in as vulgar a manner as possible. It's a high price to pay, and everyone is suffering."

"Last year they asked me to go to Bangkok. Between the lines they were saying, 'If you don't go you won't be going anywhere in this company.' It was very hard on my family, but I was being tested. They have this sink-or-swim mentality. They don't care if it's hard. If you complain or it doesn't work out, you're a failure. They'll find a spot for you in some remote corner, or not, and you'll never get another chance."

"He screamed at the consultant, in front of all of us, 'Now you work for me and I want you in my office with everyone else at 6 A.M., you little fucker!'"

"I wake up in cold sweats at night. I'm totally on my own. If I get an idea, I have to make it work on my own. That's hard enough, but when they don't give me what I need to do the job right and still hold me responsible, I feel they're holding a revolver to my head. I've tripled this company's billings and I know I can continue to make the profits come in, but I need time and support and the power to make changes. I also know I'll end up the sacrificial lamb if we continue to do things the old way."

"My old boss couldn't have protected his job. They brought in an outside consultant. The consultant was quick to earn his money and told everyone what my boss was doing wrong. Guess who got the job when my boss was fired? The consultant. Guess who the new boss wants to get rid of now? Everybody in my old boss's camp."

How "Lean and Mean" Robs People and Profits

Lesley Wright
and
Marti Smye

Macmillan • USA

MACMILLAN
A Simon & Schuster Macmillan Company
1633 Broadway
New York, NY 10019

Library of Congress Cataloging-in-Publication Data
Smye, Marti Diane.
    Corporate abuse / Marti Smye and Lesley Wright.
      p.   cm.
    ISBN 0-02-861290-6
    1. Business ethics.   2. Management—Moral and ethical aspects.
3. Corporations—Corrupt practices.   Wright, Lesley.
II. Title
HF5387.S583   1996   96-8096
147'.4—dc20   CIP

Manufactured in the United States of America

10   9   8   7   6   5   4   3   2   1

Design by Amy Peppler Adams—designLab, Seattle

To Our Readers

This book was written for you. Whether you are an employee in a small office or a leader of a large corporation, we hope it will help you to understand why your work is not as happy or as successful as you would like it to be.

If you find you have one or more of the abusive cultures we describe in your business, we believe this book will serve as an instrument of discussion. Use it to shed light on the dark side of your company and help bring about positive change.

The stories you will read are all true. However, we have changed any identifying information of those involved to protect them from any further abuse or embarrassment. It is not our intention to expose any particular individual, company, or industry as being abusive. To our knowledge no one profession or industry is likely to be any more abusive than another, nor is corporate abuse a regional problem. It is a worldwide problem.

What is important is to recognize in these accounts the behaviors, systems, and structures that lead to the soul-destroying behavior that in turn kills ideas and leads to business failure. Although there are hundreds of tales of woe, we have chosen to include those abusive experiences we felt were most prevalent in the workplace today. We are confident that the personal accounts you read won't be unfamiliar to you. In many cases you might identify with the abused; in some cases you may identify with the abuser; in certain situations you may even identify with both—after all, if society can shape us, so can corporate cultures.

We believe that in naming and identifying corporate abuse, we will help you to recognize the inadvertent behaviors in you and your organization that stand in the way of your business' success and personal fulfillment. On the other hand, if you are deliberately abusing your colleagues, we hope that this book will either help you or help others to put a stop to your ways.

CONTENTS

Acknowledgments

Writing this book required many people to bare their souls and talk to us about things they would rather forget. To those of you who made yourselves vulnerable through hours of interviews, we are deeply grateful.

We are also grateful to those who have helped us bring these words together in the most effective way. For research, editing, and generally helping us pull the manuscript together we owe much to Philipp Campsie, Karen Dawson, and Nancy Nalence. We thank Lee Downs for her special efforts on the manuscript at the eleventh hour and we cherish Zella Hayman for her ability to create harmony even in the most hectic of situations.

For helping us get our book into everyone's hands we thank Lise Hutchinson, Rosemary Reid, our agent Al Zuckerman, and our publishing editor John Michel. We very much appreciate their enthusiasm for this book.

We are both blessed with enormous support from our friends. Special thanks to Holly Hutchinson who contributed valuable information on family systems and offered constant encouragement and inspiration, to Pam Frier for an unforgettable day on Galiano Island contemplating the soul and creativity, and to Marian Marshall and Helen Ryane for confirming that our solutions are meaningful. Finally, to our families, thank you for your unconditional love. You give us the courage, principles, and heart to speak up for positive change.

THE DARK SIDE
OF WORK

THE DARK SIDE OF WORK

*f*EW PEOPLE go off to work these days with a song in their hearts. As the true stories in this book demonstrate, many people dread each day because they have to work in places where they feel abused and powerless.

What is happening to us? Why can't we enjoy our jobs anymore? Why are talented, productive people being thwarted and sabotaged? Why do we treat each other so badly? Why are tyrannical bosses tolerated? Does the bottom line really justify the frustration and the hurt we experience?

Some of the distress we feel comes from working with different personalities, under pressure, in a tough economy. This friction has always been a part of the workplace. Today, however, something much more pervasive and arbitrary is happening. It comes from autocratic or inconsistent management, illogical rules and red tape, ruthless downsizing, and a climate of hostility and fear.

The desperation to become successful has clouded our vision and skewed our priorities so much that lives and careers are being damaged. The workplace has gone far beyond being simply "tough" and "competitive." It is becoming uncivilized.

Like a shadow we glimpse out of the corners of our eyes, we sense that something is badly wrong, but we don't quite know what it is. Furtively looking over our shoulders, we feel more and more vulnerable. We are aware of our every move, every word we utter. We stop trying to excel and attempt simply to protect ourselves. Even though we work hard, we never feel fulfilled and self-confident because fear and suspicion overwhelm us.

Some of us come alive only at home, surrounded by people who love us. But for many of us, there is no respite there either. Our jobs have taken so much of our time and energy that there's nothing left to give.

3

Our tempers are too short; we are too preoccupied with problems at work; we are so exhausted when we come home that our partners and children seldom see us conscious.

We are criticized at home for not giving enough, and we're continually asked to give more at the office. One executive deals with the stress by running back to the familiar, although painful environment of the office. At 11 P.M. or 5 A.M. you can find him there, suspended between the pressures of home and the pressures of work. Another finds peace on the golf course once a week. Another finds safety in a stiff drink at the bar.

We can't go on like this. We can't compartmentalize our lives. We can't postpone the joy in our lives until after work and on weekends and cram all that is worthwhile in life into a few hours on a golf course or in a bar, or into a two-week vacation on a beach. There isn't enough time to have a work life, a family life, a love life, a life of hope and dreams, all lived separately. Nor can we do our jobs well if we are close to burnout or paralyzed with fear. Our work suffers, and the business suffers with it.

Yet jobs are so scarce nowadays that we feel lucky even to be drawing a salary. Complaining about our frustrations makes us sound like whiners, and that makes us feel guilty. There are plenty of people out there who are desperate to take our places in this jobless recovery. We are supposed to work harder and smarter in businesses that are leaner and meaner, mostly meaner. So when problems arise, we often feel that they are our problems and that we must solve them on our own. When we can't, it seems like our fault, the result of some personal inadequacy.

Our demons come in many shapes and guises. Some come in the form of unsettling changes to the work environment. Some are bosses or co-workers who make life unpleasant; others are attitudes or systems that stymie our efforts to do good work. Demons can appear as corporate tyrants who bully, intimidate, and humiliate workers, or as corporate expectations disguised as business as usual. They may be the endless demands of work that take over our personal lives. They may be feelings of guilt at surviving a downsizing that threw colleagues out of work. No one is safe from these demons. Men and women at all levels in the company, from receptionists to CEOs, know them well.

We have named these demons corporate abuse.

Although the word "abuse" sounds dramatic and alarmist, we have used it deliberately to underline the gravity of the problem and to call attention to what we believe is a crisis. Leaders today are well aware that their company's competitive edge is its ability to add customer value. In a world of increasing product parity, they know that success lies in ideas that lead to innovation. Ideas come from people, and by harming people and instilling fear, corporate abuse kills ideas. We can no longer afford to waste opportunities and sacrifice employees. The real bottom line is that corporate abuse is bad for business.

Corporate abuse has many faces. In its most obvious form it includes discrimination, overwork, harassment, systematic humiliation, arbitrary dismissal, demotion without cause, withholding of resources, and financial manipulation. Its more subtle manifestations include lack of support, penny-pinching, micromanagement, constant miscommunication, hidden agendas, surveillance, inverted priorities, and smothering corporate cultures. Abuse can be found in all kinds of companies—large and small, old and new, around the world. They may be prosperous or struggling, high-tech or old-fashioned, but all are too preoccupied with global issues to look closely at how they treat their own employees.

Corporate abuse is the dirty secret of corporations that are unwilling or unable to let in the fresh air of new ideas. This book exposes the abuse for what it is: the biggest and most under-recognized threat to productivity, innovation, and long-term success in today's business world. In fact, we define corporate abuse as *anything* that kills good ideas and innovation.

Because we are in the midst of a wrenching transition from the industrial age to the information age, the only certainty in our workplace is change. However, no one is certain exactly where that change will take us. Alas, abusive cultures thrive in uncertainty, generating fear and dependency in people when what we need most at this time is confidence and independent thinking.

We must get rid of the industrial era cultures that justified abusive behavior in the workplace. Fifty years ago, a rigid hierarchy was necessary for efficient mass production. Those on the top commanded; those below obeyed. This structure was reflected in the way our professionals were educated. For example, MBAs learned the culture of competition and the most effective ways of extracting labor from others. Engineers were steeped in a machismo culture that placed technical considerations far above human ones. The legal culture fostered confrontation, antagonism, and winning at all costs.

Today change and innovation are what drive corporations and help them succeed. Nothing is constant. What used to be predictable has become erratic; what used to be homogeneous is now diverse. Our careers and our lives are not unfolding as we presumed they would. Because of the constant uncertainty, we crave the security and balance that come from working in an environment that is safe not only physically but psychologically, at a job that is meaningful, stimulating, and productive. Most of all, we want to be remunerated fairly for our labor—in money and benefits, to be certain, but also with respect and appreciation. Corporate abuse rewards nobody. In abusive corporations, everybody pays.

THE PERSONAL COSTS OF ABUSE

Corporate abuse makes itself felt in individual lives before it appears on the bottom line. Stress, headaches, ulcers, exhaustion, insomnia, anxiety, burnout, heart attacks, panic attacks, nervous breakdowns—all have been traced to working environments that breed fear and hostility.

One personnel director reports some of the symptoms she witnessed when dealing with a group of men who had been subjected to a particularly abusive boss:

> One was very gaunt, red-eyed and unshaven. He seemed to have lost any pride in the way he looked. He was working very, very ineffectively and he appeared frightened. Another one of them constantly chain-smoked and seemed to have the shakes. A third was pale and withdrawn and seemed very uptight.

The health costs are the most obvious personal costs. But the greater costs may be the long-term effects of abuse on relationships, families, and personal self-esteem.

Abusive people and abusive cultures can put a number of behaviors in motion that attack our souls. Sometimes abuse is experienced as fatigue, when we are forced to work longer and longer hours, or as frustration, when no matter how hard we work, we cannot seem to get our ideas accepted or our contributions recognized, but by far the worst effect is fear. "Fear is to a man's soul as a drop of poison is to a well of spring water." Fear permeates our entire being. Fear turns our courage into cowardice, our passion into pain, our truth into lies, and our creative, fertile mind into a wasteland. It can slay our souls and kill our ideas.

Fear can make people lash out and transform normally reasonable people into bullies and tyrants. But the manifestation of corporate abuse is much more insidious than the terrifying behavior of a sadistic manager. Fear spreads like a virus and encourages corporate abuse to thrive in the policies, structures, and operations of a business.

In an abusive corporate culture, those in power can mistreat all employees; in a threatened company, external pressures may make life intolerable for everyone from the CEO on down. Many corporations have been caught unaware in the transition from the industrial age to the information age. The economy has clobbered them, the marketplace is a mystery, and they are moving into completely uncharted territory without a guide or a searchlight. They are scared and they are passing their fear along in the form of abuse.

Sometimes abuse manifests itself in unreasonable demands, with bosses demanding two hundred percent effort from employees even while they are cutting back on support systems reducing staff, eliminating margins for error, and gutting bonuses. Working under these strapped conditions makes it hard enough to give fifty percent effort, never mind four times as much.

Worst of all, corporate abuse is a monster with two heads—one that kills our businesses and one that kills our souls. Does it seem strange to be talking about souls and corporations in the same sentence, even in the same book? David Whyte, in his book *The Heart Aroused*, argues that "the split between our work life and that part of our soul life that has been pushed underground seems to be at the root of much of our current unhappiness." To take that idea one step further, corporate abuse has made its lair deep in that rift. Unless we root it out, we can never fully meld our creative and productive energies.

THE BUSINESS COSTS OF ABUSE

It seems obvious that dispirited, exhausted, or burned-out employees do not make up a productive workforce in the age of innovation, but for those who want statistics, here are a few to ponder.

The cost of stress to the American workplace has been estimated at between $150 billion and $180 billion a year. Stress-related illness accounts for millions of lost working days each year, and the number is rising. One study found that in 1980 no occupational disease claims were related to stress; in 1990, 10 percent of them were. A 1993 study by Commerce Clearing House reports that unscheduled absences can cost U.S. employers more than $500 per employee per year. Experts believe that stress accounts for 12 percent of all workers' compensation claims. A major insurance company has reported that on average one million workers are absent daily because of stress-related disorders.

These problems are not restricted to the U.S. workforce. In the United Kingdom, about 1.5 million working days a year are lost through stress-related illness. The Confederation of British Industry puts the annual cost of stress-related absenteeism and staff turnover at £1.3 billion. In Sweden, the problem has become a major focus, with the government paying for rehabilitation clinics for people who are suffering the effects of being bullied at work. After years of subsidizing the clinics, the Swedish government is now holding companies responsible for paying the millions of dollars in health costs that their employees need as a result of working in abusive environments.

There are even more direct costs to businesses, however. As a recent article put it, "Corporate America is only very quietly admitting the billions it loses to sabotage from bored, creatively stifled, or justifiably pissed-off employees." Given the potential of such things as computer viruses to wreak havoc in a corporation, there are very compelling reasons to stamp out abuse wherever we find it.

But those are all short-term costs. What about the long-term opportunity costs of wasted ideas? What about the innovation that is not happening because employees are too fearful, too exhausted, or too frustrated to contribute?

One of the first things to disappear in an abusive environment is the honest, open exchange of ideas—the lifeblood of the idea economy. It's the same silence that shrouds abusive homes. Without open communications, there can be no growth and no experimentation. Everybody is too worried about trying to fit into a rigid and often undefined code of behavior. This is where companies start to die.

Some corporations keep staggering along, disguising the lack of ideas with high turnover. They keep taking new people on board, swiping their fresh ideas, slowly silencing them with the abusive culture, then firing them and starting all over. In business numbers the cost of such turnover includes all the projects that didn't get finished, all the files left unexamined, all the time wasted in bringing a new person up to speed, and the growing timidity of those who survive turnover by keeping their heads down and their mouths shut.

Creativity and innovation require certain conditions to flourish. One of these conditions is the freedom to experiment and the presence of a safety net to catch you if you fail. For every successful innovation there are dozens, even hundreds, of experiments that were unsuccessful but useful. Failed experiments are how people learn, how they find out what works and what doesn't. In an abusive culture, the terror of failure is too great to allow for experimentation, which means that innovation is nearly impossible.

Anything that creates fear kills ideas—fear of failure or of ridicule, fear of criticism, fear of being yelled at by the boss, fear of being fired. Abuse creates a climate of uncertainty, suspicion, and conspiracy in which the wisest option is to play it safe. But the pace of change is such that nobody has time to play it safe.

Abusive cultures do not foster the innovation that corporations need to compete. They do not attract the best employees, particularly those in the generation coming into the workforce in the 1990s. They cannot adjust to the rapid changes that characterize today's economy, or carry out successful restructuring or repositioning. In abusive cultures, people are so busy coping with each other that they have a hard time competing with anyone else. They destroy the very qualities they need to survive.

FROM ABUSE TO CIVILITY TO COMMUNITY

This book is for people who work, whether they are managers or staff, bosses or workers. It is about changing abusive cultures in order to create an environment in which creativity can thrive and diversity is respected.

Because the only prediction that anyone can make about the future of any corporation is that change and uncertainty will continue into the twenty-first century, we need to find ways to handle the uncertainty without resorting to abuse. All of the wisdom of new management techniques, better productivity, and global theory will fall on deaf ears if companies continue to foster soul-destroying behavior. By giving a name to corporate abuse and identifying various kinds of abuse and abusive cultures, this book may enable both employees and employers to recognize and change their behaviors before they damage lives, careers, and businesses.

The book provides tools that readers can use to identify corporate abuse, then recommends specific remedies. Sometimes employees feel stressed out and unhappy, but they cannot put their finger on exactly what is the matter. Because stress often builds gradually, they do not recognize that what they are experiencing is abuse. The real test of abuse is in its effects, and its biggest effect is a decline in creativity, a dearth of ideas and open discussions.

In the information age, competitiveness and global position depend on human assets. That does not simply mean warm bodies. Warm bodies belong to human beings. They have personalities, needs, desires, ambitions—souls. If they are under continuous and excessive stress, they can't produce the economy's most valuable commodity: ideas and creativity. Ending psychological abuse in the workplace is a matter of economic survival in the twenty-first century.

We need to do more than fix individual problems, though. We have to move beyond repair jobs to design and create sustainable and nurturing cultures in which passionate and extraordinary conversations take place about the nature of work and creative ways to find solutions. Most leaders realize that an unhappy workplace isn't good for the bottom line. But their actions belie their promises and even their intentions because the corporations are locked into structures and systems that foster abuse and undermine productivity and individual creativity.

We must have the courage to look into the darker side of our corporations and recognize corporate abuse. And we must conquer it on a personal and systemic basis. Moving from an industrial-age model to an idea-generating culture is our long-term and comprehensive solution. Our hope for fulfillment lies in our ability to integrate our passionate, courageous, and creative souls with our work. Our hope for business success depends on the same thing: the continual replenishment of the corporate soul.

Before we can even begin to heal the damage that has been done through corporate abuse, we need to reintroduce the basic idea of civility in the workplace. Civility means a lot more than good manners and politeness. It is the guiding principle of the civilized organization,

> less a code of conduct than a spirit. That spirit encompasses consideration, tact, good humor, and respect for others' feelings and rights. . . . It is a variation on the golden rule, urging that you treat everyone as decently and considerately as you would like to be treated yourself. . . . Civility does not preclude intense debate, nor does it lead us to back down from principles that really matter. It only means that we conduct our debates and defend our principles in an atmosphere of reasonableness and courtesy. Where there is civility in discourse, differences can be examined intelligently. They are not resolved by the unfair criterion of which party is able to shout the other down.

Civility is out of favor these days. Rudeness and boorishness are in vogue, and politeness has become the mark of the wimp. On television, in the movies, wittiness consists of insults, while persuasion is best accomplished with a gun. In our walled and gated communities, we have lost the ability to resolve problems over the back fence. Instead of complaining about a problem to our neighbors, we call the police. We do not negotiate; we litigate. We build barriers around ourselves because we haven't a clue how to handle differences in a civilized manner. If we are especially enlightened, we might resort to alternative dispute resolution and call in professionals, but we have lost the ability to resolve everyday conflicts on our own.

Civility is a step forward, but it is not our final destination. Beyond civility lie the nurturing of individual souls and creative powers in the workplace and the sustainability of our corporations. One of the ways to have a successful economy is to have sustainable corporations, even if the form in which they continue changes beyond recognition. After all, Purolator started as a company that made oil filters, but that's not what you think of when you hear the name today. Quick-hit companies aren't in it for the long term, so another way to develop the essence of the corporate soul is to leave a proud legacy.

The soul—whether we are talking about organizations or people— is the point from which all of our actions radiate. It is our center, our citadel. It houses our courage, our passion, our creativity, our truth, our imagination, and all things sensed but unknown. It is the central source of our power. A corporate environment that feeds our souls rather than strangling them can tap into that power and creativity. It can also make the workplace a community rather than a prison. As David Whyte puts it:

> We are all aware how work both emboldens us and strangles our soul life in the very same instant. It reveals how much we can do as part of a larger body, literally a corpus, a corporation, and how much the wellsprings of our creativity are stopped at the source by the pressures of that same smothering organization.

WORKPLACE COMMUNITIES

There are plenty of magazine articles and books about the "hunger for community" where we live. But very little attention is paid to creating community where we work. Most of us don't even think of the workplace as a community, even though we spend most of our waking hours there.

Unfortunately, a lot of what gets said about "community" has more to do with nostalgia for small towns and "Leave It to Beaver" family values than with collective problem-solving, the toleration of differences, and the ability to work together. You can have a community without families and without cute little houses. You can find it in a high-rise office or a high-tech business park. It may even be possible to create it from a group of people who do not share space but are connected by fiber-optic cables and modems.

There are countless ways to make connections. That's the easy part, especially with high-speed communications, interactive television, and electronic mail. What isn't so easy, though, is using the new connections to enhance communications and build new bridges. Look at the phenomenon of sending abusive messages or "flaming" on the Internet. More communication isn't enough. There must be civility as well.

This book is about making the workplace a community, creating an environment in which souls can thrive and employees can feel a sense of belonging. It is about helping our corporations sustain themselves and create future legacies. The first step is getting rid of corporate abuse.

Before we slay any demons, though, let's take a moment to step back and see how corporate abuse has developed in the workplace. History is written by the winners, and corporate stories are usually told by the survivors. They do not draw up casualty lists of those who are missing in action. We talk about survival of the fittest without asking what these survivors are fit *for*. And we want to believe that we are more humane than our predecessors. Are we? Let's find out.

Abuse, Justification, and Acceptance

All bad precedents began as justifiable measures.

—Julius Caesar

WE ALL KNOW it exists. So why has so little been written on the subject of corporate abuse? Why does the problem seem almost invisible? The answer is simple: throughout history, abuse has been the norm, not the exception, in work relationships.

Our capacity to accept abusive behavior can be measured by the extent to which we can justify it. This formula has been proven in the past and continues to be valid today. However, once we remove the justification, either on philosophical or practical grounds, we can expose abuse as harmful, unacceptable, and counterproductive.

As a step toward understanding the connection between abuse and justification, we can begin with the ancient civilizations. According to the Judeo-Christian tradition, work is a punishment meted out by God because of human disobedience; remember Adam and Eve and the expulsion from the Garden of Eden? Work was manual work—it involved the sweat of one's brow, it was hard, and it hurt. In fact, if it didn't hurt, it wasn't considered work.

The Greek philosopher Aristotle thought that work was incompatible with noble pursuits, politics, the arts, and philosophy. It was fit only for slaves. And for thousands of years there were slaves to do it, kept in line with chains, whippings, and other forms of discipline.

It wasn't until the nineteenth century, of course, that slavery began to wane. And although philosophers, politicians, and abolitionists spoke out against slavery on moral grounds, the argument that really held sway in the end was an economic one. People realized that slaves made very bad workers. They were hard to manage because they needed to be policed, and they were justly resentful of the legal chains that bound them to their masters.

In Europe for hundreds of years, most work relationships were defined by the feudal system. Land was owned by kings, barons, and knights. Serfs were allowed to work the land in exchange for military service, a portion of their produce, and a set number of work days. Feudalism was a personal and paternalistic system, under which the serfs were offered protection against outside forces in exchange for loyalty and service to the landowners.

There were other master/servant relationships—domestic service, apprenticeship, and indentured labor—which gave most rights to the employer and few to the worker. Eventually serfs were allowed to own small strips of land and were paid for their labor, but the demands and restrictions of the larger landowners persisted.

Later, industrialization added two new factors to the equation: workers had to leave home to work in factories alongside strangers, and they had to adjust their pace to the insatiable demands of machines. Nowhere did men, women, and children do more adjusting than in the dark, satanic mills of the Industrial Revolution. People had to work twelve hours a day at machines that never stopped for a rest from morning to night, that deafened them and polluted the atmosphere, that could kill or maim unwary or tired workers.

The more appalling and inhumane the work, the more employers had to abuse their employees to keep them at it. Wages were kept at a subsistence level and, as Michael Argyle points out in *The Social Psychology of Work,* a variety of punishments were invented to force employees to be as reliable as machines:

> *In their efforts to control workers, employers used fines for lateness and absenteeism, low wages (so that hunger would keep them at work), long hours (to keep them out of the public houses), corporal punishment (especially for children), dismissal or relegation to worse jobs—and resultant starvation and prison. The discipline enforced was tyrannical and brutal, and many children died in mines and factories. . . . Despite these disincentives workers were frequently absent, late, idle or drunk, fought each other, produced poor quality work, and as a result had no ambition to become prosperous or respectable.*

One could argue that it was *because* of the disincentives, not in spite of them, that workers behaved badly. If people are expected to be unreliable, lazy, stupid, and incorrigible, and are treated as such, it shouldn't be a surprise when they behave that way.

Around the turn of the century, a Quaker engineer working in the Bethlehem Steel Works in Pittsburgh began to time factory operations with a stopwatch. Frederick Winslow Taylor published *Principles of Scientific Management* in 1911. It helped to justify the modern assembly line with its minute divisions of labor, in which workers perform short, unchallenging tasks over and over again. It helped also to bring about a new form of abuse through boredom, meaninglessness, and alienation, according to Donald A. Norman.

> *What the time-and-motion folks ignored was the person. They took a mechanistic, machine-centered point of view, analyzing every action through high-speed motion picture photography and doing controlled experiments that examined the differences among various procedures for the same task. They looked for wasted motion and inefficient procedures. . . . Time-and-motion studies do lead to enhanced production in the short run. In the long run, they can lead to diminished quality of life, diminished quality of the product.*

Efficient, routine operations are fine for machines, not for humans. The body wears out—"repetitive stress syndrome," we call it today. Just as the body can wear out, so too can the mind—a syndrome called "burnout"—wearing out the ability to create, to innovate, or even simply to care about the work being produced.

Although Taylor himself talked about the need for worker involvement and managerial responsibility and for cooperation between employees and employers, his disciples often adopted the simple, mechanistic aspects of scientific management and ignored the rest. These ideas were carried from the factory to the office, and many are still practiced by old-style managers.

Eventually, trade unions fought for and won better wages, shorter hours, more humane working conditions, and regulations against child labor. They helped create a better balance of power between the employers and the workers. The worst forms of abuse were eradicated in many factories and mitigated in others. Even so, the motto of the 1933 Chicago World's Fair was "Science Finds, Industry Applies, Man Conforms."

Of course, the trade unions didn't make much headway in the offices of corporate America, where office industrialization was creating some equally abusive situations. Stenographers were as much slaves to the typewriter as factory hands were to the assembly line, but in white-collar and pink-collar jobs, the abuse went unrecognized.

PSYCHOLOGICAL ABUSE

The mechanization of work marks a turning point in our journey through the history of abuses suffered at work, away from the physical and toward the more subtle abuses of the soul. For although factories advanced to be more efficient and productive, employees were still given very little respect. Rather than seeing them as people with dreams and needs, bosses considered them as little more than bodies to push and pull the job to completion.

The attitude that workers are lesser beings shifted from the shop floor to the office tower. Even though we have witnessed the decline of traditional industry over the last twenty or thirty years, the working models from the old industries have survived and can be found in even our most modern businesses.

Many of today's companies have been structured like a pyramid based on the military model of a general at the top. The general's orders are carried down through the ranks to a large number of soldiers at the bottom of the pyramid. To make the system work, it is necessary to break down independent thought to ensure "followship." Company leaders have set up systems of blind obedience that sacrifice the needs of the individual to corporate goals.

The problem is, information technology has turned the pyramid on its head and this approach no longer works. The whole is no longer greater than the individual parts. Our new industries need workers to use the vast amount of knowledge they have acquired to create new ideas that will improve the business. Now we need not just the body of the agricultural age, not just the body and the few minds of the industrial age, but the mind, body, and soul of the information age. Most important of all is the fulfilled soul of every worker. So the question has changed from "How can we get more efficient work out of these *bodies?*" to "What does this *person* need in order to be more productive and creative?" Consequently, any behavior that damages the soul can no longer be tolerated or justified.

The psychologist Abraham Maslow understood that people are more than bodies when he described the hierarchy of needs.

1. Self-fulfillment or self-actualization

2. Self-esteem

3. Social needs (acceptance)

4. Safety needs

5. Physiological needs (hunger and thirst)

Maslow argued that once basic needs such as hunger, thirst, and safety have been satisfied, human beings experience needs that are social and personal. We need acceptance by others in order to find a place in society; we need self-esteem to feel at peace with ourselves; and finally we need self-fulfillment or self-actualization, the "highest" of all needs, to carry out a purpose in life. Without that sense of meaning and purpose, our souls wither.

Industrial age hierarchies foster much of the subtle, soul-destroying abusive behavior we are experiencing today. In many cases we have simply inherited the abusive behaviors that came out of a need for hands rather than heads in the workplace. By accepting that legacy, we are destroying the total commitment we need to succeed in the information age and beyond.

THE TECHNOLOGIES OF CONTROL

Psychological experiments in brainwashing and the treatment of prisoners of war and members of religious cults have provided some terrifying lessons in controlling and modifying behavior in the workplace. They have proved that by destroying human reference points and undermining confidence, those in control can reduce people to obedient, unquestioning, unthinking automatons.

In the 1970s these ideas emerged in a bizarre form as part of the "human potential movement." It began with a salesman called Jack Rosenberg. He changed his name to Werner Eberhard and invented a brand of therapy called EST. He promised that after sixty hours in Eberhard Seminars Training, a person could be transformed. Cobbling together ideas from sources such as Scientology and Dale Carnegie, Rosenberg/Eberhard enticed thousands of paying people to register for four fifteen-hour days during which they had to abide by strict rules and endure a steady stream of verbal abuse. In the end, their transformation consisted of being told that they were responsible for everything that had ever happened to them—good or bad.

What does EST have to do with corporate abuse? Both are forms of control that destabilize people's image of themselves and put them under the power of another person or system. Consider the corporations that demand unquestioning obedience and go to extraordinary lengths to ensure that no employee deviates from the prevailing norms. The intolerance of independent thinking or originality in these companies is similar to that in certain cults. Sure, the employees are smiling. In some companies they can be fined if they don't. Abuse? In a way, yes.

The last few decades have advanced the technologies of control. A flight reservations service monitors the duration and content of calls. A bank reads its employees' e-mail messages. A database management firm counts keystrokes per hour for each employee at a terminal. An aeronautical engineering company issues "active badges" to its employees that not only identify them but track their whereabouts and record how long they spend in the washroom or chatting at the coffee machine. Paroled convicts who are being electronically monitored have more freedom and privacy than employees in certain companies.

Many companies in the information age seem to spend as much time gathering information on employees as they do creating value for customers and clients. When employees' output no longer consists of tangible, measurable objects—bales of cloth or papers of pins—companies often assume that the best way to keep track of how much work they are doing is to count the number of hours their bodies are sitting at desks or workstations. Employees call this "face time."

The rationale for face time assumes that if the supervisor can see the employee's face, the employee must be working. Managers who demand face time assume that something, anything, must be measured as a way of understanding productivity. They don't realize that you can't measure ideas in minutes or days and that demanding face time will not ensure that any activity is occurring behind those blank masks. It may ensure that the greatest amount of activity is devoted to updating résumés and making personal calls.

Compare face time to "discretionary time." This is the time and effort that employees put in—or don't put in—in addition to face time. Let's say that employees have 100 points of productivity in their personal commitment banks to an organization. (Nowadays most corporations are demanding 110 productivity points, but we'll set that aside for the moment.) Face time accounts for 60 of those points. Giving the other 40 (or 50) depends on how people feel about the workplace, whether they are appreciated, well rewarded, and considered.

In a face-time type of environment, supervision becomes surveillance; people are shoehorned into sterile, cramped cubicles, and threats of dismissal or demotion are used to force compliance with corporate policy. These attitudes assume that people have no more desire to work than Adam and Eve did when they left the Garden of Eden. The assumption is insulting, and the strategies it engenders are abusive. Isolating employees, reducing their work to staring at computer screens for long hours, and discouraging open dialogue are all tactics to coerce, trick, manipulate, and brainwash people into bending their wills to the corporate will.

Abuse and the Corporate Lifecycle

OMETIMES ABUSE can be hard to recognize. You feel something is wrong, but you can't put your finger on the source of the problem. You are stressed, but you don't exactly know why. There are no obvious bullies, no clear villains. Sooner or later you begin to think that you're the one who is out of step and that it is your fault. At about this point you begin to feel uncertain about your ability to do the job. You start questioning your own decisions and conclusions. Your energy flags and you can't seem to generate anything brighter than a low-watt idea. You just aren't as creative as you used to be—maybe you were deluding yourself and the company all along. As one despairing person put it:

> I don't know, maybe it's just me. I started with such high hopes. The job seemed perfect—I felt I had found the place I belonged at last. But now I get off the elevator and the doors close behind me and I feel I'm in some alien environment. It's not that the people are unkind or mean; they are perfectly friendly. I'm paid well, and I've got a nice office. But I feel like a gerbil in a cage, running and running and never getting anywhere.
>
> I'm swamped in paperwork that seems largely pointless. I have no signing authority. I have to refer all decisions to the VP, and all my suggestions are politely listened to and ignored. I spend my days in meetings at which we go round and round on the same questions we were discussing last year.
>
> Everyone else seems to find this normal, and when I say that maybe we could streamline our operations, they look at me as if I had two heads. I really am beginning to feel like a freak. At the same time, I feel that the quality of my ideas has suffered through sheer neglect.
>
> —*Lisette, human resources manager*

Abuse makes us doubt ourselves, sometimes even doubt our sanity. Everyone else is busy conforming, and we feel out of step. Abuse can make competent people feel stupid. It can do a lot of damage before people figure out that what's wrong is not their fault.

Abuse may seem like too strong a word for the misfit between what a company says and what it actually does to employees. But when employees experience the same level of stress, when workflow, productivity, and innovation suffer to the same degree, what's the difference? The fault lies not with an aggressive or bullying boss but within the structure of the organization. This is *systemic abuse.* We see it most often when stated goals ("We're a people place") are incompatible with the entrenched structure ("You're not here to think; you're here to follow the rules") or when a company repeatedly fails to deliver on promises and reneges on commitments.

> When I was hired they said, "We really need you to help turn this place around." So far I've been able to accomplish two things: a small change in accounting procedures and a contract with a new firm for supplying and watering plants! That's it. Everything else I've tried to do has been shot down in flames. I'm so frustrated I'm ready to quit.
>
> —*Andrea, office manager*

> The infant mortality rate of good ideas around here is about 90 percent, I'd say. There are still a few stubborn cusses who persist and manage to raise an idea as far as adolescence, but I don't think any of them come to maturity. As for the rest of us, we just take our ideas and drown them like unwanted kittens. It's kinder in the long run. Me, I'm just waiting to retire and I'm saving all my good ideas for that.
>
> —*Frank, insurance agent*

> Teamwork, they tell us. Great idea! Except that we're so squeezed for space that there are only about two meeting rooms left and they are always booked. Facilities management keeps saying we can't get more space. Have you ever tried to work in a team when the only place to meet is the parking lot?
>
> —*Gurvinder, software engineer*

Andrea's, Frank's, and Gurvinder's CEOs would be appalled to hear that their companies are abusive. These companies want to treat their employees well. None of them are deliberately trying to make their employees' lives difficult. Yet Andrea is ready to quit, Frank is counting the days until retirement, and Gurvinder is cynical about his company's policies. What is wrong?

All three firms are abusing their staff. Andrea and Frank have discovered that the entrenched systems defeat individual initiatives, even when the organization is trying to bring about change; Gurvinder has found that his company has conflicting priorities and that when push comes to shove, teamwork gets a lower priority than the need to save space.

At one advertising company, the employees were asked to fill out a questionnaire about the company and make suggestions for improvements and changes. People spent hours working on the questionnaires, and many of them came up with creative, constructive suggestions. Considerable time was spent collating and analyzing the results.

Then the CEO called the employees together for a meeting. As far as he was concerned, the problems that had been identified were caused by the employees themselves, and he reprimanded them for what was wrong with the company. The employees were devastated, and morale sank to an all-time low.

The cycle of hope, expectation, and disappointment is typical of an abusive culture. This kind of corporate abuse is similar to certain types of domestic abuse. Think about the distress that results from the inconsistent behavior of an alcoholic parent. The parent makes a promise to the family, either a pledge to attend AA or some other promise: a vacation, a present, or just a day out at the ball park. The family gets excited and hopeful. But inevitably the promise is broken: the alcoholic lapses after two AA meetings, the vacation never happens, the present is never bought, the day at the ball park never comes. When this pattern is repeated over and over again, all trust is lost. The family knows not to believe the alcoholic's promises because they never come true.

Similarly, in corporations inconsistency leads to distrust and cynicism. This is counterproductive both for implementing business goals and for promoting personal growth.

It is particularly hard on committed, creative employees. They're the ones who genuinely believe in the company and who eagerly contribute ideas and talents to realizing corporate goals. When these employees are turned off, the entire workplace can become cynical and demoralized.

At an electronics plant, a committee was formed to work on an ethical charter for the company. Seven people consulted widely throughout the company and spent six months working out the details of a document that they felt represented good corporate ethics. According to one committee member:

> We really thought we were doing something important, setting a new direction for the company, maybe even the industry. When it was all over, the charter was printed up nicely, circulated to the staff, and that was that. We'd wanted a splashy presentation, discussion groups, follow-up, but none of that happened. All our suggestions were brushed aside. After a while we figured out that we'd been given the assignment to take our minds off the downsizings that were going on at the same time.

Anne Wilson Schaef and Diane Fassel describe the effects of saying one thing and doing another on a group of nurses in a large hospital. The nurses were clearly upset about their work, so the researchers asked them to list what they thought the stated goals of the hospital were.

> *The goals they listed were concerned with promoting health and wellness, being responsive to the needs of the people, providing high-quality health care, and developing new forms of healing. They all felt comfortable with these goals. We then asked them to list the unstated goals of the hospital. The unstated goals turned out to be saving the city money, being a vehicle for the political advancement of hospital administrators, upholding the reputation of the hospital, and increasing federal funding. . . . No wonder they were confused, frustrated, and angry.*

The history of revolution teaches us that rising expectation sends people to the barricades more often than crushing oppression. The reason is simple: If you raise people's expectations, they begin to hope that life really will improve. In oppressive regimes the possibility of change is too remote for hope to take root. When a government makes promises and the people respond with faith and trust, the failure to make good on those promises can bring the populace to the boiling point.

That doesn't mean a CEO is going to walk into the office one Monday morning and confront a barricade of filing cabinets and credenzas defended by an angry mob of employees. The rebellion will be more subtle than that. It might show up as a computer crash or a production delay when the company can least afford it. It will certainly show up as a decline in morale. It is better not to promise something that can't be delivered. After all, we all know what the road to hell is paved with.

In a systemically abusive company, conflict often occurs between the innovative individual and the inert group, between the newcomer and the old-timers, between the outsider and the insiders. Employees who dislike change do not feel abused at all; they are perfectly comfortable perpetuating the status quo. The ones who experience stress are those who try to change the system, the ones with good ideas and high hopes, the ones who are potentially a company's best asset.

What makes companies so rigid? Why do they sacrifice good ideas to bad systems, or individual initiative to institutional inertia? One reason has to do with corporate lifecycles.

JURASSIC ORGANIZATIONS

Corporations grow, mature, age, and die, just like people. And just like people, some of them age more gracefully than others. There are crusty old codgers and spry septuagenarians, wonderful senior citizens and tiresome old so-and-sos.

Those that have not aged well we call Jurassic organizations. These corporations are more concerned with maintaining the status quo than with trying new directions that might increase market share. Playing it safe has long since replaced taking risks. For all intents and purposes, these corporations are at the end of their useful lives. That's not to say they are on the point of disintegration, but certainly they are on the path to extinction. Unfortunately, Jurassic organizations can keep going for years, propped up with creative accounting, favorable legislation, and infusions of government money. The emphasis in our discussion, however, is on *useful* life, the creative stage of an organization's existence.

Ichak Adizes has compared growing companies and aging companies in his book, *Corporate Lifecycles.*

Growing Companies	Aging Companies
Personal success stems from taking risk	Personal success stems from avoiding risk
Emphasis is on function over form	Emphasis is on form over function
Everything is permitted, unless expressly forbidden	Everything is forbidden, unless expressly permitted
Problems are seen as opportunities	Opportunities are seen as problems

continues

Growing Companies	Aging Companies
Political power is with the marketing and sales departments	Political power is with the accounting, finance, and legal departments
Responsibility is not matched with authority	Authority is not matched with responsibility
Management drives the momentum	Management is driven by inertia
Sales orientation	Profit preoccupation
Value added goals	Political gamesmanship

Let's look more closely at a few of these observations.

EVERYTHING IS FORBIDDEN UNLESS EXPRESSLY PERMITTED

Generally the reverse is true in our democratic society. You may do whatever is not forbidden by law. You may park your car anywhere except where there is a No Parking sign.

In Jurassic organizations, however, the only possible courses of action are laid down in rules. If there is no rule to cover a particular situation, the situation must be ignored. As far as the system is concerned, if there isn't a policy in place, new situations don't exist. Change is anathema.

Rules and procedures are created for situations that have occurred in the past. They are useless in new, unexpected situations. Bob Newhart does a wonderful monologue about a new security guard at the Empire State Building. The guard has been trained in official procedures, but the first night he is on duty, something happens that wasn't mentioned in the training session: King Kong climbs the building. The ape's toe is sticking through the window and the guard is still desperately trying to proceed according to the regulations.

Although rules can make an uncertain world more predictable, they can also choke innovation. As Stephen Covey points out in *Principle-Centered Leadership:*

> *People won't willingly change with commitment, with desire, unless their security lies inside themselves. If their security lies outside themselves, they view change as a threat. We must have a sense of permanency and security. We can't live on unstable ground all the time. It's like living*

through an earthquake every day. So we create something that is stable, predictable, often by forming structures and systems, rules and regulations. But rules and regulations only stifle the organization from adapting by closing off the stream of fresh ideas.

Rules, once created, are very difficult to dismantle. Every municipality has bylaws that were passed for situations that no longer exist. It is still legal, we understand, to drive a herd of cattle through the central part of Chicago during business hours. Likewise, rules that were created in the days before e-mail, voice mail, and local area networks may embroil employees in unnecessary paperwork.

Rules sometimes take the form of clock-watching and surveillance. We know an oil executive, for example, who brought his car into the office as early as he could and left it there late at night—even while he went to the movies or the theater—because he knew his CEO looked in the parking lot to see when he was in and when he left. It didn't matter how long he was there or what he was doing. So long as that car was in the parking lot, the CEO thought the executive was working. This is a variation on face time—maybe we can call it car time.

Rules can also take the form of petty budget restrictions. Joanna used to work for an insurance company where the traditional way to move up was to move around. The corporation paid the moving company bills but not the other costs of relocation. She had rented an apartment in New York, but she had to buy a house when she was transferred to Madison, Wisconsin, which meant buying appliances and other household furnishings out of her own money. Once she had settled in, she realized that three years' worth of the raise in pay she got by moving had been completely absorbed in relocation costs.

Three years later she was asked to go to Phoenix. She agreed, and the same thing happened again, even though she tried unsuccessfully to negotiate additional expenses for moving. After another three years she was asked to go to the office in London. Joanna figured out the cost of living in London and once again tried to negotiate appropriate relocation costs.

When the company remained adamant, she turned the job down; it went to someone less experienced. That was a year and a half ago. Now she is working for the competition—in London. As Joanna puts it:

Pretty soon the only people who will play my old company's moving game will be the no-brainers who haven't figured out the scam. Come to think of it, the guys who are running the scam from the head office are no-brainers themselves who went through the system. The system simply weeds out the intelligent people. It's remarkably effective in getting rid of anyone with an ounce of horse sense.

Joanna selected the route that most bright people take: She opted out and went to a company that put its moving money where its mouth was. Her former employer lost a good employee through penny-pinching and strict adherence to outdated rules.

Rules make it unnecessary for people to use their own judgment. Rules can make life simpler for employees, but after a lifetime of coloring inside the lines, employees may lose the ability to think for themselves. Most of the world's important innovations have occurred when somebody broke the rules, sometimes intentionally, sometimes unintentionally. But this will never occur in a Jurassic organization.

POLITICAL POWER LIES IN THE ACCOUNTING, FINANCE, AND LEGAL DEPARTMENTS

When the numbers people are in charge, everything has to look like a number. Everything is measured, whether it needs to be or not. And if it can't be measured, it is ignored. Economic factors are a lot easier to measure than social or personal factors, so of course economic factors are carefully tracked, while social factors are seldom written down.

For example, the CEO of a company making acquisitions in the former Soviet Union was nervous because of the size of the expansion. He wanted to have something concrete to hold onto, so he kept demanding budget presentations. The executives working in the field were getting so many requests from the head office to do budget reviews—what they call roll-up budgets—that they couldn't get on with the job. Given the nature of the acquisitions and the conditions in the former Soviet Union, they had no idea what the budget should be. Finally, in desperation, they just made up a budget and sent it off to the head office. Everybody was soothed at home, the deal went through, and the company made big profits. This is not an approach that we recommend, mind you, but it shows that numbers are sometimes beside the point.

The demand for numbers is more often found in everyday business interactions. People concentrate on numbers because it is easy to monitor sales, inventory, and production costs. They don't pay as much attention to less tangible but equally important elements because it is more difficult to get a handle on innovation, morale, or atmosphere. As management specialist Frank Sonnenberg puts it:

There is a tendency in this country to believe that if something cannot be quantified, it does not exist. It brings to mind the argument associated with Bishop George Berkeley, an early eighteenth century philosopher: If a tree falls in the woods, but no one is there to hear the sound, did it make a noise? To put it another way: If someone enhances performance in an organization using an approach that cannot be quantified, did the improvement take place?

In a Jurassic organization, the answer is no.

This kind of thinking has a predictable effect on pay and incentive programs. For example, at many magazine publishing companies, the people who sell advertising are well paid and have a long-established system of bonuses for good sales performance. The editorial staff, however, are less well paid and have no bonuses because it is not as easy to measure editorial productivity. Magazines could not exist without editors, yet their work is undervalued relative to sales, simply because it is more difficult to quantify.

AUTHORITY IS NOT MATCHED WITH RESPONSIBILITY

Giving someone responsibility for a job without handing over the authority to make decisions is an extraordinarily common form of abuse, not just in Jurassic organizations but in otherwise intelligently run companies. We see this inability to delegate, or micromanagement, all the time. Well-trained, competent professionals are expected to refer every tiny decision to a higher-up. This not only wastes their time and duplicates their efforts but also demoralizes them.

The director of a community services department in a large city used to drive her employees to distraction by demanding to see every piece of outgoing correspondence. She made editorial changes to nearly every letter. Unless she covered a piece of paper with notes and corrections, she thought she wasn't doing her job properly. Sometimes she asked to see a letter several times and changed her own editorial changes on subsequent drafts. The department became notoriously slow to respond to its incoming mail, a severe dysfunction in a publicly funded institution that was expected to serve the community.

Micromanagement is a corporate insult. It tells employees: you are incompetent, and left to your own devices, you will blow it. It also bogs a company down at the expense of strategic planning and long-term initiatives. One public official who is in charge of thousands of employees at a government agency in the Midwest has a signing limit of $25,000.

Every expenditure above that figure has to go through a bureaucratic round of approvals. Consequently, getting a new project off the ground takes forever. Even though in most cases micromanagement is a problem for a particular individual, when it is endemic, as in this situation, it's time to start looking for dinosaur prints on the floor.

THE MANAGEMENT-THEORY-OF-THE-MONTH SYNDROME

In a Jurassic organization, the only hope for change is a radical shakeup: No individual can single-handedly move the mountain. The best course for any bright spark is to move to a younger company where ideas are valued and the systems do not squash innovation. Beware. Some companies that say they value innovation are simply spouting the latest jargon. "Empowerment!" they cry, "Quality! Teamwork! Vision!" These companies will claim to value change and innovation yet never really succeed in making more than superficial adjustments to the way they work. They will flirt with ideas like employee empowerment, but they never practice what they preach.

A recent survey of top teams revealed that in spite of demands to reinvent the organization, most people maintain their traditional behaviors. Some of these people are what Eileen Shapiro would call "fad surfers." They glom onto the latest buzz phrase and throw it around without thinking through the consequences.

Michael Gaffney has proposed the Airport Bookstore Theory of Large-Scale Organization Change, which maintains that a goodly number of change programs are conceived in airports by senior managers whose flights have been delayed and who have some time to kill. Not being able to stomach another perusal of the latest financial reports, these managers wander into the management section of the airport bookstore—and the rest is history!

Louise, a battered sales manager trapped in a company that is always trying out the latest change program, has heard it all:

> When it was management by objectives, we had objectives coming out of our ears, although the management part looked much the same as always to me. Then it was that quality stuff, all about value-added, whatever that is, and the customer is number one. They retrained a couple of customer service clerks, but when they left, the whole quality thing sort of wilted. Now, I gather, we are "re-engineering" and we've got a

couple of nifty slogans, but, you know, the product is the same as it's always been, and so are the sales figures. Actually, I think we could improve the product and increase sales if we didn't have to attend all these pep talks about the latest hot idea.

Much of what companies call change management is very superficial. Underneath, the same old systems function as before. They have a life of their own, and no buzz phrase is going to change that. As Terrence Deal points out, "Just as reading diet books is a substitute for losing weight, reading management books is a substitute for good management."

The problem is one of conflicting priorities. No amount of saying that people are your most precious asset will make the statement true if every system in the company is designed to maximize short-term returns. In choosing between treating employees well or increasing sales, if you always put sales first, then you are sacrificing long-term results for a short-term gain. There's nothing wrong with short-term returns; what's wrong is mistreating the people you are counting on to work for you in the future.

In the end there will be a lot of unhappy employees and a confused boss who can't understand why everybody isn't as buoyant as he or she is about the sales figures. How can the staff be happy? They have been exploited and patronized. They have been told that they are the most important asset in the company, yet when it counts, they come a poor second to the sales targets.

What is especially tragic about this attitude is that it isn't necessary to sacrifice sales to people or vice versa. It is entirely possible to treat employees well *and* increase sales at the same time, as some very successful companies have shown. However, a characteristic of abusive companies is that they tend to pose these two options as either/or propositions.

"People values" is just one of the buzzwords heard all too often in abusive business environments. Other corporations are quick to spout the jargon of "creativity" and "empowerment." What's behind the rhetoric? What is really going on?

Creativity: Chances are, the employees are using it to find new ways to protect themselves or to circumvent rules they consider restrictive or illogical. Employees can be extraordinarily creative in finding ways to appear to be working long hours without actually putting in the time. Meanwhile, managerial creativity is expended on empire building, turf protection, and maintaining the status quo.

Empowerment: Hard to find when bureaucracy and micromanagement keep employees tied up in red tape, reporting every five minutes to superiors, justifying and rejustifying any new venture, until they decide that innovation is not worth the effort.

Obviously, any employee with a spark of creativity or ambition is going to find a more supportive environment somewhere else. The company will soon be left with workers who are too weary, too cynical, or too spineless to question the prevailing culture, and certainly too docile to risk leaving. Does this sound like the kind of company you want to work for or invest in, let alone run?

CULTURAL ANTIBODIES

Resistance to change often takes the form of "cultural antibodies" that search out and destroy innovation and change. Antibodies in the human body help fight disease, but they can also cause the body to reject essential remedies such as blood transfusions or certain medications.

Antibodies protect the status quo in the human body, sometimes at the expense of life itself. Similarly, cultural antibodies can keep a company on track in good times by perpetuating systems and attitudes and warding off digressions, but if a company has stumbled into crisis, cultural antibodies can thwart necessary change.

Resistance to change is normal. After all, asking for change implies there is something wrong with the current state of affairs. When someone suggests you should try cutting your hair or maybe having it permed, you assume that it's because your current hairstyle doesn't suit you. In fact, it may simply be that hairstyles have changed, but you still feel the sting of criticism.

Nobody wants to be told that the way they work is no longer effective or that the structures and systems they have set up aren't appropriate to today's business environment. They feel it is a criticism, even though it may be that times have changed and what worked perfectly well before is now out of date. This reaction is to be expected. However, when the resistance seems to come from the system itself, it's important to ask who takes priority: the system or the people?

LEAN AND MEAN

Our parents had it easy. Once they had a job, they could expect to stay there if they wanted to, and they were valued for their years of experience and knowledge. If they wanted to leave, they could usually find something else, so they weren't stuck in a situation that was killing them. Now we're told we can't expect job security, but we're too terrified to leave in case we can't find another job.

—Dieter, accountant

These days, it's upgrade, upgrade, upgrade, whatever worked last year is useless this year. The minute you get used to one computer system, they replace it. For crying out loud, I still can't transfer calls on the damn telephone without cutting people off, and they want me to learn how to do all this spreadsheet stuff on the computer. Honest to God, those things are giving me ulcers.

—Lloyd, warehouse supervisor

Why can't management say what it means? Like that guy who said something about getting out his gun when he heard the word "culture," I'm ready to get out my gun when I hear the word "restructuring." It means firing—everybody knows that. I'm sick of all the bafflegab. It just adds to the feeling of uncertainty and dread.

—Marta, systems analyst

THESE DAYS many of us feel like Alice Through the Looking Glass, who found she had to run as hard as she could just to stay in one place and was told by the Red Queen that she would have to run even faster if she wanted to advance on the chessboard. In the shift from an industrial age to an information age, changes have occurred in the workplace that neither workers nor management could have anticipated. Burgeoning technology, shrinking customer loyalty, and expanding global markets have sharpened competition, while production costs have risen. The scramble to stay on top of the heap gets more heated with every business quarter, as stockholders demand that corporate executives cut costs and show profits. In many cases the battle is for sheer survival.

Competition for jobs is fiercer than ever, so the closest most of us get to climbing the corporate hierarchy is swinging from one ladder to another. Gone are the days when a young graduate signed on for life at a huge corporation. Loyalty to the firm has been downplayed by jittery professionals who have no choice but to rank building their own careers over the needs of a company that will in all likelihood offer only a temporary home.

Consequently, the traditional psychological contract has been broken. Managers feel pressured to produce results at any cost while often finding their own jobs in jeopardy. They feel deserted by a workforce that seems unmotivated and unwilling to make sacrifices. Employees don't have faith that their loyalty and performance will guarantee them a job in the future. They see high-level profit-taking at the expense of thousands of jobs; they watch as fellow workers are laid off in an arbitrary fashion; they see surviving staff members overburdened with increasing workloads. And they look over their shoulders, waiting fearfully for the ax to fall. Trust is gone from the relationship, so both parties feel justified in acting in their own self-interest.

This kind of abuse is *structural*. Its sources are pressures that affect the organization as a whole: globalization, takeovers, mergers, downsizing, automation. In structural abuse, the corporation itself is often a victim of circumstances beyond its control. Inside the corporation, employees are trapped in a bubble of fear and stress. They feel they can't blame the boss or the corporation; they can't "know" the source of their distress and that compounds it.

Of course, cyclical reductions have always been an accepted method of cutting costs during downturns, but in our increasingly competitive business environment, staff cuts and plant closings are being used more and more as a restructuring *strategy*, a plan to be used even in good times to make a company more "lean and mean."

Corporations seeking to reduce operating costs and increase profitability believe that by eliminating workers they can improve profit margins and build up their revenues. The idea that "lean and mean" makes companies more competitive has established a strong foothold in the corporate world. When AT&T announced in January 1996 that 40,000 jobs were being cut as part of its separation into three smaller companies, its stocks soared. The implicit notion that workers are just another production tool, easy to replace or exchange for a newer model, is worrisome as much for what it suggests about our values as for the toll it takes in human and business terms.

"Corporate Killers" blazed the headline on a recent *Newsweek* cover. Under mug shots of four top executives—Robert Palmer at Digital, Albert Dunlap at Scott, Robert E. Allen at AT&T, and Louis V. Gerstner at IBM— the magazine ran the number of jobs each of them had slashed. Inside, writer Allan Sloan asked rhetorically:

> *How many CEOs of big, downsizing companies sacrificed some of their pay and perks to encourage a sense of community? Did they apologize publicly to the people they fired? Did they take any personal responsibility for mistakes that helped cause the problems they're solving with lay-offs? No way, that's not macho.*

At the core of the "downsizing" dilemma is the issue of *trust*. Trust is the central, unspoken element in the relationship between an employer and an employee. This relationship is the "psychological contract" between employer and employee. In the 1950s or early 1960s the psychological contract was paternalistic in its nature: It placed the welfare of the employee in the hands of the employer.

Employees agreed to put in "a good day's work" on a continuing basis and to show loyalty to the company over time. In return the employer agreed to pay a fair wage and provide certain benefits. It was understood that raises would be forthcoming based on seniority and performance. If people stayed and didn't botch the job, they were assured of a place until retirement. The advancements and rewards they reaped along the way were determined by the quality of their work and the degree of their loyalty.

That form of contract was swept away, first by the wave of mergers and acquisitions in the 1980s, then by the recession and downsizings of the early 1990s. Now all bets are off.

When a company is undergoing structural abuse, the stress comes from fear of the unknown and of the future. Nobody knows what is going to happen; all anyone knows is that it won't be pretty. Fear becomes the only motivation for action—or inaction.

In companies undergoing radical change, every corporate announcement is greeted with suspicion. Globalization means jobs go to the Third
World and people here get fired. Takeovers mean somebody else benefits
from all our hard work and the people who built the company get fired.
Automation means that computers do jobs that humans used to do and
people get fired. Restructuring by definition means people get fired.

The trouble is, most of the time these suspicions are correct. They
don't have to be, but they often are. Firing people is a lot easier and
quicker than retraining them, redeploying them, or empowering them,
so management tends to fire people at the first sign of trouble. Those
who are spared often wish they'd been let go too, because in an abusive
company they have to do several jobs without any increase in pay or
support. This is a lose/lose situation.

What is the cost of such wholesale elimination of jobs? What can
executives learn about implementing cutbacks that will make the gains
outweigh the costs? There are no simple answers to these questions, but
one thing is certain: Knee-jerk reactions hurt everybody. Besides the
disastrous effects on individuals—those who are fired and those who
survive as the working wounded—they reduce equity in the company.
Downsizing should always maximize performance both for those staying and for those leaving the organization.

A good deal of structural abuse is avoidable. Although downsizing
and restructuring are often necessary, they don't need to be carried out
in a way that humiliates those who are laid off, traumatizes those who
stay, and fails to achieve efficiency and responsiveness. There are companies that manage to treat employees well even during downsizings
and that work hard to keep up morale in tough times. It *is* possible.

GLOBALIZATION PANIC

The new global realities have got a lot of companies running scared. The
borderless economy means that people can compete with unknown and
unseen counterparts on the other side of the world. There is nowhere to
hide in the global economy, no protection for unprofitable operations
or outdated methods. No matter how fast you run, there may be someone whose name you don't even know who is running just as fast—maybe
even faster. That, at any rate, is the fear.

The international division of labor means that, in theory at least,
a corporation can locate different functions in different countries:

low-skilled work in a country with cheap labor, research and development in a country with good universities, computer operations in a country with reliable telecommunications, and so forth. Meanwhile, money can be moved around electronically and invested in any country via stock exchanges from New York to London to Tokyo.

The optimists see globalization as an opportunity to get into new markets and expand; the pessimists can't see beyond plant closures and layoffs. Both are right—but both are oversimplifying a very complex process. Also, both may be using globalization as a stick for beating employees to make them work harder and faster.

The effects of globalization are uneven across industries, and there are many locally based businesses and institutions for which globalization is essentially irrelevant. After all, in the average city, it is estimated that about three-quarters of all jobs are in sectors that provide services to local residents. As one city planner puts it, "Most of us are employed taking in each other's washing." In other words, most of us work for our neighbors in one way or another, not for faceless millions around the world.

A lot of the stress caused by bandying the word "globalization" about comes from poor communication. Too often employees are left to assume the worst. If a company is planning to compete globally, employees anticipate overwork and intense pressure to compete. If the company is likely to lose out, employees expect job loss for the front-line workers while the executive officers sail away on golden parachutes. A company that fails to state its position clearly can create a lot of free-floating anxiety.

RESTRUCTURING MARATHONS

"Restructuring: a simple plan instituted from above in which workers are right-sized, downsized, surplused, lateralized, or, in the business jargon of days of yore, fired," says reporter Erick Schonfeld from *Fortune* magazine. In theory, restructuring should mean redistributing power, resetting priorities, and reorganizing basic systems. In practice, however, corporations often resort to surgery rather than long-term therapy when times are tough. It's the top-down way of doing things: Cut first, ask questions later. Downsizing is often carried out without considering the consequences and without adequate preparation and backup from systems. As Manuel Werner notes in *Business Horizons*:

> *Flattening the organization has become a very popular pastime. By itself, however, it is probably worse than no solution at all. Without the*

wherewithal to empower, flattening only overburdens the manager while slowing everyone else down, because they still have to have approved all that they had approved in the past. Flattening has erroneously been wielded as a tool when it is, in fact, an outcome or by-product of empowerment.

A classic example of how not to make cutbacks comes from a large British publishing firm. The company was in financial distress, so a new chief executive officer was brought in to appease creditors. Stock prices were depressed, and creditors who had accepted shares in the company as collateral for extensive loans wanted someone in charge who would get the value of the shares back up.

According to an editor who worked there at the time, one of the new CEO's first acts was to fire about 100 workers without notice, justifying his actions as a cost-cutting measure. Using staff cuts as an example of a new "get tough" attitude, he went on to chop more than 1,000 workers. The survivors, one of whom was the editor, were loaded down with unreasonable workloads and deadlines. Stress was rampant, "a siege mentality" set in, and the office was riddled with insecurity. Here's how the editor described what happened during the cuts:

> Specially hired security guards were stationed on every floor and at all exits and entrances. The effect was that of martial law. The new management team was instructed to remove "veterans," "known complainers," the "disaffected," those "unsupportive of the new regime," "drunks," and "others not positively recommended by superiors." A great many people were removed for personal reasons and in some cases only after a considerable amount of bullying and torment. One contract-staffer fired by a new member of management was given five minutes to vacate the offices or be "forcibly removed" by the security guards. The manager felt sufficiently justified and safe in the circumstances to act this way—perhaps as an act of career-augmenting machismo, since it was sure to be reported back to top management. Their mission was to root out the "wrong-doers," in other words, those that management did not want. One hope was that less robust staff would simply walk away without payoffs.

The price of the company's shares went back up, satisfying its creditors and solidifying the position of the new CEO: "When the share price hit a high in mid-1993, the creditor banks got back their money in a highly successful sell-off." Despite the short-lived happy ending, the circulation figures fell, and subsequent legal costs and severance payoffs significantly ate into profits. Reflecting on the whole incident, the editor says:

> Doubtless some redundancies were necessary because of new technology, but this does not excuse the manner in which many employees were removed. By business reckoning the company was now safe. But at what cost in human terms? While it's certainly true that the company had been in real peril, the prescription put into effect involved innumerable injustices and cruelties, which were validated by the "situation," by an exaggerated sense of crisis and fear.

The picture we get of modern corporate life is not a pretty one: stockholders focused only on the bottom line; executives pressured to serve short-term shareholder interests without the tools, support, or motivation to carry out long-term goals; managers, fearful of finding themselves unemployed, sacrificing their ideals to jockey for position in a fast-paced game of professional musical chairs; and employees toiling long hours at their jobs while watching their backs.

In a paper presented to the Human Resources Planning Society Research Symposium at Cornell University in 1993, Kenneth P. De Meuse, Paul A. Vanderheiden, and Thomas J. Bergmann discussed the effects of downsizing on efficiency and profitability. De Meuse and his colleagues tracked the performance, over a five-year period, of seventeen Fortune 100 companies that had made layoff announcements and thirty-five others that had not. They concluded that "the relative performance of the layoff firms not only did not improve but generally deteriorated further."

The De Meuse findings are backed up by a more recent study of 531 companies by the Wyatt Company. The Wyatt survey found that many companies failed to meet their stated goals of reducing costs, increasing profits, bolstering productivity, and improving customer service after downsizing. The Wyatt study also looked at downsizing methods and found that a company's subsequent financial performance could be affected by the way cutbacks were handled by management. Clearly there are some valuable clues here for executives and managers looking for real solutions.

When new management is called in to fix an ailing company, or when restructuring steps are taken inside a firm, employees face a frightening uncertainty. If they are kept out of the picture about what policies will be instituted and how their jobs will be affected, rumors and fear proliferate. When the first wave of layoffs comes, the cuts can seem arbitrary and ruthless. Long-term employees, more experienced workers, high-salaried staff members, support workers without powerful allies may be among the first to go. There is no guarantee that good performance and long-standing employment will be protection against the ax.

Fear is a powerful emotion, yielding anxiety, self-protection, and resentment. Working under a siege mentality, employees are transformed into a sullen and unmotivated workforce. Demoralized individuals shift into a survival mode, producing just what is demanded of them and no more. At a time when management is struggling to restructure and boost productivity, employees are least capable of contributing. Management's efforts to save the company are sabotaged by its own misguided methods.

Consider another battle story. A major pharmaceutical manufacturer arranged an out-of-town conference for a group of researchers. They were to be housed on two floors of a hotel near corporate headquarters. When the unsuspecting employees arrived, they soon discovered that only the individuals who were given rooms on the higher of the two floors were expected to attend the conference. Those who had been assigned rooms on the lower floor were dismissed shortly after they checked in. As more people arrived and word got around, it became evident that those with certain room keys were only moments away from sudden unemployment. Those who survived the humiliating ordeal went back to their jobs shaken and appalled.

What is tragic is that these stories and thousands of similar incidents are not anomalies. They are sadly typical of how too many corporate executives depersonalize and demean their workers in the name of progress. The unhappy implication of this kind of behavior is that those at the top do not recognize the humanity of those whose lives they control. It is not surprising to find workers enraged at an eroding job economy when they see corporate heads taking home "compensation packages" ninety times higher than the salaries of their average employees. Could this irreconcilable disparity explain why some executives are hopelessly out of touch with the lives and values of the people who work for them?

Although studies have shown that most companies that use massive layoffs as a way to improve performance and cut costs seldom achieve their goals, it comes as a surprise to some CEOs that most attempts at restructuring do not work.

The business environment is radically different today, yet corporate leaders are still relying on traditional "efficiency" methods when, in fact, it's innovation that is called for, finding new solutions, new ways of approaching problems, and new ways of doing work. As we have said, the old style of work was labor-intensive—requiring muscles and endurance—while the new style is thoughtful and imaginative, requiring thinking and collaborating and endurance of a different sort. Unfortunately, too many executives believe that simply making staff cuts will be enough to improve financial performance. They don't stop to think about how the cuts should be made or how to compensate for them. A change in one part of an organization always has a countervailing effect somewhere else.

Even worse, workers are kept in the dark concerning corporate goals and are not told what programs will be implemented next or why. Often high-salaried employees, the "knowledge" workers, are the first to go, leaving the company with a disproportionate number of inexperienced or less skilled workers. The victims of cutbacks are unprepared to face the hostile job market, and surviving employees, forced to take on additional work, are left to fend for themselves in a climate of uncertainty. Middle management ranks are cut, and mentoring possibilities evaporate. The networks within the corporation are torn apart, and there is nothing to replace them. But beyond these internal problems is the question of the survival of the company as a whole when the product or the service suffers.

Retained employees may feel some relief at having escaped with their jobs, but their victory may be short-lived. According to the De Meuse study, of the seventeen companies that carried out layoffs, eleven made further cuts one year after the initial layoffs, and fourteen made more cuts two years later.

Meanwhile, the survivors become cynical, especially when spending in other areas is not cut back. Even more galling from the worker's point of view are the seemingly profligate salaries and irresponsible behavior of some chief executives. At a large energy company, a senior executive oversaw every detail of his company's relocation, personally selecting everything from carpeting to bathroom tile. After all twenty-eight bathrooms in the new headquarters had been completed, the executive decided he was unhappy with the tile color he had chosen. He ordered every piece of tile ripped out and replaced. A month earlier, two hundred employees had been laid off. Obviously, he did not consider how his actions would affect the morale of his remaining workers.

Even properly motivated, responsible company leaders often seem out of touch with their workers. Executives are bewildered when a company's performance continues to fall short. In their frustration, they often institute misguided "get tough" policies that further alienate workers. Or, out of a real desire to set things right, they institute "quality management" programs that, although well intentioned, usually don't have any significant effect, according to the Wyatt survey.

In fact, these programs usually make things worse because employees feel that they are being asked to endure yet another futile program, another waste of money by management. The paternalistic attitudes of the past, when workers were told only what they needed to know and management acted for the good of the corporation, do not work anymore. They don't achieve corporate business goals, and they also sacrifice the company's most valuable assets: the commitment and creativity of its employees.

Workers who show up and keep their heads down, plotting revenge or just hoping to avoid confrontation and hang onto their paychecks, will not be capable of leading industry into the next century. They will, in fact, have very little energy left for anything. In the end, it's not only corporate life that will feel the repercussions, but our economy, our families, and our entire society.

FEAR OF TECHNOLOGY

Like mergers, takeovers, restructuring, or globalization, technology often seems to be an uncontrollable factor in corporate life. It has a momentum of its own; it is unstoppable; and human beings are subject to it. It invades a corporation like an alien species from another planet.

None of this is true, of course, but this is how people in corporations experience technology because of the way in which technology is designed by its human creators and because of the way it is introduced into organizations. For many people structural abuse comes in the form of pressure to use new technology.

At a seminar held in Toronto recently on human-centered design, one speaker began his talk with a few sentences in Gaelic, a language not many of us understand today. He went on to explain that the frustration a great many people experience in trying to deal with technological change is the same frustration experienced by people trying to negotiate in a foreign language in an unfamiliar culture. They do not understand what is being said to them, and they cannot make their needs understood.

Technology is often frustrating because it makes skills obsolete very rapidly. Just as you get the hang of the new software system, it is upgraded and you have to learn a new set of commands. This creates an enormous amount of stress as workers struggle to keep up. Meanwhile, the use of technology to cut downtime increases the volume and pace of daily work until workers are exhausted. It is not possible for humans to work at the pace of machines without time for replenishment, but they are often expected to. This is not the fault of the machines, however; it is a management decision.

Even where employees are in control of technology, there is a compulsion to use technology just because everyone else is using it, even if it doesn't seem relevant to your job. If everyone else is surfing the Internet, you feel you have to do it, too, or risk becoming hopelessly out of the loop. Moreover, you find yourself doing things because you can, not because you need to.

Technology's bells and whistles can waste enormous amounts of time and make us feel overworked, even as our output decreases. We make draft copies look as good as published documents; our weekly reports are as pretty as our annual reports. Standards rise, expectations rise, and soon we are expected to make memos look like minor masterpieces.

Homemakers have known this for decades: Every supposedly labor-saving device in the home just creates more work because when formerly difficult tasks become easier, the standards of cooking or cleanliness rise. The effects are the same in the workplace, and office technology can create as much work as it saves. With faxes and e-mail, for example, it seems every message must be answered. Unfortunately, this work has to be done by fewer people when support staff are replaced by personal computers and voice mail.

Even more frustrating is the added burden of technology used inappropriately. Do you have colleagues and business associates who leave a five-minute voice message when they should have sent a memo? Who clutter up your e-mail with long documents you'd rather read in print? Who inundate you with faxes that are not at all urgent and could be sent through the mail? The urge to use the latest technology for absolutely everything can backfire and turn even techies into Luddites.

And, of course, technology is often cast as the spy. Big Brother is watching you. Video cameras, electronic monitoring of workers at computer terminals, tapping into employees' e-mail and voice mail, smart badges that track employees' locations at all times are examples of the way technology can be used to abuse workers.

Surveillance invades the privacy of employees and creates a climate of suspicion and unease that can fragment the workforce. Who can employees trust if no one trusts them? We have seen many instances of employees suffering nervous breakdowns from the pressure of having their work monitored too closely or too often. An airline reservations clerk in San Diego collapsed because of a system that tracked how long she spent on each call. The pressure to work faster and faster made her so nervous that she needed eight months of therapy. "I am supposed to have a digital clock in my head," she complained. "I'm not a machine." Besides the monitoring, she was distressed because she had to sacrifice accuracy to speed. In the end the company had to pay, not only for sick leave but for costly mistakes.

MIT professor Robert Thomas has looked closely at technology in the workplace and come to some important conclusions about the way in which technology is designed, adopted, and used. He points out that technology is chosen either to reinforce or to change the power structure in an organization. Think about the technology in your workplace. Who really benefits from it? Whose work does it save and whose does it increase? Who does it include and who does it exclude? Has it changed the reporting structure? Whose status does it enhance?

Thomas also notes that those who design the technology rarely ask for input from those who are the objects of change, which is why most employees experience technology as something imposed from outside, over which they have little control.

We have to remember that technology is designed by humans, chosen by humans, implemented by humans. It doesn't come from outer space; it is a human creation and an instrument of human political power. Because we live in a technological age, we tend to assume that if machines can't do it, it is not worth doing. Donald A. Norman at the University of California contrasts the human-centered view of the world with the machine-centered. This is the machine-centered way of looking at life:

People Are ...	Machines Are ...
Vague	Precise
Disorganized	Orderly
Distractible	Undistractible
Emotional	Unemotional
Illogical	Logical

All this is quite correct in its way, but it puts a value on the machine's way of doing things and discounts the human way of behaving. The machine-centered approach overlooks the fact that there are times when precision is not useful or necessary, when logic ignores qualitative factors in decision-making, when being undistractible means carrying on operations normally in abnormal times. Machines cannot make intuitive leaps in thinking. They can process only the information they are given; they don't go looking for additional information when it is needed. They don't have hunches or gut feelings or any of the very important human qualities that lead to innovation.

When you frame the same categories in a different way, the comparison looks like this:

People Are ...	Machines Are ...
Creative	Dumb
Compliant [flexible]	Rigid
Attentive to change	Insensitive to change
Resourceful	Unimaginative
Decisions are flexible because they are based upon qualitative as well as quantitative assessment, modified by the special circumstances and context.	Decisions are consistent because they are based upon quantitative evaluation of numerically specified, context-free variables.

Same categories, different value systems. Corporations often get hijacked by engineers and technocrats who have a machine-centered view of the world, and employees find themselves at the mercy of apparently impersonal forces they do not understand.

Research has shown that it is possible to humanize an automated workplace by letting employees participate in decisions about the design and choice of technology. When employees have autonomy and a sense of control over the technology, when they have a variety of tasks and access to information, training, and support, they generally stop hating machines. Not only does this reduce their stress levels, it also makes it easier for managers to implement new work systems using technology. Technology does not need to be a source of abuse. Only people can make it so.

THE TERRIFYING WORLD OF CHANGE

Globalization, takeovers, restructuring, technological change—it's scary out there, all right. The normal human reactions to such changes include confusion, unrealistic expectations, and a variety of coping strategies ranging from the severely dysfunctional, including substance abuse, to acceptance and adaptation.

What really hampers our ability to adjust is the fact that we do not have a legacy of capable organizations that can respond adequately and intelligently to the challenges of change. Instead, we have de-skilled workers using scientific management methods, so that they depend completely upon their role as a cog in a machine; they have forgotten how to think for themselves.

We have trained managers who can crunch numbers but who have not risen up through the ranks, so they have no idea what life is like for the front-line workers and they cannot understand the social consequences of economic decisions. Top management is often completely out of touch, preoccupied with political games, status, and perks. Hardly anyone in the corporation is equipped to deal sensibly with change. The result? Abuse. From ignorance, from fear, from knee-jerk reactions to perceived threats.

Individuals who are on the receiving end of corporate abuse are struggling to survive in a workplace that has become uncivilized. It doesn't have to be like this. Corporations are the creations of human beings, and human beings can reinvent them. Unfortunately, some of the biggest obstacles to needed change are human beings. We cannot overlook the fact that certain kinds of abuse are personal, carried out by individuals who for one reason or another find it necessary to mistreat the people around them. Before we go any further, we should grapple with abuse on an individual, personal level.

Sorcerers and Tyrants

Connors [John Connors, CEO, Hill Holliday Advertising] kicked the man's chair violently—with the executive still in it. Recalls a manager who was present: "There was Jack kicking the chair with this guy hanging on like a fighter pilot."

Wachner [Linda Wachner, CEO, Warnaco] lashed out at a meeting of executives from the women's clothing group. Angered by their performance, she declared: "You're eunuchs. How can your wives stand you? You've got nothing between your legs!"

After roughly two minutes, Jobs [Steve Jobs, CEO, Next Computer], his face turning red, cut the startled man off and began screaming that the [computer] shell had to cost $20, that the manager didn't know what he was talking about, and that he was going to ruin the company. The expletive-laden tirade lasted three to four minutes.

THIS IS THE LANGUAGE of our corporate heroes, the eminently successful business leaders of our era. These examples come from an article in *Fortune* magazine, "America's Toughest Bosses." The article goes on to describe how these very successful corporate leaders continually bully the highly talented people who work for them.

One executive recalled how two engineers had been slaving nights and weekends for fifteen months (including toiling over Christmas break) to meet an important—and impossible—deadline. For all their effort, the boss publicly and viciously berated them before the entire company for not working faster.

Another remarked how his boss puts on "his drooling psycho face . . . [which] features, among other things, bulging veins and narrowed eyes. He follows up with some fist pounding and verbal lashing. . . . I've watched [him] tear people to shreds and make them leave the room in tears."

Almost as shocking as the appalling behavior we've described is the reaction it provoked. Instead of revulsion, there was an aura of acceptance for the outrageous behavior of these high-powered bosses. Certainly the bosses seemed quite unashamed of being exposed as tyrants in a high-profile magazine. Even more bizarre, their abused employees appeared almost to relish their position as illustrious survivors, like soldiers talking nostalgically about how tough it was in boot camp.

Why is this?

The obvious reason is that many abusive people are extremely rich and powerful. Somehow, we think that gives them license to be bullies. Our research brought us in touch with people who worked under the tyranny of Lance, a very successful and very wealthy CEO of a stock brokerage firm. Everyone who came into contact with Lance, whether in a professional capacity or simply as a neighbor, had a tale to tell.

Barbara, his second-in-command, reported that Lance "constantly humiliated me" in front of her team.

> He would tell me I didn't know what the f—k I was doing and that I wouldn't be anywhere without him. At one meeting he called me a V.I.C. and then asked if I knew what it meant. I said no, and he said it stands for Very Important C—t!

Barbara endured this kind of behavior from Lance, as did her colleagues, until he left the company to become a consultant.

> Lance has some serious personality problems and he really put me through hell. I am amazed I survived, but he is the most brilliant man I know, and he did help to make me a millionaire.

Lance dished out his abuse to men as well as women, to outsiders as well as colleagues. A male real estate agent told us:

> When I was selling Lance's home, he would call me regularly from wherever he was on business just to scream at me and ask why I hadn't sold his house yet. He would threaten me by saying he had documented all of my activities and I was under surveillance. He was extremely threatening and verbally abusive, but you have to admire the guy, he's so successful.

It was hard to find anyone who didn't admire Lance because of his personal wealth, but no one ever mentions his company's performance.

Nobody admired Lance for what he achieved in the workplace, only for the money he amassed.

Lance's ex-wife remembers that people would want to get close to Lance because they thought that somehow he could make them rich too. Regardless of how he treated them, they still wanted to associate with him and to work with him. Even a neighbor said, "Oh, he is really disgusting, but very successful!"

Lance's financial success blinded people to his abusive behavior. Like sorcerers, people like Lance seduce us with their success and wealth. In exchange for a chance to share that bounty, we suffer their abuse and do their bidding.

Barbara is now a millionaire, thanks at least in part to Lance. What has she learned from the experience? That bullying and abuse get you money, if not respect. And money is apparently what she wanted, since she put up with Lance's abuse to get it.

Lance may have left the company, but we'd be very surprised if Barbara suddenly turned into a consensus-building, empowering boss herself.

Just as children who have been abused often turn into abusive parents, abused employees who claw their way to the top often have so much built-up resentment about the way in which they were treated that they repeat the abuse as soon as they have a little power.

People like Lance and Barbara are typical "self-maximizers." To hell with the rest of the firm, they just want their millions. Some firms encourage this behavior, assuming that corporate success will somehow emerge as a byproduct of personal ambition and greed. Sometimes they do get good short-term results, but this kind of policy is a recipe for long-term disaster.

The way people relate to Lance and Barbara has a deeper psychological meaning than mere kowtowing to bullies. It indicates a worrisome shift of values in which people prize success and wealth above civility. This shift in values is what permits the kind of abuse that we call *deliberate abuse*.

With the possible exception of Mother Teresa, it is difficult to think of a man or woman today who is both celebrated and poor. It is also just as rare to hear about a sports hero without mention of the salary he commands. Wealth has always been valued in our society and it always will be. It is possible, however, to encourage civilized behavior in addition to wealth.

We can restore balance by proving that abusive bosses, no matter how successful and wealthy, are of little long-term value to corporations. The damage they do to the individuals they abuse will reverberate throughout the organization. But first we need to take a closer look at the causes and effects of bullying.

BULLYING

In her book *Thick Face, Black Heart,* Chin-Ning Chu tells us of an old Chinese story:

> *Years ago in China, when a monkey was disobedient, the trainer killed a rooster in front of it. Witnessing the poor rooster's death agony served as a powerful teacher to the monkey.*

The practice of instilling fear by abusing and ridiculing employees is a misguided but all-too-common notion of how to motivate workers. The monkey wasn't expected to be creative, innovative, or risk-taking. In fact, those were the very qualities the trainer was trying to suppress. The monkey was required only to obey. This was also what was demanded of the Light Brigade, and we all know what happened to them when they were given the order to charge.

Many of the people who hire bullies find their behavior acceptable and even seek them out to "whip their companies into shape." One executive told us, "The holding company decided that what they needed to improve the company's productivity was someone to kick some butts, so they hired a nasty ex-submarine commander."

People who hire bullies don't seem to realize that hatchet men and women offer nothing more than quick fixes and short-term solutions. They rarely act in the long-term best interests of their companies. Nor do they consider the ongoing effects of bullying. Once the butts have been kicked, the company whipped into shape (or into submission), what then? Some people have sunk, some people are swimming, and the swimmers are starting to look a lot like sharks.

Tyrants, of course, seldom accept that there may be anything wrong with their behavior, let alone their psyche. Most of them find their behavior totally acceptable and have little or no empathy for how their actions affect others. At some level they feel people exist for them and that their feelings and wishes come first; how dare we question or criticize them?

In her book *Bullying at Work*, Andrea Adams reveals that bullying is often seen as a more crippling and devastating problem for employees and employers than all the other work-related stresses put together. The term "bullying" suggests children and immaturity. We've all seen it at daycare centers and in the schoolyard, but it can be found creating havoc in workplaces too. It includes destructive behaviors that range from the use of abusive and vulgar language and humiliation to stealing ideas, sabotaging efforts, and failing to promote and reward.

Ten Ways to Recognize a Bully

1. Displays uncontrolled anger, often shouting and using vulgar language.

2. Humiliates others in front of colleagues or in private.

3. Persistently criticizes and uses sarcasm.

4. Deliberately ignores or isolates people and excludes them from taking an active part in discussions.

5. Sets impossible deadlines and changes instructions without consultation, for no other apparent reason than to make life difficult and failure inevitable.

6. Has difficulty delegating because of a belief that no one else can do the job to the required standard.

7. Takes credit for other people's ideas and success but never shoulders the blame when things go wrong.

8. Repeatedly refuses reasonable requests; cancels holiday leave at short notice.

9. Continually undermines others' authority.

10. Blocks promotion.

In addition to the straightforward havoc that bullies can wreak on the workplace, they generally do considerable damage to our souls. Earlier, we described the soul as being the citadel that houses the essence of who we are. It is our vital core from which our emotion, action, and energy emanate. Our self-image and our self-esteem, how we think of ourselves, all live at the center of our soul. Our work and our place in the work community play an important part in making the connection between our souls and the world around us. Doing our work well nurtures our soul. Earning respect from doing good work feeds our self-image and our self-esteem.

Our self-image exercises a controlling effect on our behavior. In simple terms, we act in ways that are consistent with our image of ourselves, and we resist performing in a manner that is inconsistent. That simple credo is the basis for all self-help seminars on the benefits of positive thinking.

If we believe we are great, we will do things that support that belief. If we believe we are less than great, we will do things that are consistent with that belief. If we are high in self-esteem, we tackle tasks and social situations with confidence and have good social skills. If we are low in self-esteem, we will be subject to depression and a number of other demotivating aspects.

By their actions, tyrants negate the value of our work and ultimately our sense of self-worth. They dispossess us of our rightful place in the community of work.

Bullying can throw us into a downward spiral until we start to doubt our worth and abilities. McGill University philosopher Charles Taylor has written an essay called "The Politics of Recognition," in which he says that a person can suffer "real damage, real distortion, if the people or society around them mirror back a confining or demeaning or contemptible picture of themselves." He calls this "non recognition" or "misrecognition," and he says it can "imprison somebody in a false, distorted, and reduced mode of being."

This diminished sense of self, whereby a person actually comes to believe that the bully's lies and distortions are true, can be extremely damaging. It is part of a syndrome of self-victimization that many rape victims fall into, where they think the sexual assault must somehow have been their fault.

Sometimes a bully will select one worker to victimize. Being isolated makes it easier for the person being abused to feel that he or she is the problem. Otherwise, why doesn't the boss pick on the other workers? This leads to the feeling that "I am constantly being chastised and pressured because I am inadequate." Colleen, a government social worker, reported:

Every morning before I entered the office, I would feel the blood drain
from my head. . . . I felt lightheaded, as though I would faint. My palms
were always sweaty. I would go into the ladies toilet and sit in a cubicle
with my head between my knees. I'd stay there for as long as I could,
trying to get the courage to face her. It was worse when we would have
a group meeting because then I would be singled out and interrogated.
I had joined this office from another office virtually around the corner
in the same town. I was so happy in the other office and assumed the
new office would be more or less the same, but from the day I started I
was criticized by the boss. I always felt so helpless. I just didn't know
what I was doing wrong. One day I discovered I could get to my office
through the back door. This was so much better but it didn't last long.
She insisted I go through the front door so she could check the time I
came in. I took more sick days than I had ever taken in any other job.

Colleen is not alone in feeling inadequate and guilty. Who wouldn't
feel that way, given the persecution she was enduring? Invariably, people
absorb the negative messages and feel confused about their self-worth.
Losing your self-esteem translates into a loss of confidence and leads to
lower performance.

Research tells us that bullies are bullies usually because of experiences in infancy or childhood. If a child has been treated harshly and is
profoundly affected by it, he carries the experience with him into adulthood. In his subconscious the child who experienced aggression looks
for opportunities to relive the experience, but this time instead of being
the victim, he becomes the powerful aggressor. The process of recogniz-
ing what happened to him as a child and resolving his pain from the
perspective of an adult has never occurred, so the child within reasons
he must continually even the score.

Knowing all this is well and good. But what do you do when you are
confronted with someone whose face is contorted with rage, who has
the power to fire, demote, or harass you? When it comes to bullies, knowing that your soul is being sapped because there is a Wounded Child
Within, who has been unable to resolve his pain from an adult perspective, doesn't seem as significant as the immediate task of dealing with
the Loathsome Adult Without.

Reporting an abusive boss means breaking the taboo of going
over the boss's head. It is difficult and not always successful. Going after
a bully is a troublesome process, even for the bully's supervisor. Yet it

must be done. Otherwise the bullying will never stop and everyone in the company suffers.

A bully's stock in trade is sniffing out vulnerabilities and capitalizing on weaknesses. That's why they strut and shout and broadcast messages like "If you can't stand the heat get out of the kitchen." This makes us feel ashamed to admit we cannot cope. We are afraid of confrontation, so we avert our eyes and let them get away with it. So they do. And the bullying goes on. As Edmund Burke is supposed to have said, "The only thing necessary for the triumph of evil is for good men to do nothing."

BUDGET BUSTERS

Bullies are the most obvious form of abusive individuals, but there are other types who make life miserable for those around them. Consider the tightwads. The miserly spirit of Ebenezer Scrooge (before the ghosts of Christmas past, present, and future visited him) lives on. Scrooge was at least consistent: he was miserable and stingy in his home life as well as on the job. However, there are more upper managers than we like to think about who scrimp on their employees while paying themselves lavish bonuses. The employees get understandably angry and resentful. You can be certain that if they have a good idea or a new way of doing things, they aren't going to waste it on a stingy employer. They will flush it down the toilet sooner than hand over another profitable or cost-saving measure to their bosses.

In one extreme situation, a legal firm that was trying to cut costs was squeezing every penny, shortening vacation allowances, refusing to pay reasonable expenses, and removing some of the facilities formerly available to the support staff. The point of this stinginess was a deliberate plan to irritate the employees so much that they would quit voluntarily and the partners would not have to pay severance. At first glance this sounds simply mean-spirited, but with a little more thought the sheer stupidity of such a plan becomes apparent: who is likely to stay in such an environment except the ones who can't get a job elsewhere?

Oddly enough, it does not take a great deal of money to assuage the frustration and irritation caused by stinginess. Small rewards are usually as effective as large ones, as long as employees are noticed and appreciated. Of all the forms of abuse we have seen, stinginess is probably the most moronic, because the company loses far more than the employees do. It sacrifices loyalty and productivity, and eventually good employees simply leave, taking their ideas and experience with them.

———————

These, then, are the sources of abuse: the persistence of outdated systems that take precedence over human needs, which we call systemic abuse; the wrenching changes in industrial and economic structures that put an entire company under pressure, which we call structural abuse; and the dysfunctional behavior of individuals, which we call deliberate abuse.

Shining a light in the face of the monster brings the issue of abuse into focus, but there is still one question to address before we move on to practical advice and suggestions: why, when we hate what abuse does to us and to our companies, do we still allow it to occur?

WHY DO WE TOLERATE ABUSE?

E KNOW THAT MANY CORPORATE tyrants are hired and their behaviors sanctioned in a misguided attempt to rescue failing businesses, but why do we, as individuals, tolerate abusive people and abusive working cultures? Much of the answer to this lies in our individual and social conditioning.

Just as children learn how to cope with abusive parents, adults modify their behavior so they can tolerate abusive bosses in the business world. It's simply a question of survival. The imbalance of power between employer and employee, or boss and subordinate, puts abusive bosses in control and sets up employees in docile, submissive roles.

Some of us learned how to cower and to smile from our parents. If they shouted and threatened, we assumed that was normal and appropriate behavior. As far as we knew, all parents behaved that way. "Do as I say or else you can't go out to play." "Do as I say or I will stop your allowance." "Do as I say or I'll beat you." If our parents spoke in these harsh terms, we grew up in relationships based on ultimatums, intimidation, and humiliation. Our feelings were subordinated to theirs; our needs, desires, and opinions were irrelevant.

Many people go into the workforce with vivid memories of this kind of direct control from when they were growing up. In her book *Toxic Parents*, Dr. Susan Forward gives an example of direct control by relating how one of her clients described her father:

> He'd have these screaming fits if I dared disagree with him. He'd call me terrible names. He was really loud and scary.
>
> When I was a teenager, he started using money to keep me in line. Sometimes he'd be incredibly generous, which made me feel really loved

and safe. But other times he'd humiliate me by making me beg and cry for anything from movie money to school books. I was never sure what my crimes were. I just know I spent a lot of time trying to figure out how to please him. It was never the same two days in a row. He kept making it tougher.

It's easy to substitute "boss" for "father" in this scenario and see how we come to the workplace predisposed to accept abuse because it seems normal. Abusive bosses who wield their power by threatening us with loss of status, reduced opportunities, heavier workloads, or the possibility of being laid off or fired mirror the behavior some of us have experienced and learned to live with from childhood. The abuse of direct control is so familiar that it may not even occur to us to object.

There are many parallels between the family system and the "work family" culture. Parents who enjoy high levels of self-worth have expectations that are realistic and flexible. They set rules that reflect those qualities. And they exude positive feelings about themselves and others. In the workplace leaders like that set realistic goals and are able to adapt to changing circumstances—even negative ones—without panicking. This kind of boss encourages employees to feel a sense of control and entitlement, bolstered by positive feelings about themselves.

Parents who suffer from low self-esteem frequently manifest their sense of inadequacy in behavior that is rigid and demanding. Often they are perfectionists, setting impossible standards. Inevitably, the unrealistic goals can't be met and the children feel less and less confident about their abilities.

When this kind of person is given a managerial function in the workplace, he or she often becomes a boss who sets the staff up for failure and who passes along negative and destructive feelings. No matter how hard employees work, it is never good enough. With every new crisis, the demands increase and they feel less able to cope.

This kind of leader governs by criticism and blame. Even if, despite obstacles, a employee does a stellar job, that success is downplayed. He or she may even hear the words "You were just lucky."

In the work environment, as in the family system, people with power make the rules. They design the system in their own image. If it is dysfunctional, the "work family" takes on a group identity that begins to display the psychological symptoms of the abuser. Frequently contradictory messages are given, ones that mask the real emotions seething underneath.

Underneath the contradictory messages lie a variety of reasons for abuse. These beliefs and motivations are at the root of abusive systems, guide the design of abusive structures, and are used to justify abusive behavior.

A Genuine or Perceived Crisis

Anyone who has ever taken a course in cardiopulmonary resuscitation knows that in a real life-or-death situation there is no time to observe the social niceties. Whoever takes charge can do whatever bullying is necessary to get the job done. "You, call an ambulance! You, get a blanket! Don't stand there staring, give me a hand here! Get out of the way!"

There are, however, fewer life-and-death crises in the world of work than the amount of bullying would suggest. As one consultant wisely says when the level of hysteria builds up, "Hey, relax! We're not shipping serum to the Congo."

Although there will be times when the need to work quickly will override other considerations, this should be a temporary condition. When crises become permanent, so does abuse.

The really ugly thing about contrived crises is that people start to believe in them. In one well-known experiment conducted by Philip Zimbardo at Stanford University in the early 1970s, students were asked to play the roles of prisoners and guards. The roles were assigned randomly to the students, who were an average bunch of college-age kids. Zimbardo made the experiment so realistic that the "prisoners" became violent and the "guards" became brutal and he had to call the whole thing to a halt because of the threat to the students' safety and emotional health. Whipping people up into a frenzy is a dangerous—and sometimes altogether too easy—business. They start to believe in the roles we have assigned to them. When people start to believe that they really *are* shipping serum to the Congo, they may use this belief to justify all kinds of ethical shortcuts.

Ambition or Greed

Abuse may emanate from one person in particular, as it did in the case of Lance, the wealthy CEO of the stock brokerage. Everybody, from his ex-wife to his colleagues and competitors, admired Lance's ability to make money, but they all had shocking tales to tell of his wrath and his brutality. He constantly humiliated his subordinate, Barbara, in front of her team, but she put up with his abusive behavior at least partly because he made her a millionaire.

People who are intensely ambitious often enjoy the feeling of power and control that they get from treating others badly. Dishing out abuse becomes addictive, a drug for the ego. These people can never have enough money or enough power; they crave more and more, and like other addicts, they lose all interest in the welfare of others when they need a "fix."

When the power-addicted person is the founder or CEO of a company, personal abuse may become embedded in the system, and the climate of abuse percolates throughout the company.

ABUSERS WERE ABUSED THEMSELVES

Corporate abuse often creates abusers out of victims. No doubt Lance's second-in-command, Barbara, has become abusive in her turn. In part Barbara wants to repeat Lance's financial success, but she has built up a lot of resentment over the years as well. She can't get back at Lance for all that he put her through, but she can take it out on *her* second-in-command now that she is in charge.

This is a well-known phenomenon. The punisher may not be particularly hostile toward the punished individual but may actually be taking revenge against someone else or against society at large. The classic example of this is the grueling work schedules to which medical students, interns, and residents are subjected. One commonly offered explanation for this dangerous practice is that the doctors in charge were forced to work those hours when they were in medical school and so they get their revenge by doing the same thing to the students under them.

This is the inverse of the golden rule: "I'll do unto them as they did unto me." When you hear old folks talk about "When I was a lad . . ." or "When I was a girl . . ." followed by tales of walking five miles through the snow to school every morning or some other hardship, you are hearing a mild form of this very human feeling. "It was tough for me," people tell themselves, "so why should the next generation have it easy?" Once a tradition of abuse has been created, it may be perpetuated in this way.

A particular form of this kind of abuse is known as the Queen Bee syndrome, whereby a woman who has broken the glass ceiling and clawed her way to the top refuses to hold out a hand to help others scrambling to follow the same route.

In some companies employees accept abuse as part of "what it takes to get ahead." It is similar to the hazing that passes for initiation rites in many fraternities, sororities, and other secret societies. Unless you have been humiliated in public, you are not considered part of the team. Employees pride themselves on taking what is dished out and look forward to the day when they can do it themselves. This kind of culture appears to be in decline, but it can still be found in a number of companies.

ABUSE IS CHEAP

Treating employees well requires some investment in time as well as money. The payoffs will more than cover the costs, but not all companies have figured this out yet. When Ebenezer Scrooge had his change of heart on Christmas Day, he found himself paying for a large goose and at least an extra shovelful of coal on the fire for Bob Crachit. We expect that Crachit's productivity probably improved considerably after this modest investment on Scrooge's part.

People need good working conditions, including well-designed and well-lit work spaces, equipment and furniture that help prevent repetitive stress injuries, meeting spaces for teamwork, recreation areas, and so forth. They need these conditions whether they are working in an office or out of their cars or their home offices—as one large telecommunications company found when it tried to decentralize its workforce. They also need to take vacations and time off for their families. They need privacy and a feeling of control over their time. All these things cost money.

Some companies claim they cannot afford to provide top-quality working conditions, that they lose money when employees are not at their desks, that rigid centralized control is cost-effective. Rather than follow the adage "an ounce of prevention is worth a pound of cure," they scrimp on prevention and pay dearly in burnout, turnover, absenteeism, and lowered productivity.

MANAGERS DON'T KNOW HOW ELSE TO MANAGE

Many people are promoted to management positions because they are good at something else. They are whizzes at accounting, they understand the intricate workings of the local area network, or they are hot salespeople. As a reward they are cherry-picked from their area of expertise and dropped into management—with only a jot of training: a seminar here and there, a half-day workshop on motivating staff, and whatever wisdom they have gleaned from the paperback they picked up in the airport bookstore when the flight to Brussels was delayed.

Maybe it was something like *The 30-Second Manager Teaches the Stegosaurus to Waltz* or *1,000 Tips for First-Time Managers*. The title doesn't matter. The point is that no management book is a substitute for training and experience. Without a solid foundation and the chance to try out the ideas in a training situation, managers simply cannot apply the ideas in these books.

Of course, people who don't know how to manage may try bullying. Bullying produces quick results. Throw a tantrum and people snap to attention. When it has worked once, it is tempting to do it again. And again. And since most companies value and reward short-term performance, there is little incentive to stop.

ABUSE CONCEALS IGNORANCE

Some managers come from management schools without having had the experience of working on the front lines. They don't really know what is going on, but they know they must look as though they are in charge. They need to feel in control and to hide their ignorance about the work.

Bully the workers, and nobody will ever dare ask you if you know what you are doing. You will make a lot of stupid decisions, which nobody will point out to you, but you can always kill the messenger who brings news of your latest foul-up.

Effective leadership requires a combination of training, experience, and confidence, particularly confidence. You cannot build up your employees' sense of competence if you have none of your own.

ABUSE IS A TRADITIONAL MANAGEMENT STRATEGY

In the industrial age, many abusive techniques were recommended, practiced, and taught as part of the training of professional managers. Nowadays this is called "Theory X Management."

Back in 1960, Douglas McGregor suggested that management tended to make one of two assumptions about human nature. These assumptions, McGregor argued, determined how a company was run and how employees were treated. He called the two assumptions Theory X and Theory Y.

According to Theory X, most workers are lazy, unmotivated, and immature. Management based on this assumption uses carrots and sticks to get employees to work, provides strong control and direction, and offers workers little autonomy and responsibility.

Theory Y, on the other hand, is the assumption that people need to work to achieve genuine self-fulfillment and that they are willing to accept responsibility if it is offered. This approach leads to a management style that encourages employee participation and the exercise of individual initiative and creativity.

Management theorists have argued back and forth about these assumptions and whether or not they work in practice. Abraham Maslow conducted experiments in an electronics factory and found that Theory Y has a few holes: People are not motivated in all situations; their readiness to accept responsibility varies depending on the tasks they do and the circumstances under which they work.

What is interesting about McGregor's work is not the actual content of the assumptions about human motivation and maturity. There are times when human beings are lazy and do not care about their work, and there are times when they are so committed that they will gladly go above and beyond the call of duty.

What Theory X and Theory Y say to us is that the assumptions we make about people, *whatever those assumptions may be,* affect the way we treat employees and thereby create a certain kind of corporate culture. Pick an assumption, any assumption. Let's call it Theory Q. It says that all workers, given the opportunity, will steal from their employer. This leads to a corporate culture that relies heavily on surveillance and the deterrence of crime, even when this interferes with the work being done.

Where do we get these assumptions about people? Let's take an example from a psychology course. The professor asked students to complete the statement "People are . . ." The responses from different people in the course ranged from "People are complex and unpredictable" to "People are incapable of real change" to "People are basically honest."

After a certain amount of head scratching, one student wrote "People are not good and evil; they are good and scared." The instructor then told everyone to cross out the first two words and substitute "I am . . ."

The students stared at the results: "I am complex and unpredictable," "I am incapable of real change," "I am basically honest," and, of course, "I am good and scared."

We assume people are like us. Managers who treat employees as lazy, unreliable good-for-nothings are probably trying to overcompensate for their own faults by suppressing these traits in other people. When this abusive style permeates an entire corporation, you can be sure that the people who designed the structure and systems are trying to replicate the structures and systems *they* need to feel secure and able to function as managers. That's what structures and systems are for. If we are forgetful, we create systems that build in timely reminders. If we are disorganized, we make systems that impose organization. If we are sloppy, we make the system precise. People build counterweights to their own failings into the system.

Management consultants, who are human, too, often make the same mistake, recommending solutions that solve their own problems, not the client's. Quite a few of them have a grab bag of familiar solutions, and they go from company to company looking for problems that fit them. This shows up again and again in our work, especially in companies that have been "consulted to death." Likewise, the management gurus who write the books about excellence or quality or leadership tend to analyze their own problems in these books, just as Sigmund Freud's books describe nobody quite as well as Freud himself.

MANAGERS HAVE UNRESOLVED PERSONAL PROBLEMS

Alcoholic bosses, depressive bosses, manic bosses—we've all worked for one or two. At one rather old-fashioned company, the VP of sales used to spend every afternoon in his favorite bar. The waitresses knew him well and took messages when employees needed to get hold of him quickly. Although he was a fairly gentle drunk who got progressively sentimental as the afternoon wore on, the department was demoralized nonetheless because he would never authorize any changes or unusual expenditures and because he was blocking the promotion of a number of hardworking subordinates.

In other companies dysfunctional bosses don't have the decency to take themselves to a bar; they stick around and make employees miserable as a way of dealing with their own inner demons. Abusive behavior is often the symptom of some deeper problem, such as a feeling of help-lessness, low self-esteem, or fear. The dysfunctional way to deal with these problems is to act the opposite of how one feels, thereby repro-ducing the same problems in other people. We call this the Cycle of Abuse.

Abuser's True Feelings		Abuser's Behavior		Employee's Feelings
Low self-esteem	→	Criticism	→	Low self-esteem
Helplessness	→	Controlling	→	Helplessness
Fear	→	Aggression	→	Fear
Hurt	→	Abusiveness	→	Hurt
Self-hatred	→	Blaming	→	Self-hatred

This kind of abuse can be seen in families as well as corporations and is familiar to family psychologists and therapists. The abuser's feelings are passed on to "family" members at work, and they come to demonstrate the abuser's psychological systems. However, since corporations are bigger than families, cyclical abuse has the potential to do even more widespread damage.

RIGID MANAGEMENT SYSTEMS ARE EASIER TO MAINTAIN

Think back to the professors you had in college. Chances are, you can remember several good lecturers. Now try to remember those who knew how to run effective seminars, in which everyone spoke up and contrib-uted and real debates took place. At most, you will probably come up with only one or two names.

Lecturing is one-way communication, and it isn't that hard to do, particularly if the professor is recycling last year's material. Leading a seminar or tutorial, however, requires getting other people to contrib-ute, drawing out ideas and information that students have locked in their heads. Those who are shy or who find speaking out difficult must be encouraged to participate. Students must be allowed to make mistakes and even discuss their wrong answers before the professor jumps in with the right answer. This is how students learn.

It is also how employees learn. Unfortunately, many managers are no better at encouraging participation than most professors. It is much easier simply to tell people what to do and then punish them if they don't do it. Allowing people to make mistakes and learn from them is time-consuming and risky. That's why so many managers have trouble delegating work. The problem is that this type of management breeds employees who can't make decisions and who won't take on responsibility.

UNCERTAINTY CREATES FEAR

The world of work is changing rapidly and unpredictably. What worked yesterday doesn't work anymore. Obvious solutions have gone the way of hen's teeth. This makes many managers extremely nervous. They feel that events are slipping out of their control. The only way to regain control is to bear down on employees and force them to follow orders, even if the orders are wrong.

Abusing employees doesn't make the uncertainty go away, even if it makes some people feel a bit better for a moment or two. One freshly hired insurance executive met with his managers for the first time and gave them what he thought was a pep talk. "The one thing I won't tolerate is fear," he thundered. Not surprisingly, his team responded to the mixed message by shifting their eyes and consulting their briefing notes. Where before they were welcoming, now they were wary. This was an uncomfortable start to a new working relationship, but finding functional ways to cope with uncertainty is going to be one of the biggest challenges of the twenty-first century.

ABUSE IS THE PREVAILING NORM IN
A CORPORATE CULTURE

Changing an individual is hard work. Changing a company is extremely hard work. And changing a corporate culture is such hard work that, if it weren't a matter of corporate survival, few people would have the nerve to try.

Corporate cultures may embed abusive behaviors in a way that perpetuates abuse. Sometimes people who have been in an abusive culture for a long time stop noticing that it is abusive because the suppression of ideas or the squashing of individual initiative and innovation has become the norm.

In the next section we will take a closer look at corporate cultures, three kinds in particular: the Culture of Sacrifice, the Win/Lose Culture, and the Culture of Blame. These are the kinds of cultures that kill ideas. The Culture of Sacrifice does it by exhausting and depleting employees' resources until they have nothing left to give. The Win/Lose Culture kills any idea that can't outshout, outgun, and outmaneuver the competition. The Culture of Blame kills ideas by the direct approach: Anything new is hammered down like a nail that sticks up in the wrong place.

What follows isn't pretty. It may, however, be all too familiar.

Working in an Uncivilized World

WORKING IN AN
UNCIVILIZED WORLD

Humans live in communities and each community has its own culture. Cultures are "historically created designs for living. . . ." Culture also embraces forms of social organization, rules and laws, ideas and beliefs, morals and religion. Within each culture certain types of personality and certain forms of motivation are encouraged and become prevalent.

—Michael Argyle

fOR THOSE OF US who spend most of our waking hours at work, the workplace has become our world. The company we work for has become our community, a community with its own culture, rules, and systems. The culture of a company dictates what is acceptable behavior and who or what will be rewarded or punished.

Although companies are often compared to complicated machines, they are much more like a town or village. Since a company is a living entity, made up of people, this may seem rather obvious, but it is important to understand the significance of what happens when people, rather than jobs or functions or parts, come together to work cooperatively.

Just as one village will have customs that differ from those in a neighboring village in the same region, various companies and even individual offices of the same corporation can differ substantially from each other. If you have ever traveled through Europe, you have probably observed how vastly different cultures can exist within a small geographical region. Some of the differences are instantly recognizable, such as language or local dialect, but you may have to live in Europe a very long time to pick up the more subtle distinctions between cultures. Acceptable behavior in one region may be taboo in another.

In our corporations the cultural differences between offices can be so subtle that we can't even articulate them. That doesn't mean we don't absorb and accommodate them. Just as getting off a train in a new town entails struggling to find our bearings, hiring on at a new company or undergoing a dramatic leadership change means getting to know the people and the way they do things in "their little corner of the world."

A cog in a wheel is predictable—what you see is what you get. An individual is the opposite. The individual is not a measurable entity. He or she can react in an infinite number of ways to a multitude of stimuli. What determines how we behave is a combination of what we have learned and absorbed from each day of our existence and what lives in the mysterious region of our soul.

No person walks through the doors of a company without baggage. We come with a lifetime of experiences, both positive and negative, which, thread by thread, have created the fabric of who we are. Similarly, company cultures are initially created by the founders of the company, but they change over time and successive leaderships.

Advertising guru David Ogilvy is an example of the entrepreneurial spirit, forceful character, and strong opinions that you often find in the founder of a successful company. He built an empire of multinational advertising agencies. Fifty years later, the culture he put in place still thrives. If you walk into an Ogilvy & Mather agency today, you will probably see some young men wearing the same red suspenders David Ogilvy favored.

If the company prospers, eventually the founder will be succeeded by other leaders who put their own stamp on the company culture. The evolution of the industry will also transform the company culture over the years. Thus, while you will still find red suspenders at Ogilvy & Mather today, you will also find cultural attitudes that differ from those in the days when the company was run by Ogilvy.

Corporate culture is one of those concepts that everyone intuitively understands as "the way we do things around here." In their book, *Corporate Cultures: The Rites and Rituals of Corporate Life,* Terrence Deal and Allan Kennedy define it as "a cohesion of values, myths, heroes, and symbols that has come to mean a great deal to the people who work there."

Corporate cultures became news in the 1980s, in part because of Japan's increasing dominance in world trade and finance. Suddenly people were fascinated by Japanese methods and wondered if the secret of Japan's success lay in corporate cultures that were strong and rigid. Another reason for the interest in corporate cultures was the glut of mergers taking place during that decade. Some very different corporate cultures collided during mergers, and more than half the mergers failed as a result. It is easy to take a culture for granted when one is inside it, just as a fish takes water for granted, but when mergers bring two different cultures together, culture suddenly becomes obvious, an issue to be dealt with.

Corporate culture is a form of control whereby rules and regulations are internalized by employees. Self-control is the strongest and most reliable form of control possible, so a strong corporate culture with committed employees who effectively discipline themselves makes for a very tightly controlled organization. Not surprisingly, it is notoriously difficult to change corporations with strong cultures.

The strength of a corporate culture can also be its weakness. One problem with culture is that it is easy to become a victim of one's own success. What worked in the past gets repeated over and over, even when everything else in the world is changing. Moreover, some cultures are based on faulty notions, and once these are embedded, they are perpetuated as surely as correct ones.

A centralizing belief in quality or integrity or in putting safety first unifies employees and gives them a common sense of purpose. This is the vital function of a culture. Problems arise when the culture becomes more important than the individuals within it. When this happens, diversity is obliterated and independent thinking is smothered. When innovation is restricted to certain jobs and is not welcomed from frontline workers or anybody else within the organization, an enormous source of useful and profitable ideas is suppressed and wasted.

There is a school of thought that suggests that success comes with a culture that is all things to all employees, whatever that culture may be. The business bestseller in the early 1980s, *In Search of Excellence*, seems to endorse this view, although by now we all know that some of the "excellent" companies are a little battered and bruised. This quotation from *A Passion for Excellence* always sends a chill down our spines:

> We have found that the majority of passionate activists who hammer away at the old boundaries have given up family vacations, little league games, birthday dinners, evenings, weekends and lunch hours, gardening, reading, movies and most other pastimes. We have a number of

friends whose marriages or partnerships crumbled under the weight of their devotion to a dream. . . . Excellence is a high-cost item.

Most people would react to this kind of obsessiveness with a shudder. Still, many people are deluded into thinking they are working for a kinder, gentler corporation simply because the firm organizes all sorts of extra-work activities. The question to ask is what purpose the activities serve. Are they designed to give employees an opportunity to relax and socialize, or are they intended to absorb their nonwork time until they are stuck to the corporate culture like bugs on flypaper?

It is important to remember that people experience cultures differently. For example, Pierre, a graphic designer, moved from a government bureaucracy to a small advertising company. He found his job much more interesting, but he was bothered by the non-work-related activities that seemed to be an essential aspect of life at the new company. Pierre didn't want to join the baseball team; he was bored by the family picnics; he dreaded the motivational seminars at which emotional outpourings seemed to be expected. He began to feel more and more isolated, since the culture seemed to demand participation in all these activities and his avoidance of them was regarded as a form of disloyalty to the company.

> The pressure to conform was enormous. I mean, people there seemed to think that if you didn't play baseball, you didn't care about your work. They couldn't separate work and play; everything was part of the culture, even casual Fridays. When I came in wearing a suit one Friday because I was going to a wedding after work, I spent most of the day explaining myself. Perhaps it seems odd that these things were stressful to me, but they made me feel claustrophobic. I felt my privacy had been invaded. There was no "outside" for these people. Everything had to relate to the company. Eventually I moved to a job in a larger company where the culture was looser and more open and nobody asked what I did with my evenings and weekends.

For Pierre, the culture was abusive because he felt it was invading his privacy and pressuring him to conform to a stereotype he did not fit. However, most of the other people in the advertising firm probably did not experience the same problems, although we have a suspicion that this culture was not as open to diversity as it might have been.

Perhaps the most famous example of a strong corporate culture that can be intensely stressful is the Disney Corporation. In her book *Inside the Mouse,* Jane Kuenz describes working conditions for the people who wear the costumes and project the happy, smiling image that the tourists see. The pay is good, the benefits are excellent, and there appears to be an extensive network of clubs and sports teams. Yet employees talk about working at the "Rat." Rules are ruthlessly enforced, surveillance is routine, and socializing occurs within very narrow bounds in a highly stratified society. As one worker put it:

> You've got to keep your mouth shut. You can't tell them your opinion. You have to do everything they say. The Disney way. Never say anything negative. Everything's positive. There's never a no. You never say I don't know. If you don't know something you find out fast, even on your own after work.

Another employee remarked:

> They look for someone who can follow the rules, be a team player, never rock the boat no matter what the circumstances.

This is where strong corporate cultures become abusive. They go too far in the demands they make and kill individual initiative.

For a great many employees, dominant corporate cultures are a security blanket. They want to belong, and if that means putting up with rules, discipline, and a lack of privacy, then so be it. By complying, of course, they are sending a message that this kind of corporate behavior is OK. Companies that fit this profile often claim that employees accept the culture as one of the conditions of work. Abuse? Not us, the companies say in hurt disbelief.

In fact, this is abuse at its most insidious—manipulative under a sugar-coated guise of caring. The family atmosphere is really a sham to control employees. It is interesting to see how closely the observations from people working at the "Rat" fit in with Robert Subby's description of manipulation and denial in the addictive family system.

Nine Rules for Dysfunctional Families

1. It is not OK to talk about problems.

2. Feelings should not be expressed openly.

3. Communication is best if indirect.

4. Be good, strong, right, and perfect.

5. Make us proud.

6. Don't be selfish.

7. Do as I say and not as I do.

8. It is not OK to play or be playful.

9. Don't rock the boat.

In the context of the dysfunctional corporation, these nine "rules" might look like this:

1. do not discuss the undiscussable;

2. feelings are undiscussable in the workplace;

3. never say exactly what you mean to the person who most needs to hear it;

4. one mistake and you're out;

5. we'll take credit for your good ideas and punish you for your failures;

6. everything you are belongs to the company;

7. do as we say and don't ask questions;

8. you're not here to enjoy yourself; you're here to work;

9. don't try to change anything.

Some people feel they have no choice, that they must tolerate abuse to keep their jobs. Others may be vulnerable for personal reasons: they go looking for a family substitute in the work world and accept the dysfunctional corporation as normal because their own family was dysfunctional. Certain corporations are not above exploiting the weakness, dependency, and vulnerability of their employees.

The glue that holds many of these cultures together is ideology. At its best, ideology can be a unifying force that gives a company focus and direction. But there is a downside. Management professor Henry Mintzberg notes: "Ideologies cause people to look within the organization for direction. Too much of this and the organization loses touch with its context, closes in on itself. . . . We have no need for the extreme example of a Jonestown to appreciate the negative consequences of ideology."

Strong corporate cultures forestall diversity in the workplace when they become monocultures. As Hugh Willmott of the Manchester School of Management puts it, "Cultural diversity is dissolved in the acid bath of the core corporate values." Many of the most intolerant political regimes in history have been based on strong national cultures. Even apparently benign cultures can trample individual and cultural differences if they are allowed to become too strong. Diversity in the workplace demands open cultures, a readiness to accept differences and to allow different approaches to work.

Many people and companies that are mired in an abusive culture are profoundly affected on a daily basis. In the next chapter we will look at true stories of corporate abuse and how they affected people and their families. Make no mistake: just as you take family pressures into work with you in the morning—no matter how well suppressed or camouflaged—you take work tensions back home in the evening.

The stories are grouped according to the characteristics of the abusive culture in which they occurred. Defining corporate cultures is not as simple as black and white because many different kinds of abuse can be found in a single organization, but after studying the different cultures of abuse, we found they generally tended to take the following forms:

- The *Culture of Sacrifice,* in which excessive demands are made of employees. Over the last decade the restructuring of companies has left many holes for the remaining workers to fill, leading to the abuse of overwork. Often these organizations operate in a continual "crisis mode," and employees are expected to make great personal sacrifices for the survival of the company. Employees burn out, and absenteeism and high stress levels take their toll on business sooner rather than later, resulting in poor performance levels. These all-or-nothing workplaces demand such complete identification with the work that nothing is left of the individual. Employees can work as hard as they like as long as they don't think for themselves.

- The *Win/Lose Culture,* in which employees are forced to compete with each other for pay, promotion, and perks. Abusive cultures can even come out of national values that have shaped countries.

In North America the competitive spirit is so highly valued that many companies have created teams of individuals to compete with one another in the same organization. But the competitive spirit can make people forget who the real competition is. In the process competition can damage lives and whole industries. It is time to explode the myth that the best man or woman wins. It is the best at winning who wins, and sometimes winners' ideas are real losers.

- The *Culture of Blame,* in which somebody is always at fault. Typically in this culture the company rewards or punishes individual performance rather than group effort. This type of company is likely to operate day to day on an informal "star and demerit" system that puts a number of behaviors in motion. From the employee's point of view, the objective is to be seen as the person doing the good work or conversely not to be seen as the person who has made a mistake. If the Culture of Blame is in place, scapegoats are found and employees spend a great deal of time protecting themselves from the inevitable finger-pointing that ensues. Conforming and following rules becomes the order of the day—no matter whether the rules make sense or not.

These are not mutually exclusive definitions. Aspects of two or three different cultures emerge in some of the following stories. However, these distinctions may help you to sort through your own experiences.

THE CULTURE OF SACRIFICE

SUPPOSE YOU GO for an interview with a company that you've always admired. This company seems to have it all: interesting work, great opportunities, hard-working professional people, and prestige.

The president of the company is very affable. He shakes your hand, offers you coffee, and proceeds to tell you about the company. He is extremely enthusiastic about the possibility of you working for them. He says to you:

> We really need someone with your skills here. You're the kind of person who can help this company soar. There's no limit to the amount of profit this company can make with people like you giving 150 percent every day, morning, noon, and night, seven days a week if necessary. If you join us you'll become part of a team that never says "I can't" or "No." You'll be able to test your limits and go far beyond what you ever thought possible.
>
> To be successful here, all you have to do is work hard and put the company first, before your family, before your friends, your hobbies, and your dreams. Everything in your life outside the company has to be put on hold. If you're not prepared to do this, don't come to work here. It's a demanding job, but as long as you perform, you'll be rewarded. Of course, we can't guarantee how long we'll need you, but that's a risk you take anywhere these days.

He stands up, shakes your hand again, and says he hopes you'll join the company. It will be a privilege and a great opportunity for you to work there.

What the president has just described to you is the essence of the Culture of Sacrifice. Unfortunately, few of us who find ourselves working in such a culture have been so clearly warned. The demands and the expectations are much more insidious and are only revealed over time.

Initially, it is easy to be seduced by the challenge of sacrifice. We concur with the philosophy of "no pain, no gain" and we pump ourselves up to meet our responsibility to the company. After all, we're well paid, and the more we do for the company, the more we'll share in its success.

Greater success will mean more money to enrich our lives and fulfill our heart's desires. So we work until late at night and on weekends. We give up vacation time. We uproot our families and go wherever in the world the company needs us to go. We rise to the challenge to pull the company out of yet another crisis, and we jump higher every time the company decides it's time to raise the bar.

Many workers can't shake the feeling that they have to keep producing, regardless of the time of day or how many hours they've put in. They feel as if they're not meeting employers' expectations even though they're putting in as many as ninety hours a week. An executive we know complains of getting faxes and phone messages from workers at all hours of the night. It may be pressure to live up to actual standards, implicitly or explicitly understood, or it may be that workers are not given a clear sense of exactly what is expected of them from management.

In many cases the time crunch is driven by the struggle to keep up with expanding workloads. For many others it's a basic matter of survival. Not able to meet expenses on the salary provided by a single job, many workers are resorting to part-time employment to supplement their incomes. Even though their full-time jobs may have reasonable time requirements, these people are getting overextended trying to make ends meet.

Ironically, the growth of technology is also responsible for ballooning work hours. Many companies are taking advantage of current technology to move employees out of the office—a cost-cutting move—and into their own at-home or mobile workplaces. While this development may seem like a way of freeing workers by allowing them more flexibility in controlling their time, in fact the opposite phenomenon is being observed, if the case of John is any example.

John works for one of the large management consulting firms. The firm has time-stamped voice mail that records both the time of the message and the interval before a response is registered. John's boss sends him messages at all hours of the day and night. Because John wants to show his boss he's listening, he sets his alarm for 5 A.M. so he can get out of bed to answer his voice mail. What's really happening is that John's boss is keeping him under surveillance by voice mail.

With everyone working flat out in a Culture of Sacrifice, the company is initially very productive, but ultimately the quality is unsustainable. Over time we realize we have made a commitment with our minds and bodies that our souls can't keep. The long hours rob us of time with family, friends, and the world outside. Without time to replenish our souls, we can't work as effectively and powerfully as before. Our ideas grow stale, and we stop caring about the quality of our work.

A company with a Culture of Sacrifice seldom recognizes the needs of individuals. A former executive at Texas Air blamed the company's "rampant divorce rate" on bizarre working hours that saw people regularly putting in fourteen-hour days and six-day weeks. If people don't perform, the pressure is increased. Any request to lessen the pain is regarded as an inability to cut the mustard, and any employee who attempts to take time off to attend to personal or family matters is seen as weak and uncommitted.

The worst examples of a company invading family time come from Jim Miller, CEO of Miller Business Systems and author of a book called *Corporate Coach*. He organized a national contest in 1993 offering a free trip to Hawaii for two for the person who submitted a written description of the most gruesome boss. The winner was a sales manager who said his boss demanded that employees produce obituaries to verify their relationship to the deceased if they wanted to take time off to attend a funeral. This boss also wrote a memo threatening to fire anybody who adjusted the office thermostat. The runner-up in the worst-boss contest was a woman who claimed her boss called her at home while she was in labor and continued the conversation for twenty minutes even though she "alerted him each time a new contraction was beginning."

In a Culture of Sacrifice, people are driven by feelings of responsibility to the company. This is particularly true for those who link loss of performance with loss of self-esteem. These people become the company workaholics. Workaholics get caught up in a never-ending mission to gain control by devoting more and more time to work, to the exclusion of virtually everything else. If they slow down or relax, they worry they will be seen as slackers or incompetents. In their quest to be "good enough," they draw themselves and others into a working frenzy that focuses on quantity rather than quality, aggressively pushing the company and fellow workers to the point of collapse.

Failure is inevitable in this culture. These companies operate on the assumption that the company is more important than its workers, and they are prepared to sacrifice excellent workers to prove the point.

When employees have been with the company for some time, they begin to realize that perhaps the sacrifices are too great. The time and effort the job demands and the strain of corporate transfers on their loved ones reveal a picture far different from the one they imagined. Finally they understand that the rewards the company offers are not enough. How could they be? What would be worth losing their souls?

In his book *The Age of Paradox,* Charles Handy defines productivity as "more and better work from fewer people." If we accept this definition, then employers have to ask themselves, are they really getting more for their money by driving workers to pick up the slack created by downsizing and other efficiency measures? Or is the exhaustion and demoralization of a spiritually starved workforce costing them in creativity and output?

The stories in this chapter demonstrate the various abuses found in this culture, from the soul-destroying day-to-day demands on personal time to the ultimate pain of sacrificing careers. The business case is clear. Exhaustion does not leave energy for creating ideas, and self-doubt saps people's confidence for taking risks. And those are two key ingredients for success in the information age.

THE RAVAGES OF TIME

Beth, thirtyish, is a lawyer who left her profession to raise her family. Her husband, Tom, is also a lawyer and was recently named a partner in a prominent, nationally known law firm. Beth gave up her career, she says, partly because she didn't enjoy practicing law but also because she and her husband realized it would be impossible for them to meet the responsibilities of family life and the demands of two law careers.

Tom's firm requires its partners to bill a minimum of 2,100 hours a year. According to Beth:

> Billable hours don't include the time you have to spend on client development, instructing associates, interacting with your secretary about day-to-day business, or just going to the washroom. It's not

uncommon to put in one-third or one-half again as much time on unbillable work as on client hours.

In real time that means Tom leaves the house at 7:00 A.M. and usually returns at around 11:30 P.M. His weekends are spent working at the office, traveling, or at client meetings while Beth takes on the challenge of caring for three young daughters.

> I didn't intentionally buy into the job of being the single mother of three children, but that's the way it's worked out. I'm pretty resigned to the fact that I'm a "work widow" and that I'll spend a lot of time alone with my children.

For ambitious young professionals there has always been some sacrifice required in terms of time and toil But this phenomenon, and the extremes to which it's carried, is growing. In the law profession, for example, it has traditionally been expected that young associates put in long hours to pay their dues and earn their partnerships. The partners, having sacrificed so much in their youth, could pace themselves and enjoy more hard-earned leisure time. But today even partners are on the line, and they must constantly keep up their billable hours or even make a surplus to hold onto their positions. Beth says:

> I've noticed that among the older partners, the ones who choose to have more of a life are the ones with less power and influence. That's a hard choice for an ambitious young person to make.

What happens to individuals who are driven to give up any respite from the pressures of their jobs? Beth relates the toll it takes on her family:

> Your family is more than just a beautiful picture on your desk. We want Tom's company; we need him around more. It's rare that the two of us get to have an actual conversation, and theres no time to just sit and play with the girls. Instead, we wind up trying to enforce these artificial bonding sessions. If he's got a Sunday at home, we have to seize the moment for "family time" because he's available, regardless of how the girls are feeling or what we really want to do.

For Tom, there's a double price to pay. The pressure is on, of course, to spend any free time with his wife and daughters. He misses being part of the day-to-day, easy routine he sees between Beth and the girls. On the other hand, Tom has a serious interest in the outdoors and fishing; these activities give him a deep sense of satisfaction and fill him with a sense of peacefulness and balance. When those rare moments of downtime present themselves, he feels a genuine conflict between the need for a real connection with his family and the need for solitude. What happens to people who are forced on an ongoing basis to give up the things that define them as individuals, the things that keep them grounded, that provide satisfaction and solace? We've reached a point where the notion of having fun seems contradictory to making a living.

For Beth and Tom and for too many families, the conflict cannot be resolved without facing the real issue. Says Beth:

> When he's frustrated, Tom winds up feeling like it's his family that's keeping him from doing the other things he loves to do. I have to remind him how little of his time we really have. If he wants more time for himself, it will have to come from his work hours because he can't cut us back much more and still survive as a family.

Even so, Beth recognizes her husband's dilemma, having worked in the profession herself.

> I know what he faces there. You're either in the game or out of it, and if you choose to be in it, you do whatever it takes. It's competitive. You're getting pressure from the firm because if you don't kill yourself for them, some other lawyer will. And the whole world operates on a tight clock these days. Clients want it done yesterday, and if you can't do it they'll find another firm that will.

ANALYSIS

Cultures of Sacrifice use employees the way Pony Express riders used ponies: they ride them until they drop and then get a replacement. Those who are not prepared to offer unlimited hours to the job are considered unprofessional, uncooperative, and unwilling to renounce their self-interest for the greater good of the company. In the nineteenth century, bosses could say with impunity, "Don't show up on Monday if you don't come in on Sunday," keeping employees in line with the naked fear of losing their livelihood. Today the threat is more veiled, but workers know if they aren't willing to put in the hours, they could risk losing advancement, pay raises, and their very jobs.

In the battle to keep down costs, companies wind up understaffed and overextended. Under pressure to meet expanding workloads, employees are expected to put in overtime or stay at their desks until the work is done. In the United States the average employee puts in forty-seven hours a week, and the figure is rising. Some estimates say that figure will reach sixty hours a week in just twenty years. This may well be a false economy, for without time and relaxation for replenishment, ideas grow stale. As the quantity of hours goes up, the quality of the work goes down.

Despite the high cost of sacrificing rest, replenishment, and relationships, employees have been willing to keep their noses to the grindstone for increasing periods of time for pretty compelling reasons. In many cases the additional hours are necessary just to stay on top of their jobs; decreased staffing means increased workloads. Also, the competitive climate demands that companies respond to client "needs," including unrestricted availability and fast, often unreasonable deadlines.

The competition for advancement is so overheated that anyone who expects to rise to the top has to perform well above the level of co-workers. And in an environment where the indiscriminate axing of competent employees is the accepted norm, workers feel compelled to demonstrate their loyalty and dedication as a means of gaining whatever advantage they can.

Burnout, depression, fatigue, mistakes, and divorce can be the consequences of time abuse. For families like Beth and Tom's, the result is estrangement, conflict, and tension. But for many, the cost escalates far beyond anything that can be justified by business or human standards. The body and mind can literally break down. Exhaustion leads to illness. Depression leads to despair. When the cycle goes uninterrupted, the consequences can be extreme. In Japan they call the syndrome *karoshi,* or "death from overwork," and the condition isn't confined to the Japanese.

> Five years ago I was working for a law firm in Philadelphia. One night, a senior partner came in and dumped a huge load of files on my desk and told me he wanted an analysis done by morning. I worked through the night. At about six in the morning, when I thought I was nearly finished, I found a document that changed the entire complexion of the case. I nearly went crazy. I was really tempted to hide the document, even though I knew it wouldn't be ethical. Eventually I explained the problem to the senior lawyer. He was furious, but he told me that he'd stall the client while I fixed up my brief. I finally left the office at ten the following evening. I'd had about half an hour's sleep in more than thirty-six hours, and I could hardly focus, I was so exhausted. I remember

standing at the train station, staring at the tracks, thinking vaguely that it would be so easy to step off and just leave all my problems behind.

I didn't do it. I went home, slept around the clock, came in at noon, and resigned. Now I have a job selling office furniture to offices, including several law firms. In my job, I sometimes get glimpses of young lawyers who are going through what I went through, and I wonder how many of them stare at train tracks, thinking how easy it would be . . .

—*Ingrid, a former lawyer*

For other people, the long hours lead them to cram in the fun part. Some people drink too much or party too much. Others spend every weekend on the golf course or the ski slopes, every lunch hour at the fitness club, trying to wear out their bodies to match their worn-out minds.

Time abuse leads to some very vicious circles. People have to pay for the things they no longer have the time to do themselves—things like preparing meals, caring for children, walking the dog, cleaning the house. Then they have to work even harder to continue to pay for all these services. Meanwhile, latchkey children come home to empty houses, meals are eaten on the run, and simple, everyday chores are neglected. The fabric of the family and of social interactions begins to unravel. Simple joys and pleasures get lost in the scramble to beat the clock. Children don't get hugged, gardens go uncultivated, conversations are left unspoken, porch swings sit unoccupied. Lest the busiest among us dismiss all of this as so much unsophisticated nonsense, let's not forget that humans are spiritual beings, not machines. We need more than a paycheck to keep us running.

For the business, the implications of time abuse should be obvious. Exhausted employees are prone to making errors and bad decisions, which can cost the business money and client loyalty. At one company the lawyer with the largest number of billable hours was found to have taken a few ethical shortcuts in order to keep up the pace of his work. The resulting news stories cost the firm several high-profile clients, and it had to make severe cutbacks in order to survive. Last we heard, it was still on the critical list.

Until these kinds of firms recognize the simple fact that time abuse does not increase long-term profitability or ensure sustainability, the best solution for individuals will be finding a firm that does not make unreasonable demands or starting a new firm with like-minded colleagues who have a more balanced approach to family and career. For young lawyers, desperate for a job in a tight market, the choices seem to be few.

If you are caught in a Culture of Sacrifice, try to scale down your lifestyle or negotiate work-at-home arrangements whenever possible. This may not cut down on your work hours, but at the very least it saves commuting time and allows you to eat more meals with your family. If you are able to schedule a vacation or even a short weekend break, choose a location where work cannot interfere. A cottage with no telephone. A remote bed-and-breakfast that will not take messages. Do not check your voice mail. Cultures of Sacrifice encourage employees to become defined by their jobs and discourage outside connections and interests; do not be drawn in. Always keep part of you for yourself.

WHAT'S THE REAL DEADLINE?

Cultures of Sacrifice often manufacture crises as a way of keeping up the pressure. They set unnecessarily tight deadlines, hint at nonexistent competition, tell employees that clients are unsatisfied even when this is untrue. Employees are hard-pressed to know which crises are real and which are simply created to force the pace of work. If they slack off, they may risk missing a real deadline.

Clients can, in fact, have as big an impact on time tyranny as employers. Nora, a young producer working for a production company in New York, found herself at the whim of her supervisors, driven by the unreasonable demands of their clients. Commuting to work from twenty minutes outside the city, she would catch the last bus home at 1:00 A.M. and the first bus back in at 6:30 A.M. This schedule would continue for months at a time with short lag periods in between.

> My friends joked that I would have to have my briefcase surgically removed from my hand. The trouble was that clients would say, "I need that videotape by Tuesday," and the bosses would never say, "No way." They were so afraid the clients would go to another production house, they just kept saying yes, no matter how ridiculous the request. And then we, the grunts, would have to deliver. We all got to be really close because none of us had lives away from work. The ones who couldn't keep up with the hours or the pressure got dumped, and a new, energized body would be brought in to fill the gap.

The crowning insult, in Nora's eyes, was the sheer futility of it all.

Sometimes we were working to meet a real show date or something concrete. But most of the time we'd kill ourselves to deliver a program, only to have it sit on some middle manager's desk until he got around to showing it to his boss. It seemed like they created this sense of urgency just because they could. Their priorities were never questioned because they called the shots. Meanwhile, we were dropping like flies.

ANALYSIS

Sooner or later it is time to ask what all the work is for. What are we really getting out of it? Unless the work itself is deeply satisfying, we are not in a position to enjoy what it brings: money, reputation, material comforts. And on the rare occasions when we do get to revel in our wealth or possessions, the enjoyment is often short-lived. Jaguars and Jacuzzis don't really fill the void when our souls are worn threadbare and our family lives have fallen apart. If wealth and possessions were really a substitute for satisfying relationships, the Princess of Wales wouldn't have become a bulimic. If fame really meant more than self-esteem, Marilyn Monroe would not have been so unhappy and desperate for affection.

Roger von Oech, in his book *A Whack on the Side of the Head,* advises: "Going to a junk yard is a sobering experience. There you can see the ultimate destination of almost everything we desire." Perhaps even more pathetic and depressing are the yard sales of couples on the point of divorce. Try driving around a residential area some sunny summer Saturday if you need to be convinced that VCRs and food processors cannot glue a relationship together.

Get your priorities straight. What do you want your tombstone to say? "Top salesman of 1999" or "Devoted father and loving husband"? "The woman who produced a 380-page report in two weeks" or "Sorely missed by everyone in the community"? Remember Faust, who sold his immortal soul to Mephistopheles in return for youth and worldly knowledge? What are you getting in return for your soul?

In *The Age of Paradox,* Charles Handy states that modern commerce has turned time into a commodity. "Organizations are now re-thinking time for their own advantage, as if they had finally realized that there are actually 168 hours in the week, not 40. Sleeping assets make no money, so why shut them down for 128 hours a week when half of the world is awake?"

Increased working assets may seem to weigh in favor of the corporation, but are ever-expanding work hours really the most efficient way to boost productivity? When people are fatigued, the quality of their work drops and they're more likely to make costly or dangerous mistakes. Exhaustion can trip an individual's "survival mode" switch, wiping out ideas and creativity. Resentment at loss of control can turn workers into damaged souls who are not working at their optimum levels, despite their long hours.

Employers must begin to acknowledge the value of *creativity* above mere *activity*. Workers who are simply going through the motions or who are running twice as fast just to stay in the same place are being devalued as humans and as business assets. Cultures of Sacrifice fail to recognize that overwork actually reduces productivity and innovation and that long hours have nothing to do with an employee's value to a firm.

Cultures of Sacrifice tend to focus on short-term results, oblivious to the fact that their demands often increase staff turnover and decrease client loyalty. Moreover, with an exhausted workforce, there is little opportunity for establishing a unique difference from competing companies. Energy is expended on mere survival, not on long-term goals and strategic positioning.

In the meantime, employees must create their own survival strategies. If you find yourself in a Culture of Sacrifice, keep your wits about you and don't try to do everything. Network with colleagues and clients to find out what crises are real and which are manufactured. Design work tasks and activities so that you are always learning new skills that will benefit the company and you. Learn what is important for the business and concentrate on those jobs. In other words, if you have to select which tasks to tackle first, do those that fit into the corporate agenda. Be ruthless in turning down nonessential work.

Also, the more time you have to spend in the office, the better the environment must be. Don't settle for an uncomfortable chair, a desk that is the wrong height, or inadequate lighting. You have a right to demand the tools and equipment you need for your job.

Finally, keep up your profile outside your company. If you must stay at your desk, use the time to write articles for journals, research topics that interest you, plan seminars, do work for industry-wide committees. This will make your résumé more attractive when the time comes to move to a less insane company.

LOST IN THE SHUFFLE

Sometimes the maneuvers of a large corporation can seem like a game in which employees are moved from one position to another to benefit the company. In the process of grooming individuals for key positions, it's not unusual for large corporations to try to keep as many people as possible in the game and on the move, even if certain functions are duplicated in the process. Employees may be asked to move around the corporation or even around the world to broaden their experience, only to find their personal investment and sacrifice negated in the next corporate shuffle.

The effect of these transfers on employees, on their families, and on their co-workers is seldom a consideration in deciding who goes where. Employees are suddenly thrust into unfamiliar cultures, their families are uprooted, and coworkers must deal with constant reshufflings. Even when an employee is enthusiastic about the move, there are always problems of adjustment.

Gary was the president of the Australian branch of an international company. During his five years in Sydney, he had increased profits and built a strong client base. After being successful in Sydney, he lobbied to be transferred back to New York in hope of becoming president of the New York office.

Roger, the co-CEO of the company in charge of North America, thought highly of Gary and considered him something of a protégé. The two had kept in touch regularly, and Roger knew Gary wanted to return to New York. In January 1992, Gary got a phone call from Roger asking him to come to New York to talk about an urgent matter. Present at that meeting with Roger was Kurt, the other co-CEO, who was in charge of worldwide operations. They said, "We need you to become head of our largest account in Europe, Russia, and North Africa."

The account represented a huge amount of business—more than $250 million. Roger and Kurt stressed the importance of being a worldwide manager to Gary and how this type of international post was a better move for him than being president of the U.S. office. Gary would be based in Frankfurt and was to start immediately. He talked it over with his wife, Debbie, that night:

> We were unsure if it would be a good move from the business point of view . . . there were so many unknowns . . . but to be in Europe in 1992 was always talked about with great promise. From a personal point of

view, we thought it would be a terrific experience to live in Europe for three years.

Debbie said:

> We went back and forth about it. Should we go? Do we, or don't we? Gary would come home and say, "What do you think about this or that?" My intuition was, let's not do this and so was Gary's, but we got caught up in what it could be. All along Gary was getting the green light. The bosses were doing a real sales job on him.

A move to Frankfurt would have a great impact on Debbie:

> I was giving up everything I'd accomplished. I had become involved in local municipal politics and I was doing community work that was very important to me. I would have to start all over again in Frankfurt. I was concerned that there might not be similar community organizations in which I could make a contribution.

Within days Gary and Debbie were invited to dinner in New York to talk about the move. Roger focused a lot of attention on Debbie, and she thought the purpose of the dinner was to make her feel as comfortable as Gary. At the dinner Gary's boss told Gary that he believed in him and this would be the right thing for him. "You'll be doing this for me," he told Gary. "When I was asked, I went, and look what happened to me . . . CEO!" But Debbie was worried:

> Underneath I got the feeling he was saying, "If you don't go you'll regret it. You'll be saying no and letting the company down and digging your own grave." No one said this—it was just a sense I got. Kind of a veiled threat.

After the dinner in New York, Gary and Debbie talked about the move and what a great opportunity it seemed to be. A lot of the growth opportunities for the business were in Europe, and being successful there would mean Gary could return to New York in a very strong position. Debbie still wasn't convinced.

> My gut feeling was something about the job was bothering Gary. I think deep down he realized he was really happy in Sydney . . . he had an incredible career there . . . and deep down I don't think he wanted to leave. But neither of us communicated our gut feelings. And Gary was really being seduced by his bosses. On another level, the thought of living in Germany was really appealing to us. We started to get excited about experiencing a whole new way of life. Our friends were getting

excited too. They'd talk about how they would visit and we'd all have a great time. Everyone seemed to think it was a glorious opportunity and a real career move for Gary.

Gary went to Frankfurt to meet the president of the European region. The European managers wanted him to start as soon as possible. "We needed you yesterday!" they said. Gary felt he got on well with both the staff and the clients he met. Debbie went to Frankfurt also, to look for a place to live and to figure out how she could work there.

> When we went over to Frankfurt, I sought out various English-speaking community groups while Gary was in meetings. After a few meetings, I felt reassured that I would be able to make friends and find my place in Frankfurt through these groups and everything would be OK. Everything seemed to be OK for Gary too. . . . He liked the clients he met with and most of the people he would be working with. . . . There were a couple of people who were less friendly and forthcoming, but they really didn't alarm Gary, so he decided to accept the position.

Upon his return to Sydney, Gary started to write a formal contract with the New York office.

> I put in my contract that I wanted a guarantee that I could come back to a suitable position in New York and that I didn't want to take a financial hit with this move; in other words, I wanted it to be at least at the same salary or better. New York was slow to pull together a final agreement. I think they wanted to keep things loose and flexible, but I would have been foolish to expect things to get sorted out in Frankfurt. I pushed for a formal agreement. A couple of days later I got a fax with a very sketchy contract. It seemed to me to be so vague as not to have any value. On top of this they had chipped away at some of the things we had previously agreed to. For example, let's say my salary was to be $100,000; it became $95,000 in the contract. There were a number of things like this that were a little less than we had previously agreed to. I guess the alarm bells should have gone off at that point, but I knew these guys, so they didn't.

While Gary was negotiating his contract, Debbie was negotiating the move to Frankfurt.

> When I got into the logistics of the move, I asked to meet with some of the human resources people in New York. My sense when I talked to them was that they hadn't really done a lot of work in helping people to relocate. I had this niggling feeling that we were really on our own. When

I asked for some guidelines on living accommodations, they casually said, "Just go ahead. We'll back you." I felt uneasy about their lack of formality and structure about this whole business.

The next step for Gary was to appoint a replacement in the Sydney office. He felt confident that his next-in-command would do a great job as president of that office. He was an excellent manager and motivator of people and had the loyalty of the clients.

I went public and announced I was going to Frankfurt to be manager of Europe on a key piece of business and that Bruce would take over as president of the Sydney office.

Soon after making his formal announcement, Gary joined his wife in Frankfurt and they continued their search for an apartment. They found something that was comparable to the apartment they had in Sydney and reported to the Frankfurt office, asking them to help do the initial paperwork involved with the lease. At this point the president of the Frankfurt office told Gary that New York wasn't ready to commit to Gary taking the position.

I called New York immediately. I couldn't believe my ears. "What is going on?" I asked. They said that Kurt, the worldwide co-CEO, had been fired and the guys in Europe were upset about this because he was European. They saw Kurt as "their man" and now they didn't feel well-represented. In addition, they didn't like the idea that New York was sending them this expensive American—me—to run things.

When Debbie heard the news, she was in shock.

We went from green light to red light with no yellow light. I was very angry right away. As soon as we heard, we flew out of Frankfurt. I had previously arranged to have an operation, so I went right into the hospital and Gary flew directly to New York for meetings the next day.

When Gary got to New York, he was furious.

When I told them I was being treated very badly, they said, "Well, the CEO in Frankfurt didn't care for you anyway." I said, "So this is over?" and they said yes.

Debbie's take was that there was a turf war going on between the United States and Europe, and when the senior guy was ousted, it gave the European managers a chance to change the plan.

Gary had no idea this would be the case. He felt the strategy would be the same, but it all changed. When Gary came back to Sydney and said it was completely off, it was very hard for us. He couldn't believe it and he keep saying he was sorry.

On top of all these feelings was the fact that the company had arranged a going-away party for us, with clients and staff members there, and insisted we attend. It was very hard for Gary to stand up and say, "It's all off. We're not going and I don't know what is going to happen next." Everyone there was shocked and appalled. It was awful. The head office even sent a guy from New York because there would be clients at the party, and he was very blasé about everything. He really couldn't understand why we didn't feel like wining and dining him.

The bosses in New York never said they were sorry and never expressed any sense of concern. They have no sense of the toll this sort of thing takes on people. Afterwards, friends told us stories of how this person or that person was packed off and forgotten about. I was glad the whole thing blew up before we actually unpacked in Frankfurt because I have no doubt we would have just been cut loose in Frankfurt with our boxes and New York would have forgotten all about us.

When Gary asked, "What now?" Roger, the CEO of North American operations, told him to move to New York and they would try to find him a position.

I asked how long that would take, and they said, "Maybe a year or so." I was so upset. I said, "No, I want you to fire me. Pay me my salary and whatever else I have coming and just fire me!"

They agreed to this, but the impact on Gary was severe.

I felt hurt. I didn't know what was next. I lost some confidence and wondered how others would see this. How was it going to affect my career?

Debbie said:

Gary was shocked and sad. He just kept saying to me over and over again, "I'm sorry, I'm sorry." I was so wrenched by his saying that, so hurt for him.

As it happened, Debbie and Gary had booked a week's holiday on a faraway beach before they learned of the changes, and they decided to go ahead with their vacation. Debbie said:

It was just what we needed. We were both so wounded, and like wounded animals we went to ground to heal. It worked out very well.

Even on vacation, Gary kept asking, "What could I have done?" and kept saying, "I'm sorry." My response was "What could you have done differently? You did the rational thing at the time. Things were going on at different levels that you couldn't do anything about."

Gary went inward. He had experienced a death. The death of his career. He was "what he did," and he couldn't come to terms with who he was now. He didn't want to do anything and he didn't want to think. He just wanted to decompress. Next, we had to decide, do we stay in Australia or do we go back to New York? We decided to go back to New York because the opportunities there seemed more to our liking. Our apartment in Sydney wasn't selling, so we just started from scratch.

Gary took a job as a senior vice president and director of another large multinational company based in New York. When he accepted the new job, he asked for a month's delay in starting because he needed to relax. He liked the man who hired him and liked the fact that the company was still privately owned.

Debbie feels it was important for Gary to get back to work.

He was damaged by the Frankfurt experience and needed to get some confidence back, but I think the fun is gone for him. He wonders if the business has changed so much that he can't fit. Although he is working for a wonderful human being, he is doing a lot of soul searching. Even though he's back in the saddle, he's not sure he wants to ride anymore.

I think the business is cruel, and I'd like Gary to get out of it. Six years ago when he saw that I was struggling with a deep lack of fulfillment with my career, he gave me the luxury of finding out what I really wanted to do and what would make me happy. Now that I'm very clear and focused and know what a difference that time out made to me, I want to give him that luxury. I want him to stop and think and not be abused by the business anymore.

ANALYSIS

When we first approached Gary to tell us his story, he said, "I don't know whether my story could be called abuse or not." Many of the higher-level people we interviewed, particularly men, seemed unsure whether they had been abused. They have bought into the "all's fair in business" attitude so completely that they suppress their normal feelings and reactions. Yet many of them are so emotionally damaged by their experiences that they cannot continue in their careers. They assume that abuse consists simply of bullying or other obvious forms of unpleasant behavior; they do not realize that abuse is anything that kills ideas and creativity and ruins careers.

When we mentioned this observation to Gary, he said:

> I think that comes from two areas. As you climb up the ladder, you are put in the position of having to do things to people that are unfair, and you justify it to yourself: "Oh well, that's just business." The other problem is that your ego won't let you "grieve," as my wife puts it. Debbie has done a lot of counseling in her career and has constantly been at me to allow myself to grieve, but I just can't.

Women are usually socialized to reach out to others in times of crisis. They tend to express feelings of hurt or betrayal in the workplace more freely than men. A 1976 study asked 434 Americans, "Would you try very hard to control the way you showed your emotions in public?" Among men, 80 percent responded yes, a significant difference when contrasted with 70 percent of women. When Debbie heard the job was lost, she expressed her anger and grief right away. It is very clear to Debbie that Gary must acknowledge his pain in order to move on.

Gary was suddenly thrust into the middle of a complicated political game without realizing that he was a pawn, not a player. Obviously, the company needed someone to fill a very important position in Europe. When Gary voiced his interest in returning to New York, Roger and Kurt seized the opportunity to use Gary to fill their immediate need and overrode Gary's request. They seduced Gary into taking the Frankfurt job, and they did it without getting the full support of the company leaders in Europe.

The company was acting globally without thinking locally. Roger and Kurt showed a lack of respect for the European team by appointing Gary without giving the European team a chance to offer their own candidate or have any input in the selection process. Then they failed to take the time to convince the others of Gary's abilities and his appropriateness for the job. Consequently, they created a hostile environment ready to reject Gary on sight.

Gary was given just enough information to make him receptive to playing his role. However, by not making him fully aware of the big picture, Kurt and Roger rendered him powerless to help solve the discord with his European working partners and defenseless to protect himself and his own interests.

When Kurt was fired, Roger was left with a greater need to capitulate to the European team. The music had suddenly stopped in this game of musical chairs and Gary was left without a chair. He had given his Sydney seat to another, Roger had taken away the place in Europe, and there were no more chairs in sight.

Gary made two mistakes, however. First, he didn't listen to his own gut feelings. He told us that "alarm bells should have gone off"; they did, but he wasn't listening. Second, he took the irrevocable step of announcing his successor before the contract for his new position was signed, witnessed, issued in triplicate, and sealed. Never announce a move until you have a legally binding commitment from your new company.

This is particularly important in a culture like this, in which conflict does not occur in the open. In conflict-averse cultures, no one wants to confront issues openly in case there is disagreement. In order to side-step conflict, complicated webs of avoidance and deception are created. In this case the company didn't make a single clean decision all the way along the line. Initially they ignored Gary's request to return to New York. Then they didn't bring the European team into the process of filling the position in Europe. Then they avoided telling Gary that the Europeans were not keen on him for the position. Finally the web became so tangled that there was no choice but to make an abrupt and callous decision.

A conflict-averse culture can appear to be helpful, even friendly, on the surface, but refusing to deal with the initial confrontation in an open and honest manner often belies very selfish motives. In this case, as in many others, keeping everyone in the dark had some benefit to the people withholding information.

This company's indecisiveness was reflected in a number of ways. When asked why there were two CEOs of the company, Gary explained:

> Whenever they had a big job to fill, they would put two people in the position—co-chairmen, co-directors, and so on—then whoever turned out to please them more they would keep and let the other one go or move him somewhere else. I think in Kurt's case he was pushing for the job of sole CEO, and being such an intense guy, maybe he pushed a little too hard and fell out of favor somehow. Roger, on the other hand, was easygoing.

Roger's "easygoing" attitude is typical of a conflict-averse culture. It is, however, important to be able to distinguish between a leader who is sensitive and one who is simply trying to please everyone because he is afraid of confrontation.

Ultimately, this type of leader will avoid taking responsibility and being held accountable. His conflict-averse nature will repeatedly lead him to take a "Let it work itself out" approach. The problem with this thinking is that a situation often works itself out at the expense of someone else.

What has the company lost? It has lost an experienced senior employee with a good record of performance and sent a message to the remaining employees that good work and good faith mean little in the culture. It has wasted time and money on political charades that have soured relationships with overseas offices. Once again we see how Cultures of Sacrifice fail to consider the long-term implications of their demands. In this case we might even say that the company exchanged short-term pain for long-term pain. Not much of a bargain, is it?

"A BUSINESS DECISION"

Robert built his career within a large telecommunications company in the system sales management area. He sold systems to large retail companies and businesses throughout North America. He was always highly rated and was placed consistently as one of the top three sales managers in the country. Eventually, in addition to his region of New Jersey and New York City, Robert added the New England region and worked half of the time out of his Boston office. On one of these trips to Boston, Robert's life and career changed forever.

In May 1993, Robert took a cab from Logan airport, bound for a client meeting. As the taxi sped along the freeway, the driver suddenly lost control of the car and slammed into a dividing wall. Robert's body hit the heavy plastic divider between the back seat and the driver's seat with such force he broke several bones and suffered internal injuries. He was rushed to Massachusetts General Hospital, where he was operated on and stayed for three weeks.

The doctors estimated Robert would be in recuperation for six months. Fortunately, he had relatives in Boston, so it was convenient for him to stay there during his recuperation. While Robert was in the hospital, his colleagues and friends phoned regularly, as did his clients. However, his immediate boss, Ken, never spoke to Robert and never came to visit, even when he was in Boston on business. Robert was perplexed by this. He felt hurt and a little angry that his boss didn't seem to care about him.

Ken had joined the company as Robert's boss in February of that year, and Robert felt they had a good relationship. He also felt Ken trusted him and would often leave him in charge of serious business matters. So why was Ken the only one who didn't at least phone to see how he was feeling? Robert put these feelings aside and tried to focus on getting better. He was able to keep tabs on what was happening with his clients because his account executives called daily to ask him questions and discuss business. Although the doctors estimated that he wouldn't be able to return to work for six months, Robert felt strong and hoped to be back after four months.

A month before he planned to return to work, Robert wrote to Ken to say he hoped the doctor would give him the OK to return to work within a few weeks. He asked Ken to send him recent sales reports and other papers to bring him up to speed on what had happened during his absence, and mentioned some commission payments that were owing. He signed off, "Looking forward to getting back to work!"

About ten days passed and Robert hadn't heard from Ken, so he called Ken's secretary, who said he had read the letter a few days earlier. After a few more days, Robert called Ken to say that the doctor had told him that he could return to work immediately. But Ken seemed surprisingly evasive:

> He kind of hemmed and hawed and said, 'I'm not sure what I'm going to do. I need people who can give 120 percent and I don't think you'll be able to. I'm concerned from a business perspective." I couldn't believe my ears. I told him I was fine and could give 120 percent if I had to, that I always had and always would. I suggested that I stay in Boston and work out of the Boston office, but Ken said absolutely not and told me to come back to New Jersey. Then I asked him if he had read my letter and he said no.

A week later Robert went back to work. Ken smiled and shook Robert's hand and the two went straight into a staff meeting together.

> When we were back in Ken's office, Ken said that he had intended to put me back into my old job but that things had changed. "I've put Jack in your job and he's doing well; I don't want to change everything again." He suggested that I speak to the staff director and find another

position in the company. I said I thought that this was rather unfair, and he said, "It's just a business decision." I realized he had made up his mind.

I talked to the staff director, who was a friend of mine, and he found me the best job he could, but all the positions available were dead-end jobs that would probably be cut in the next round of layoffs. I worked in the marketing department, and I did a good job, but I wanted to be back in sales because that was where I really excelled. Some of my clients were upset about the change, and at this point in my career, I didn't want to start all over again.

I became extremely depressed for the first time in my life. I kept thinking how unfair it was. What had I done wrong? I couldn't think how I could have done a better job. I kept thinking that there had to be justice, but when I couldn't get any action out of human resources, I realized that I wouldn't get it.

My wife was understanding, but her attitude was "Just get on with it." But I couldn't; I was too devastated. My confidence was shattered. I guess to a large extent I was defined by my job. I had been with the company since 1965, I was Mr. Company Man. I had helped the company grow into its present position, and now I was being discarded. I alternated between bouts of despair and anger.

I went to human resources, and when I told the assistant to the director what had happened, she was appalled. She said she'd talk to the director immediately and get back to me. I never heard from her again. No one would answer my calls.

It became increasingly clear that there would be no further opportunities for Robert within the company. He visited a psychologist to help him deal with his pain and consulted a lawyer, who is helping him sue the company. The lawyer believes that the company has violated the Disabilities Act and that its treatment of Robert is a form of discrimination on the basis of age. Meanwhile, Robert still works at the company in the marketing department.

I'm not openly shunned, but my lawyer warned me I may be seen as a pariah. I never thought my career would end like this. I stuck with the company because it was the kind of place that cared about employees and rewarded those who did their jobs well. The culture used to be paternalistic. They wanted you to do everything with the company—from company health care to company picnics. Sometimes the line between home and work got a little blurred, but it was all one big happy family. It could be a little claustrophobic at times, but the attraction was the feeling of security, the cradle-to-grave culture. Even though it didn't pay as much as some of its competitors, it was secure. Being a family man, I went for the security.

And it used to treat workers over fifty well. Employees who had been around a long time were valued for their experience. Now the younger managers seem to feel threatened by the older ones. At the same time, there is still a huge bureaucracy. Sure, there has been some downsizing, but all below the fourth level of the hierarchy. They are just getting rid of the Indians and keeping the chiefs.

I didn't intend it to end this way. I thought I'd get my gold watch and have a party, just like everyone else. But it's not just me who suffers in all this. Every time a company mistreats someone, they hurt the ones who stay. My colleagues know what happened to me, and some of them are worried about their own jobs. An accident can happen to anyone. They have lost my ideas and my experience; they may be about to lose the loyalty of others like me.

ANALYSIS

Robert is a company man. The thought of going to a different company to do the job he does well has never occurred to him. Unfortunately, Cultures of Sacrifice tend to eat company men and women alive. They thrive on a diet of dependent employees who cling to the old-fashioned idea of staying with the same company throughout their careers.

In the industrial age this was the accepted model for employer-employee relations, but in the information age the individuality of employees, their experience, knowledge, and skills, should be seen as company assets. What Ken called "a business decision" was simply a matter of convenience for Ken, not necessarily a decision that was made in the long-term interests of the company. It was easier for Ken to push aside an older man than a younger, perhaps more ambitious colleague. Obviously, Robert's replacement, Jack, wants to move up and gain experience, but in the meantime, the company has squandered the valuable experience that Robert has gained.

Now the company has a competency problem: a less experienced salesperson in charge of a key territory, which will have an effect on customer relations, and an employee in the marketing department who is frustrated and underperforming. Other arrangements were undoubtedly possible but would have required Ken to do more than follow the line of least resistance. Genuine business decisions are those that put employees where they can work effectively and where the company can benefit from their ideas and experience. The company has also sent a message about its attitudes to other experienced senior employees: "Don't expect any help from us if you have problems."

Robert's problem is that this wrenching change in his life has come at a difficult time for him. He is fifty, an age when people often go through a period of doubt and self-examination. If he hadn't had the accident, he might be wondering if his job was all there was to life and feeling depressed about facing another fifteen years doing the same work. The accident has pre-empted this normal process, so change is being forced upon Robert without giving him much time to adjust. Because his body has been battered, his spirit craves something familiar, so what now seems like such a desirable job might have begun to feel oppressive if he hadn't had the accident. He has regained his health, but not his confidence.

Robert has certainly been abused by his company, and he is within his rights to fight back using legal means. Discrimination on the basis of age is not only illegal but illogical; it wastes the experience of knowledgeable people. Exhausting and expensive as they are, lawsuits are a way to fight back, and fighting back is sometimes psychologically necessary for people who have been kicked when they are down. However, Robert should sue the company only as a last resort. Litigation is a painful process in which everybody can lose.

Robert has overlooked new opportunities available to him by trying to move back into sales rather than accepting his new position in marketing. He mentions in passing that he is doing a "good job" in marketing, and presumably his skills are being put to use there, even if not in the way he would have chosen. But he's so anxious to get back to the familiar work of sales that he forgets that he is actually making a contribution in marketing. Sometimes we spend so much time wishing we were doing a different job that we fail to notice the opportunities in the job at hand. So-called dead-end jobs are not always blind alleys; sometimes it is possible to climb over the wall at the end of the road and move on.

In *New Passages,* Gail Sheehy talks about a "second adulthood" that often starts when people are in their fifties, but first they must go through a period of mourning for the old life. Robert is in mourning and has not yet embarked on his second adulthood. His decision to get professional help is sensible and should help him through this crisis and enable him to see that his life is far from over.

It is healthy and normal to mourn for a job that is gone irretrievably, but it is counterproductive to try to get it back. Even if we did get it back, we would probably find that we had outgrown it. Change is traumatic, but the alternative—clinging to the past—is infinitely worse.

ROLLING STONES

Ben was a senior executive and partner of a large international accounting firm. He joined the firm straight out of college in the fall of 1973. At that time it was the fourth-largest accounting firm in the country and one of the largest in the world, with more than 10,000 employees. Unlike its main competitors, which were all based in New York, Ben's head office was in the Midwest. The company prided itself on its midwestern values, hard-working people, and conservative image.

That reputation was about to change. During Ben's fourth year with the company, a new chairman was selected who wanted to take the firm in new directions and make it more prominent and aggressive in the industry. The corporate culture began to change just as Ben was promoted to management.

Soon after, Ben was selected by the firm's international group in New York to work for the company's office in Caracas, Venezuela. Such a transfer was unusual in that the U.S. and international firms were separate, but the international group asked for Ben because, in addition to having excellent accounting skills, he was born in Argentina and had the language and cultural skills they needed. Ben was excited about the move and felt that it would be a good career decision.

Ben and his wife, Sally, went to Caracas. Although Ben could speak the language, he was far from familiar with the city and had hoped for some help from the company to get settled. There was none. The most the head office did was rent them an apartment, sight unseen, near the airport. This was to be their home for the next five years.

The family had to make sacrifices in Venezuela, but the overall experience was a positive one. Even though Ben was the only American in the Caracas office, he was sensitive to the attitudes and cultural differences of his colleagues, and over time he gained their trust while he substantially changed and improved the business.

After five years in Caracas, Ben was transferred to San Francisco to work in the banking sector of the practice. This was to be a two-year posting while he was groomed for a position in Argentina. Once again the company did not help with the relocation. In fact, even though Sally was nine months pregnant, the company insisted they move to San Francisco immediately. Two days after arriving, Sally had her baby, and two days after that, she was trying to care for her family in yet another hotel room. Sally remembers:

> We found an apartment to rent in a few days, but it was almost as difficult to adjust to being back in the U.S. culture as it had been in Venezuela. The company's attitude was anything to do with home or family was Ben's problem, not theirs.

When the two years in San Francisco expired, Ben prepared to move to Argentina to oversee banking operations there. However, just as things were coming together, the international branch asked him to go to Mexico City instead. He and Sally were disappointed, but they considered moving wherever the company needed them as their duty. "We pretty much did what they told us to do," says Sally.

At this point, Ben was made a partner, which meant he had "arrived" in the firm and in his career. With this new feeling of accomplishment and recognition, he and his family moved to Mexico City in 1985, ready to start the next phase of their lives.

In Mexico City, Ben was well received by the Mexican team and was seen as the problem solver and the intermediary with the New York office. The international group of partners were impressed with his performance and were also fond of him, particularly when he took on the job of taking care of expatriates who went to Latin America.

The situation in the United States was not so positive. In 1989, during the last year Ben was in Mexico, the firm merged with another large accounting firm. Upper-level management at the head office changed to younger, "more visionary" managers. This resulted in changes in the overall operation of the company. The firm as Ben had known it disappeared. It went through an identity crisis. Two distinct cultures were merged, with two separate management organizations. Ben began to see things that disturbed him ethically: there was a great deal of over-billing; the rules seemed to change. When the firm was implicated in the savings-and-loan crisis, the legal staff grew from 40 to 180 to cope with the litigation claims that the company was facing.

Ben was advised by the international group that if he didn't return home soon, he'd have to spend the rest of his career overseas. At the same time, colleagues began calling and making references to "excess baggage" and the "housecleaning" sprees that had taken place during the merger. For the first time, Ben became wary.

Nevertheless, he and Sally wanted to return to the United States. They had four children now, two of whom were teenagers, and they wanted them to go to school in the States, so Ben requested a transfer. He was offered a post in Atlanta, Georgia.

Shortly after they had settled into a new house in Atlanta, the recession hit. In Atlanta the company was growing, but elsewhere it was stagnating. At one meeting a partner announced almost offhandedly that there would be a 10 to 15 percent cutback at the partners' rank, but he did not say when or who. Ben felt particularly vulnerable. He had not had a chance to establish himself or develop a client portfolio, and he didn't have anyone in Atlanta to champion him.

Within two months he was called in and asked to resign the partnership. He was not given the chance to go back to Mexico. Normally, partners are given special consideration, but now they were dealt with in a very impersonal way. Six partners, including Ben, were let go in Atlanta. Four of them had recently been transferred to that office.

> We could have survived as partners if we had taken a reduction in earnings and profits. That option was never presented to us. Now I wonder if that may be too utopian an idea in this business environment.

When financial compensation was proposed, it did not reflect Ben's seniority and experience. To receive the package, Ben and the other partners had to sign a waiver about age discrimination claims. Most people signed and took the compensation in order to support their families. One partner refused to resign the partnership and spent years in litigation.

> It all came down to greed at the top. Two hundred partners were laid off so those at the top could maintain high profits. In the same year, by contrast, a large oil company did not give raises or hire new employees and was able to avoid layoffs.

Ben maintained his equilibrium for the first three months after he left the firm. He was certain he would find an equivalent job somewhere. Unfortunately for Ben, the entire profession of accounting was going through a downsizing. When frustration and anger set in, he found it difficult to direct his anger at any one thing or person. The family was very hard hit.

We had to put our new home up for sale. It took two months before my wife had the courage to allow the FOR SALE sign in the yard. We had finally got our own place after living overseas for twelve years, and now we had to give it up.

Ben has had very little contact with the local partners. He still feels angry and resentful and insecure. He finds himself thinking frequently, "Nobody wants me." Sally says:

I guess I'm still angry about the situation. My husband is forty-seven years old and is overqualified for anything that comes up. He's willing to take something for one-third of his previous salary, but in job interviews no one will hire him. They can't believe he would work for so little when he is qualified.

Ben is now trying to put together business partnerships in the United States and Mexico, but so far none of these have yielded much financial compensation, and he is nearly out of money.

ANALYSIS

This story shows the clash of old-fashioned norms and new realities. Ben became the property of his firm, which picked him up and put him down anywhere in the world. Ben believed that it would be worth the dislocation his family would endure because as long as he did everything he was asked to do, he would ultimately be rewarded. Of course, there were advantages to him and his family in gaining international experience, but there were also difficulties of adjustment both abroad and back in the United States. Still, Ben believed that he was keeping up his side of a bargain. Then the rules changed, and the company got out of its side of the bargain.

These days a lot of people have been caught between the old bargain of unquestioning loyalty in return for corporate longevity and the new reality in which there are no guarantees and each individual must strike a bargain for himself or herself.

In larger terms we are talking about a business situation that is unstable and unpredictable, as old values are set aside by certain companies and nothing better than short-term self-interest emerges to replace them. Eventually, we believe, new models will emerge that will help people order their working lives, but in the 1990s everything is in flux.

Transfers, moves, even promotions—all these are known as "churn" by the people who carry out the arrangements: human resource personnel and facilities managers. Churn signifies downtime, lost productivity, time spent bringing newcomers up to speed, time spent getting new offices redecorated, phones hooked up, computers put in place, business cards printed—all the minutiae that occur when employees move to a new position or location. These problems have always existed for companies, but in recent years, with restructuring, downsizing, and globalization, churn seems to affect more and more employees.

Churn is usually evaluated in financial terms by companies, but rarely in terms of lost productivity or opportunities. Nobody can measure the time spent by executives thinking about selling houses and finding good schools for their kids when they could be thinking about servicing new accounts.

It is important for employees to grow and tackle new challenges. Moving up and around is part of the experience of learning, but when a quarter to a third of a company is on the move at any given time (as is the case with certain "high-churn" companies), an enormous amount of experience is squandered.

Companies can reduce the waste by making the rewards and the sacrifices of moves and transfers explicit, so that employees can make independent choices and feel as though they are part of the decision-making process. This is important for others in the company who might be next in line for a transfer. They will be much more willing to move if they can observe that the company is open about the advantages and the disadvantages of relocating, as well as sensitive and helpful to the needs of the family.

There are thousands of people like Ben who have suffered from the rash of corporate mergers in the late 1980s. Doubtless many of their jobs could have been saved if there had been less greed and more willingness to look at alternatives. Ben's story serves as a testament that deleting names from the payroll does not mean these people vanish into thin air. They are still affected on a daily basis. Whether they have found new employment or not, they have suffered and so have their families. Lives can, and have, been destroyed by the cavalier attitudes of business leaders who feel their only obligation is to the bottom line.

Cultures of Sacrifice are cultures of control. They demand everything an employee has to give and then waste most of it. They face a paradox in which demanding more and more means getting less and less because the company is asking for the wrong things. They insist on obedience, time, and an unquestioning attitude, and in the process they exhaust and exploit their employees. These cultures may succeed in the short term, but eventually their employees are so spent that they can't give the one thing that the company needs most: creative ideas.

THE WIN/LOSE CULTURE

IVING WITH THE ENEMY is the expression that comes to mind when describing life in a Win/Lose Culture. From the moment you walk through the door in the morning, you feel as though you're fighting not only for your career but for your life—and against the very people who should be your allies—your colleagues. The Win/Lose Culture ties in with our fondness for litigation, high-stakes professional sports, and mud-slinging political speeches. Everything is competition in this culture; it's an all-or-nothing contest. You win or you lose; you're in or you're out; you're up or you're down. Winner takes all; loser gets nothing. There is no middle ground, nowhere to rest.

Regardless of how professional you are or how well you do your job, you are continually thwarted and undermined by the competition inside the company rather than by the real competition on the outside. Somehow you find yourself caught up in contests you don't want to be part of, and almost without warning you're on the defensive.

Imagine you have been selected and specially trained to perform a new function. Your new role means a shift in authority and poses a threat to people above and below you in the hierarchy. The better you look, the worse they look by comparison. They respond by discrediting you and your new role. They maintain their control and diminish you in the process.

Or imagine that you find yourself used as a pawn when two leaders are jockeying for position. Everything you do that benefits one of them is regarded as disloyalty to the other. You cannot make both of them happy no matter how hard you try. You are forced into taking sides in a battle that has nothing to do with you and from which it is impossible to extricate yourself.

The Win/Lose Culture fosters internal competitiveness that pits individuals, teams, and even functions against one another. Employees view each other not as teammates working in tandem to accomplish the company's goals but as potential obstacles to their personal success. As long as there are hierarchies with fewer and fewer positions for people at the top, there will be competition among workers to fill the coveted spots. Similarly, if there are limited rewards, such as bonuses or privileges, people will tend to vie for them, sometimes to the death of a workmate's career.

The Win/Lose Culture is supported by the entrenched notion that competition makes everyone work harder and ultimately leads to better results. In the United States, for example, the competitive spirit is so valued that people find it hard to believe that competitiveness can have any negative effects. One executive insists that internal competition promotes "rigor." Rigor mortis, perhaps—the anxiety and hostility that comes with abusive competitive behavior shuts most people down.

At Sheetrock Inc., a construction company located in the Northeast, company chiefs tried to position the firm as an industry leader in the 1970s by recruiting individuals who would do anything for money or power. They looked for aggressive, acquisitive types, assuming that their need for dominance would benefit the company. Sales grew at first, but when the home-building industry slumped, the company fell into disarray because it was staffed with self-maximizers who could not work as a team. The politics of self-interest is not a sustainable strategy for growth.

Managers at the Sheetrock company obviously belonged to the snake-pit school of management. As one consultant puts it, "Throw people in a pit and see who crawls out." Whether called a sink-or-swim mentality, a survival-of-the-fittest culture, the-cream-rises-to-the-top theory, an if-you-can't-stand-the-heat-get-out-of-the-kitchen environment, or any one of a number of names, the principle is the same. Employees must compete with each other for turf, perks, assignments, recognition, promotions, and sometimes just plain survival. Each employee is essentially on his or her own.

A number of leaders deliberately create a climate of competition. They assume that the best people will thrive in such an environment. One political leader used this policy with his cabinet. He met with them individually, and he often gave two or more of them the same task, hoping that each would try to outdo the others. In fact, cabinet members spent more time trying to sabotage the efforts of their colleagues than in coming up with good policies and programs. This was in the 1970s; the government came unglued in the recession of the early 1980s, lost power, and didn't regain it for more than ten years. By that time, of course, the leader was long gone.

At one company the vice president of operations demanded a business plan that would show 10 percent growth at a particular subsidiary. Privately, however, he made a deal with the subsidiary's head of production to give him a bonus if production increased by only 5 percent. By setting two separate agendas, the vice president drove a wedge between the interests of the head of production and the interests of the company.

The president of a large publishing company also used this approach. He terrified his acquisitions editors with fears of layoffs and sent them all out to compete for big-name authors. Some authors wondered why more than one editor from the same firm was approaching them—and in such clandestine ways. A few savvy authors played one editor off against another, so that the editors ended up paying far too much for the publishing rights to a book. But most authors recognized the publishing house for the snake pit it had become and took their manuscripts elsewhere. Meanwhile, the editors who found the process distasteful had left the company, taking several top authors with them. The president eventually retired, but it took years for the company to recover from the damage.

The sink-or-swim mentality creates a fragmented workforce. Teamwork? Forget it. There is no loyalty to the company, to co-workers, or even to the product and the work itself. Money or fear of being fired are the motivators for work. Maybe the thrill of competition works for a while for the rare souls who need hourly goals to get through the day. In this kind of work environment, daredevils and gamblers do particularly well.

The people who thrive in the Win/Lose Culture—and there *are* people who prefer to work in one—require enormous amounts of stimulation to make it through the day. "I'm an adrenaline junkie," says one twenty-nine-year-old bond trader at Scotia McLeod Inc., an investment brokerage house. "When it's quiet, I get bored shitless." Bond and currency traders, stock dealers, and certain kinds of salespeople enjoy the excitement of the chase, with its pressure and tension. They like high-risk situations; they're prepared to gamble everything on the chance of one big win. Their jobs seldom call for teamwork; they do not have to manage other people; they are simply responsible for themselves. In the army these people would be given jobs as snipers, and they'd be good at it. Most of them are under thirty; after that age many of them burn out.

The Win/Lose Culture leads to rumors, spiteful gossip, and negativity. There is no trust, so there is no positive exchange of information and therefore no chance to build on ideas. Some workers in a Win/Lose Culture are like children in a classroom who protectively cover up their test papers and homework from the pupils sitting next to them. Then they wave their arms like eggbeaters when the teacher asks a question, demanding the first chance to answer. People who willingly share information in this kind of culture may find themselves exploited. It's a credit-snatching rather than a credit-giving environment.

There is a kind of social Darwinism associated with the Win/Lose Culture, which assumes that the strongest workers will survive and the weak will fall by the wayside. But the only thing this theory proves is that we have not yet evolved to the point at which we understand our true natures and what motivates us to do our best. Nothing in a Win/Lose Culture helps us to achieve the internal peace we need to promote creative thinking or build and maintain the positive relationships that promote optimal learning and performance. Instead, the abusive behavior of those who think they can be successful only when someone else is losing engenders a climate of fear, suspicion, envy, and hostility.

This kind of behavior can only lead to the suppression of effort among most of the people in the company. If, as a leader, you promote a Win/Lose Culture, you're paying for the contribution of all the employees, but you're relying on the efforts of a few winners. To find out who the overtly competitive people are in a group, ask them what they would rather do: come in second place running a four-minute mile or first place running a four-and-a-half minute mile. The people who want to run the mile in four minutes are focused on achieving their personal best, which translates to better work, whereas for the highly competitive others, the object is simply to win.

It's time to explode the myth that in business the best man or woman wins. In reality, it is the best person at winning who usually wins, and as the following stories prove, that may not have anything to do with his or her ability to perform a task. Nor does it mean that the winner's solutions are the best solutions for the business. Let's look at a few examples.

THE WAR ZONE

Ross is a chief engineer with a large exploration company that specializes in offshore drilling. He has seventeen years of experience and is considered one of the best and most experienced engineers in his field. During his career he has remained loyal to one company, and although he has suffered a lot of abuse, he is determined to stay because he hopes that eventually things will change for the better.

According to Ross, the culture of the company changed dramatically when a man called Brad was hired to head up international offshore projects with a view to globalization. Brad was a graduate of West Point Military Academy, a decorated soldier in the Vietnam War, and had graduated from Harvard at the top of his M.B.A. class.

Everyone, including Ross, was very impressed with Brad's skill at negotiation. When he managed to secure a contract to build a huge oil rig, he earned enormous respect in the company. But anyone who worked with Brad had to pay a hefty price. As Ross explained:

> Brad took pounds of flesh at every opportunity. He was extremely demanding. He would make you jump through hoops, give you some kind of impossible deadline, and then when you delivered on time, he'd have forgotten about the whole project. He'd browbeat you constantly and threaten you with your job if the pace of your work did not meet his expectations.

As designer and chief engineer on the project, Ross was often the one who suffered the consequences of Brad's ego.

> I remember one instance. There were five of us on a plane coming back from making a major business presentation about the rig. It was midnight and we were all completely exhausted. We'd spent the entire day in meetings trying to convince the clients that they should hire us, a fairly small U.S. company, to build one of the largest offshore platforms in the entire region.
>
> Their response was fairly predictable: "Why should we use you when we have a much bigger and more experienced national company that could do the job?" Naturally, we were all disappointed but confident the door was not entirely closed and we'd get another opportunity to repitch our proposal. However, it was clear that the rejection took on a far greater dimension with Brad.
>
> As our plane flew back to headquarters, Brad accused us all of being assholes and roared orders at us. "Do this, completely redo that,

all the plans must be totally revised, and I want all of you in my office in the morning at 6 A.M.!" We had already been working eighteen-hour days for weeks, and all of us had had less than six hours' sleep the night before. But any refusal to comply would have been seen as insubordinate in Brad's eyes, so we opened our briefcases and started to work immediately—except for one guy, Pat.

Pat was a young contract lawyer Brad had hired to work with us on this project. He said, "No way. I don't work for you, and you couldn't pay me enough to put up with this!" Brad came up to his face and said, "OK, how much would it take? How much would I have to pay you?" Pat came up with an outrageous amount five times what could possibly be reasonable and Brad said, "OK, now you're working for me, and I want you in my office at 6 A.M., you little fucker!"

In the end we won the contract based on political issues that had little to do with our added pain. But it was all a war to Brad. There was always a gun pointed at our bellies. Winning was everything.

When the company won the contract to build the platform, Brad hired an army pal, Parker, to lead the project. Parker was the quickest study Ross had ever met.

You'd sit down with him and show him a design and he really seemed to understand what you were talking about. He asked the right questions. But later, in the middle of negotiating contracts, he'd become overwhelmed by the process.

About this time Ross was being considered for a more senior executive position, but Parker brought in people he knew to help him. They had two things in common: they didn't know the job and they didn't treat anybody with respect.

These people were all from the military, and none of them knew anything about our business—or any business. Their attitude was, this isn't brain surgery—how tough can it be? One ex-colonel was overheard boasting, "I don't know shit about business, but here I am getting paid a hell of a lot of money to make contracts and talk deals!"

The Win/Lose Culture was now firmly entrenched in the company. Parker even put up a plaque in the head office that read, "Take the message to Garcia!" This was from a popular book written about an incident in the Spanish American war. A U.S. general needed to get a message to General Garcia that he would support him in his efforts if he decided to advance. The general chose a young officer, said, "Take this message to

Garcia!" and dropped the soldier on a beach without any supplies or any indication of where he could find Garcia. The soldier had no help; he was completely on his own. The soldier eventually found Garcia and delivered the message. This story was held up by the company as being the ultimate in performance. Don't ask any questions, don't ask for help, just do it and do it on your own. Salute the flag and get moving.

As the huge project got under way, Ross had to report to another ex-colonel, Dwayne. He was as demanding as Brad but not as smart, and his requests were often inappropriate. His main interest was in keeping costs down and impressing Brad and Parker. More and more supplier contracts had to be finalized, and it disturbed Ross greatly that Dwayne was renegotiating contracts in ways that would affect the quality of the project and actually increase cost. Dwayne's attitude was "I'm in charge. I cannot be wrong."

Dwayne was taking his military training into the workplace, but the blind obedience that is essential on the battlefield has quite the opposite effect on a daily basis in a corporation. Ross and his team were not simply foot soldiers whose job it was to charge a hill or march around a parade square to commands barked by the company sergeant. They were qualified engineers who were experts in their fields and who could predict when something would work and when it wouldn't. It was very difficult for them to sit back and watch the potential disaster or failure of what was supposed to be "an absolutely marvelous drilling rig." Conscientious objection is OK in business and politics but not in the military. American business has thrived on the conscientious objections of loyal employees who have provided valuable input to corporate leaders in the past.

> We would say, "Look, Dwayne, we are professionals. We've all got twenty-five years in the industry and yet you don't want us to question something even if we can see it doesn't work?"

Not only did Dwayne not want their input, but he began to take more and more control himself and punish those who questioned anything he did. He refused to take the advice of experienced engineers and moved Ross from project to project into difficult situations that seemed to have no beginning and no end.

Ross felt very much out of control of the work he was told to do. With Dwayne controlling the money and the staff, Ross and the team were unable to put the right solutions in place. Over and over again, Ross had to sort out problems that Dwayne had created. As soon as the situation was controlled, Dwayne would move people onto another project and take credit for solutions. It almost appeared that Dwayne would often create problems so that he could be seen as a hero when he solved them.

When anyone challenged Dwayne, he kicked them off the team. Ross would have been thrown out of the company altogether if it had not been for colleagues on another project who said they could use him. Ross transferred to another division, and although he was a senior engineer, he was not given anything to do for several months. This was torture for him. He felt ostracized from the rest of the engineers because they were afraid to show any loyalty to him.

In the meantime, more and more army or Harvard buddies who had little or no industry experience were hired. In the end the contracts that were signed and put in place bore no resemblance to the ones originally formed by Ross and the initial team. The project went well over budget and was a year behind schedule. Dwayne's decisions were all bottom line driven, and Ross was genuinely concerned about the quality of the workmanship and the components of one of the world's most innovative oil rigs.

> I felt miserable about the project. It had so much promise and I had worked so hard in designing it from the very beginning. Now it's all been taken from me, and even worse, I'm seen as the failure or the problem while Dwayne is still seen as a great leader. How can they see him any other way? If Parker and Brad admitted he had been a problem, they would be going against their own man, and this is not the way things are done in the military.

In addition to protecting its own, this particular corporate culture rewarded its "top brass" with huge bonuses in the millions of dollars. But the rewards didn't filter down to other workers who had contributed, such as Ross. Although Ross feels he was paid very well for his job, he notes: "The pay of these guys was way out of line with their contributions and even immoral. They created a system of rewards and elevated their own kind into it."

Ross is still with the company, but working far away from the competitive brinkmanship that almost ruined his career. He now is in charge of designing and building platforms for South America. He feels he has definitely lost stature in the company for questioning the top brass and not simply "taking the message to Garcia."

The devastating thing to me is that I've spent a good portion of my career refining my expertise. Now I'm sitting here watching these people destroying our industry. It's only a matter of time before something goes very wrong . . . and our company is already being considered among our competitors as a joke! Yet there we were on the top just a couple of years ago.

The way we work has changed completely. We used to spend about 85 to 90 percent of our time on project work and about 5 percent on tracking and reporting. And we were successful. The military system we now have in place is 85 to 90 percent tracking, and the time is taken from the real project groundwork. There are also more people doing fewer things. For example, I used to supervise seven areas; now there are at least seven people supervising these areas. Again, the military model has an abundance of people of about the same caliber to spare, so everyone can have a task. The military model cannot accommodate multi-tasking of people but assigns one pigeon hole per person. Now this approach has been adopted in the corporation. You have a whole bunch of people reporting micro bits of information to the leader. It's called micromanagement.

Ross says he has friends in other industries who are experiencing the trend to hire ex-military personnel. One friend works in a company that has ventured into the waste management industry. Although only in business for two years, the company was holding its own in a tough market. The holding company decided that what they needed to improve the company's productivity was "someone to kick some butts." So they hired a retired military officer. He knew nothing whatsoever about their business; he just knew how to "kick ass," and it was thought that if he could drive a submarine, he must know how to handle people.

With so many military bases closing, it is estimated that over half a million military people will be let go, and many will filter into our corporations. The question will be, how can we take advantage of these disciplined and potentially powerful leaders and ensure they understand the value of shared power and nonhierarchical management structures—both for employees and ultimately stakeholders.

ANALYSIS

The Win/Lose Culture is one in which doing what is asked is much more important than doing what is right. There is no room for dissenting opinion, diversity of opinion, different values or thinking. It is also a culture in which only a few get credit but a great many lose out. It is an extremely hierarchical model, with people at the top of the pyramid who embody the motto Kill the Enemy! The enemy might be the business competition or simply anyone who disagrees with them. If good ideas get killed in the crossfire, all is fair in war.

In Ross's story, one of the significant differences in value systems between the long-term, quality-oriented employees and the generals is that the former were concerned with quality and reputation and were caught up in the excitement of their work, while the generals were interested only in control, power, and winning. It didn't matter what business they were in; they just wanted the biggest deals, the most credit—and obedience at any cost. And that's where the business case is really clear in this story. What would be the cost in lives and to the environment if there were an accident, if the rig collapsed, or if there were an oil spill? The compromises in quality are just not worth it.

The ruthlessness of a Win/Lose Culture may work for getting contracts, but it doesn't work in following up on those contracts and carrying out the work. In hiring Brad and letting him hire people like himself, the company was obviously following a policy of aggressive expansion and globalization. A lot of companies are forced into this position. They have no time to build up a reputation for competence and quality; the corporation simply makes deals anywhere, everywhere, and hopes that the rest of the staff can cope with them. It's a risky way to do business, but it is quite common.

This story is like a brushfire out of control. One bully hires another bully who hires another, and soon the culture is perpetuated. This significantly alters the quality of work, the values, and eventually the image of the company. Because of the rewards that the generals were receiving, they had absolutely no reason to alter their behavior. Whoever hired Brad was obviously of the opinion that the company needed "whipping into shape," that competing for the European contract was going to need bullying tactics.

Brad is not a typical military leader. Military training means teamwork as well as following orders, and real wartime stories are more often about camaraderie than about lone heroes—or would-be heroes like Brad. Putting him in a management position where he was supposed to get results by working through other people was a disastrous combination. Lone wolves should not be put in charge of the pack.

Brad's biggest problem is his bullying, competitive personality. The acquisition, the deal, and coming out on top are more important to him than anything else, even if it means paying a young, probably inexperienced lawyer five times what he is worth just to win a confrontation on an airplane. All that matters to Brad is winning, and if that means people are hurt, projects are compromised, and public safety is undermined in the process, so be it.

Brad is not the only problem at the company, although he is undoubtedly the most obvious one. Even the people who hired Brad are only symptoms. The disease is a wrong-headed strategy, carried out through hiring decisions that affect people like Ross. The problem starts with the CEO and the board, who have chosen to impose an expansionist policy on the company without getting the rest of the staff to buy in.

The "message to Garcia" ethic is quite consistent with a Win/Lose Culture. The top brass are concerned with deals and conquests; they are not particularly interested in the mundane business of how an oil rig actually gets built. The foot soldiers can do that, as long as they don't keep running to the general with tiresome questions that the general can't answer. By now Brad is off to woo another client. The European client has been won; let someone else sort out the messy details.

Ross's company is trying to develop an innovative technology with an outdated organizational structure, which is a bit like trying to build a computer using wood, hammer, and nails. The company is trying to do something new and unusual without shedding the straitjacket of an old-fashioned structure. Hierarchies and large bureaucracies had their place in the industrial age, when consistency and careful following of procedures were important. Now that production work has been largely mechanized and information is more easily available to leaders, this structure is giving way to flatter organizations in which people are needed for their ideas and ability to develop strategy, not for routine paper-pushing and mundane supervision.

Many of the jobs that are disappearing these days are bureaucratic jobs. Although job loss always creates hardship, it is difficult to justify keeping some of the unproductive, meaningless jobs created in the days of bloated budgets and expanding workforces. Creating meaningful, useful jobs is a much tougher challenge, but it is the only approach that makes sense in the long term.

Meanwhile, Ross's company has created a bureaucratic culture that creates more work instead of allowing necessary work to be done more productively. Bureaucracies manufacture work, although it consists mostly of paper-pushing and little of it contributes to the bottom line.

Obviously, with flattening and downsizing, this kind of reporting structure is becoming an unaffordable luxury. If the number of contracts decreases, this style of management won't be able to sustain itself, and the hierarchy will start to fall apart. If a disaster occurs, the downsizing will happen even faster.

Ross's company is typical of the Win/Lose Culture, which throws everyone into a pit to see who will crawl out. Ross has survived, but he feels battered and resentful. For people like him it is essential to develop survival skills. The key is not to wait around for someone to notice your performance and reward you for it. Make sure people know about your ideas. In a Win/Lose Culture, if you don't promote yourself, someone else will take credit for your work.

Ross may feel that he's lost status in the company, but he has all the necessary ingredients for a job that is more interesting and challenging than ever. In today's economy we have to take responsibility for planning our careers without assuming that a particular company will take care of us until we are ready to retire.

Ross is extremely intelligent and highly qualified. He can take on the competition and win in this culture if he has to, although he would no doubt prefer to work as part of a team. Now he has an excellent opportunity to work in two growing markets—South America and the Far East—where he can learn and gain valuable experience.

He shouldn't waste time repeatedly covering up other people's mistakes; if the mistakes continue, let their perpetrators suffer the consequences. There is a time to cover up someone else's mistakes if the mistakes are minor and a rare occurrence, but to do so repeatedly is irresponsible. Never, ever compromise your professional ethics, whatever the situation. Public safety must always come first.

This last point is extremely important for those in Win/Lose Cultures, which are often dominated by people who put winning ahead of everything else, including ethics. Whistleblowing may seem like an extreme step, but it is one of the most effective ways to stop an out-of-control Win/Lose Culture from destroying itself and blameless others through its dangerously self-destructive behavior.

NOT INVENTED HERE

Karen was speeding along in her career as a software developer in her own small company in Chicago. As inflation continued to balloon in the windy city, Karen was persuaded by her family to join them in the more affordable Southwest. The thought of warm weather and proximity to her family convinced her to move.

Rather than moving her company, she decided the time was right to join a larger firm with more industry clout and better marketing possibilities. Two companies in particular interested her, and she received offers from both. They seemed on a par with each other, so she took the one that made the better offer. The company prepared customized accounting packages for a number of firms in the aeronautical industry.

While Karen was winding up her company in Chicago, she received a bizarre but prophetic anonymous letter:

> DON'T GO. YOU WILL BE HURT AND DISAPPOINTED. YOU WILL NOT BE TOLERATED. STAY IN CHICAGO. PLEASE READ AND HEED. A FRIEND.

One copy of the letter went to Karen's home address, and the other went to her company. There were no clues as to who had written the letter, other than the southern postmark. Needless to say, the anonymous letter created quite a stir with Karen, her friends, and family.

> We were all trying to solve the mystery of who wrote it and why. My first thought was that it was a joke sent by one of my friends who didn't want me to leave Chicago.

After several days with no one owning up to sending the letter, the episode took on a rather ominous quality, but not enough to make Karen worry or change her plans.

Six weeks later Karen showed up for work at her new company. On the first day she was introduced to the staff by her immediate boss, Will, the director of development. Will was an older man who seemed pleasant, though quite reserved. Before joining the company, she had met Will only briefly to negotiate her salary. He didn't spend much time talking to her on her first day either.

It was Will's boss, Sam, the president of the company, who had taken the lead in hiring Karen, and he was the one who took her out for a welcoming breakfast. Sam was a likable fellow of about fifty, who described himself as "a real pioneer." He wore cowboy boots under his suit and had a ranch out of town that bred "paints."

Karen told Sam about the letter she had received.

> I thought he would be intrigued and a little concerned, but instead he just said, "Oh that, I know about that, it's nothing. Someone found the original, which had accidentally been left on the copier, and brought it to me."
>
> "Who sent it?" I asked.
>
> He just casually said, "I don't know," and changed the subject. He reassured me that everyone was excited about me joining the team and I should just ignore the letter. I told him obviously I had.

Sam also filled Karen in on some of the background of the company. He and Will had been working together since the 1960s, originally in a company that produced business forms. The move into software development was fairly recent. Karen got the impression that Sam and Will were very close—perhaps neurotically so—even if they didn't seem to agree on much.

After three months at the company, Karen realized she had made a big mistake in accepting the job. The company was grossly understaffed for the amount and importance of the business it was doing, and employees were working around the clock, many of them doing not only their development work but also a lot of support functions.

> The people were morose, and there was a general feeling of hopelessness and resignation. They didn't like their jobs, but there was only one other firm that did software work in town, and most of them thought it would be the same, or worse, and not worth the loss in equity to move. There are always people who feel a little job dissatisfaction in any company, but this was deeper and more prevailing than anything I had seen before.

Karen was particularly confused and disappointed by her immediate boss, Will. Even though she had the office next to his, he rarely spoke to her. When she tried to initiate conversation or involve him in her ideas, he seemed uninterested. She realized that although he had nominally accepted her appointment, he resented her presence.

Karen's relationship with Sam, the president, was better from a personal point of view, but still she began to wonder if he had hired her at least partly to thwart Will.

We would go to a client in the morning to get briefed, and when we got back to our office I would go into Sam's office to talk about the project. He would inevitably say, "I'm going to get us all together in my office at 7 P.M. to talk about it." At first I thought these late meetings were necessary because Sam was so busy that 7 P.M. was the soonest he was available, but I discovered this was just when he liked to work.

He would take long business lunches, return to work for a while, leave for dinner at around 5 P.M., then come back to the office to work. His day seemed to start at 7 P.M., and he made it clear that if you didn't stay you'd miss the meeting and it wouldn't be rescheduled to fit anyone's schedule. Eventually, after a few of these meetings, we would have defined the problem and divided up the work. The next step would be to plan another meeting with Sam. Sometime that night we would sit down with him and present our work, to which he would often say:

"That dog won't hunt, 'cause what you don't know is back in 1992 we tried that and it didn't work" or " 'cause what you don't know is that the client wants this to work on their older equipment and this needs too much memory." It was always " 'cause what you don't know is . . ."

It was very difficult to agree on anything except very conventional solutions to problems. I was working well into the night regularly and often on weekends. I was exhausted and felt totally worn down. I wasn't able to do any of the things I thought they had hired me to do. I felt I was working very hard and getting nowhere.

On one occasion Karen and her team were due to make a presentation about a new system she had developed for a client on her own time, a system that would radically streamline the client's accounting procedures. Before the presentation, however, Will made them wait outside the meeting room until he called them in. Once inside, she could see that Will had made a different presentation to the client about an idea of his own. He sat there visibly not supporting Karen's presentation of the new system.

There seemed to be a feud going on, not just with me but with all of the other software people. I felt the people in my group had been worn out years ago. My initial optimism never really worked on them, and now I understood why. There was no way to change the company as long as Sam and Will were there, and Sam and Will were determined not to go anywhere.

During Karen's fourth month at the company, Will hired a man with far less experience to fill a senior position Karen had been promised.

> When I asked Sam what was going on, he said, "Will wanted a partner to work with him with a different kind of background." When I told Sam this was not what we had agreed to and that I had another offer and intended to accept it, he spent the next two hours trying to convince me to stay. But it was clear to me that the situation was hopeless.

Karen's experience was like an old western movie in which the hero rides into town and gets caught in the crossfire between two gunslingers—one wearing a white Stetson and the other a black one. After she left, Karen was told by a friend that the mysterious letter she had received had probably been sent by Jerry, another out-of-towner who had quit just before her arrival.

> Sam and Will had been playing management poker like this for years, using their employees like chips, and they weren't interested in changing the rules to accommodate a stranger. The company was being finessed by its own cardsharps and couldn't go forward unless changes were made at the top. Without some fresh dealers and some new players, the company was almost as useless as a folded hand.

ANALYSIS

One of the most confusing things about this story is that Sam seems like a pleasant, affable man. Not all competition is fostered by bullies. Some of the most difficult bosses we know are "nice people." They do not overtly abuse their employees. They seem friendly and welcoming, and they may even appear to solicit new ideas from their employees, but when it comes to accepting those ideas, they become evasive. Even when they turn ideas down point blank, they still sound friendly or folksy, like Sam. It is a way of being patronizing and dismissive. The competition is made to appear like friendly rivalry, but it is still competition, as the effects on the employees show. At this company, Sam's team and Will's team are running neck-and-neck, and nobody is getting ahead, although the goal of winning keeps people running.

Will and Sam were clearly in disagreement about hiring Karen and probably about hiring her predecessor too, if the telegram is any indication. But instead of working through their disagreement, they suppressed it. Sam and Will should have sawed off a compromise on what they wanted in a software engineer long before Karen was hired and certainly before she arrived. Their covert feuding has fostered an abusive environment that was obviously destructive for Karen and bad for the company.

In a company like Sam's, nothing can be brought into the open and debated objectively because everything is subjective. The culture is personal, shaped by Sam and Will, so that anything that criticizes it is a criticism of Sam or Will. If one wins, the other loses. The idea that they could cooperate and both win seems never to have occurred to either of them. Sam and Will are an old-boy network of two people. Although Sam seems to have sensed that new players were needed, he is too evenly matched with his old poker rival to force change on the company. He keeps it profitable by overworking his employees rather than by innovation.

We were surprised that an ostensibly high-tech company could actually be so stagnant, but Sam and Will came from a conventional industry and brought their conventional ideas and approaches to problem-solving with them, along with their long-standing feud. The software they produced worked well enough for their clients—it did what the clients asked for—but they never challenged their clients' thinking or made suggestions of their own. Karen's attempt to present a completely new system that would have changed the way the client handled certain kinds of work was out of line with the way the company operated.

Firms that are still being run by their founders stagnate if the founder is unable to promote change. Loyalty to the company becomes personal loyalty to the founder, whether he or she is right or wrong. Many once-strong businesses falter because the founder does not groom a successor or because the designated successor is a follower, not an innovator or leader.

Karen and the culture of the company were clearly mismatched. Ambitious, confident people enjoy a good argument and can take criticism, but constant evasion and procrastination drives them crazy. Karen was used to having some of her ideas shot down by clients, but she always got a fair hearing and the criticism she received challenged her ability to come up with new solutions to problems. Sam's negativity gave her no feedback that she could use in coming up with alternative proposals, and Will's habit of pointedly ignoring her was humiliating.

This kind of misdeal sometimes occurs when an employee makes a move that is designed more to get away from something than to take a step forward. In her haste to leave Chicago, Karen ignored some warning signals and let her professional instincts doze.

The anonymous letter was peculiar, but she also discounted the evidence of her own impressions. She hoped that the company would allow her to use her talents, but if she had done more research on the two companies that made her job offers, she would have found out that their work was severely limited in scope. Chances are, she wasn't the first person with bright ideas to work at one of these companies. And the fact that the two companies were so similar indicated that there wasn't much incentive for either company to be innovative.

Karen also allowed circumstances to dictate her choice of company. Although the other company is probably no better than Sam's, accepting the best (or the first) offer is not always a good career strategy. She didn't ask herself what was really important to her: salary or satisfaction, perks or responsibility, location or job content, the size of the company or its morale? In a tradeoff, what is negotiable and what is essential?

Not getting to know Will before she started work was another error of judgment. It is very important to spend some time with the person who will be supervising you most closely before you start any job. The personality of your immediate boss can make an enormous difference to your job.

Will and Sam are losing bright, intelligent employees because of their lack of common goals. This is an expensive and foolish game. Relocating and hiring is costly—doubly so if the person leaves within six months and somebody else must be hired. Meanwhile, the other employees are keeping their heads down. They know by now that coming up with an idea that Will likes will surely displease Sam and vice versa. The only way they can "win" is by not letting either Will or Sam lose face, which means following instructions to the letter and not rocking the boat. In Win/Lose Cultures, if you listen hard enough, you will hear the death rattle of ideas.

THE NEW BROOM

The expression "A new broom sweeps clean" is often used in business to describe a new manager who comes into a company and immediately starts to "clean out" people hired by his or her predecessor. Too often careers and self-esteem are swept away in the process.

In many working structures, particularly pyramidal ones, it's not unusual for people to try to get ahead by choosing a mentor. However, if the mentor is replaced, everyone in the mentor's camp may be sacrificed by the successor. After restructuring, this is often rationalized as simply a question of "style" or "fit." Sometimes changes like these can be made with sensitivity and even produce positive outcomes, but more often than not, the situation turns into a power struggle, with the abusive successor creating an adversarial environment. Jane, a marketing executive, was not one of the lucky ones. She was constantly undermined and punished because of her perceived allegiance to her former boss.

During the 1980s, Jane was about as happy as anyone could be in a career. She worked as a marketing manager at the Seattle branch of a large American packaging company. She liked her job and she was good at it. Over a ten-year period she was able to contribute greatly to the success of the corporation. She worked with a terrific team and admired and respected her boss, John, whom she continues to think of as a brilliant and very inspirational man.

> He was a great mentor for me. We shared an inexhaustible optimism. I believe it was our combined positive attitude that made our work so enjoyable and contributed greatly to our success.

Then John was promoted to executive vice president for marketing at the head office in New York. It was a bittersweet event for Jane. John's replacement lacked his inspiration and enthusiasm, and his pessimism crushed Jane's optimism.

Unfortunately for John, he arrived at the head office in the midst of a leveraged buyout. The company was in a state of upheaval, and after a round of appointments and dismissals, John became president of a company that consisted of half the old regime and half the new one. The hybrid structure was unwieldy and couldn't perform effectively in a highly competitive market.

John wanted to create small business units for each product. He believed they would be more manageable and more responsive. He asked Jane to come to the head office to take charge of one of the products that was in decline. She jumped at the opportunity.

For three months, from August to October, Jane commuted to New York from Seattle and focused on building her department and developing a marketing strategy for her product. Upon her arrival, Jane became aware that all was not as she had anticipated.

The stress from the recent buyout was palpable. Employees at all levels were afraid of losing their jobs. Morale was very low. Uncertainty and fear led to cynicism and internal strife. Opposing camps were formed. The old guard tried to preserve what remained of the former company and collectively resisted the changes John was trying to put in place. Even though the CEO and others paid lip service to the idea of small business units, John's efforts were being thwarted because he was not getting the practical support he needed from the company's leaders.

Jane's immediate boss at the head office, Tom, was reclusive and neglected to help Jane "break the ice" with her new colleagues. He didn't arrange any of the customary dinners or get-togethers to introduce Jane. She thought it was unusual, but instead of worrying about it, she focused on building relationships through her own resources.

The initial feedback about Jane was good. She was seen as a breath of fresh air. Her natural enthusiasm, good humor, and openness were a welcome change, particularly to the CEO of the company, who commented: "You know, Jane, I only want to hire people like you. It's been a long time since anyone around here was positive." It was true that the CEO seemed to spend most of his time amongst squabbling executive vice presidents; nevertheless, Jane sensed that the CEO's appreciation of her "was more than the executive VPs could bear," and as time went by she felt more and more on the outside.

Jane was becoming aware of a fundamental difference between the approach of the organization she had left in Seattle and the one she had joined in New York. They were both part of the same corporation, but the Seattle branch worked as a team and depended on close liaisons with sales and manufacturing units. The staff might disagree on issues, but the focus was always on the company's goals.

The corporate culture in Seattle was entrepreneurial in style and task-oriented. It was made up of about 75 employees who ran the manufacturing plant and led by 10 key people who routinely discussed direction and policy. Meetings led to clear decisions about what had to be done, how to go about it, and who was going to do it. Having a clear understanding of the problems and her role in solving them had given Jane a sense of security and freedom at the same time. Under John's leadership, experimentation had been encouraged and good ideas rewarded and prized. An "idea person" like Jane thrived in this environment.

The head office in New York had 1,000 employees and 10 leaders who made corporate policy. The bureaucracy was the epitome of a Win/Lose Culture. It prized individual heroes at the expense of teamwork. Jane called it an "Ivory Tower" culture.

> The company was well established, traditional, and arrogant. Little attention was paid to what was going on outside the company. Entrepreneurial thinking was not appreciated. The head office had a pyramid structure with the checkers checking the checkers, making sure they didn't stray from the rules. It was a company of watchdogs.
>
> Everyone knew there was a problem that needed to be fixed and everyone was expected to fix it, but no one knew how to get information and ideas organized. They were afraid to do something and they were afraid not to do something because the problem wasn't getting fixed.

The lack of interaction made Jane's job more difficult, but she realized that if she were to repeat the success she and John had achieved in Seattle, she would have to pull her team together so they could work collectively toward their business goals. There were two obstacles in her way: key team members didn't believe in the concept of small business units, and people were closing ranks against John, which meant against her too because she was so closely identified with him.

In the meantime, resistance to John's vision took a new tack. After John confronted the CEO and asked for his support of the small business unit concept, the CEO brought in an outside management consultant group without consulting John. This group was led by David, a young man Jane describes as "very smart, analytical, with a photographic memory, but also very arrogant, crass, and a shameless bully." John felt undermined by the CEO's action but cooperated with the consultants.

In contrast to John's spirit of cooperation, David masterminded John's ouster over the next two months. In meetings that included Jane, John, the CEO, and senior executives, David berated John, insisting everything he had done was wrong, and humiliated him by saying, among other things, "John has absolutely no idea what has to be done here!"

The two men had very different views about what was needed to make the company more successful. John's approach was a long-term one of total quality management, building people and systems to a level of optimum performance. David's approach was that bottom-line delivery was all-important and quality was not an issue. While this conflict was being acted out, Jane tried to communicate with John to get a sense of what he could do to protect himself from David.

Surprisingly, he seemed to be turning a blind eye to the whole situation. If he did feel betrayed, he did not confide in Jane. He continued to "toe the party line" with her, which made her feel even more adrift and alone.

In October, the same month that Jane and her husband relocated to New York, John was fired. His replacement was David, the outside management consultant. To the executives, David was the hero who was going to make everything work. This was the kind of solution they were used to, and this was what they wanted.

John's leaving made Jane acutely aware of being on her own in the company. Nevertheless, she worked very hard to motivate her colleagues, who were "like walking zombies."

> Everyone seemed to be on the edge of a nervous breakdown. They had gone through eighteen months of hell during the leveraged buyout, and they were clearly struggling with the insecurity and bureaucracy inside the corporation. The company's human resource group was of no support to me either. Their policy was to "lie low and duck the bullets" rather than challenge the corporate culture.

Jane worked hard, and as the market share for her product increased, people in her group became more supportive and actually started to have a good time. But nothing was good enough for David. Jane worked harder, but one night when she didn't get home until 2:20 A.M., she realized things couldn't go on the way they were.

Two incidents made it clear to Jane that she was fighting a losing battle. First, as she was planning a new advertising campaign for her product, David told her to run the new ads without pretesting them to evaluate their effectiveness. The ads ran, and when they were tested later, the campaign's performance was only average. When Jane presented these results in a meeting, David attacked her. "That's a fucking disaster," he yelled, "and it's your fault!" As the tirade continued, no one came to Jane's defense.

The second incident was at a meeting at which it was decided to reposition the product completely. It was an enormous task and would require huge commitment and effort to succeed. Jane could see that it would be easy for her to fail if she didn't have the whole-hearted support of upper management. She confronted the issue immediately and asked the CEO, David, and her boss, Tom, to support her efforts or fire her. Their responses were noncommittal.

A few days later Tom informed her that David wanted to replace her with one of his followers and move her to another position, which was essentially a demotion. Before Jane had the opportunity to discuss the change, David informed everyone that she was moving to the new position and would be replaced. This was the last straw for Jane. Even though the CEO offered her other positions in the company and more money to stay, Jane realized she could not work in the existing corporate culture.

The company gave Jane a generous severance package but nothing could compensate her for the emotional damage she had experienced.

> I was tortured by self-doubt. I couldn't understand what was doing wrong. Everything I had learned, everything that had worked and been successful in my professional history wasn't working for me in this situation, and yet the tasks and the problems were the same. It should have worked. I drove myself harder and harder to the point of exhaustion and put my work before everything else in my life, but the message I got from David was it wasn't good enough. I was on my own. In Seattle there were always people around who knew me, knew my past performance, knew what I could do, but in New York I had no history. My past successes were negated by David, "So what if you turned around a product in Seattle; that doesn't mean anything here."
>
> A part of me began to believe that what David said was true. Maybe it was just through good luck and being associated with good people that I had been successful. David was a very smart guy; maybe he was right. Fortunately, my husband, Bruce, gave some balance to my life. It was clear to him that I was becoming a victim of a ruthless and cruel organization. He was tremendously supportive. I had dragged him to New York with me, away from his job and his friends to a place where he was unable to work and where day after day he watched me and my job security fall apart. But he understood what was going on and helped me keep some perspective. When I woke up in the morning in tears and said that I had to get out of this situation, he said, "Do whatever you have to do."
>
> After I left, I didn't look for another job for three months. I was more crushed than I had ever been in my life. I just couldn't understand what had happened to me.
>
> When I did start to go on interviews for a new job, I knew what to look for. I had a new appreciation of what makes a difference in an

organization. I wanted to know what the corporate culture was as much as what the job description was. I was looking for an environment that was full of trust and a safe place to have new and different ideas.

When asked why she didn't go back to Seattle, Jane said it was important to her to succeed in New York. She knew her personal growth depended on "getting back on the horse" in New York.

The job-hunting process was a humbling experience. She had never had to get a job by herself before. In Seattle she had moved from position to position pursued by employers. She did not use the references offered by her old company, and sometimes it seemed to Jane, as far as New York was concerned, she had no previous work reputation. Even when her new employer checked her references, he couldn't appreciate how impressive they were nor their value in Seattle terms.

Jane is now working as vice president of marketing at a furniture manufacturer in New Jersey. It's a much smaller company, and she is not at the level she was at previously, but she was persuaded to take the job because the company was committed to total quality management.

> The president said to me, "I can't match the money, the perks, or the position you had at your other job, but I really want you because you can make a difference here." I believe he is the kind of leader I want to work for, and I have had the opportunity to witness his commitment to providing an empowering working environment. I wasn't in the company long before I realized the man I reported to was as abusive as David but not as smart. My new boss would humiliate his executives by calling them "Dogshit" and threaten to throw them out the window. I was able to handle this situation. I made alliances around him. I made sure that I was seen as separate and did not subscribe to his values. Through my professionalism and teamwork, I was able to gain the respect of the other executives, and his behavior stood out as destructive to the goals of the organization.

Eventually Jane's boss was asked to leave and Jane took his position.

ANALYSIS

It is not unusual to have a different culture in the branch office than that at the head office. Many branch offices must develop different systems to operate in a different region and culture, and this often means creating a more fluid organization.

True, the ivory-tower culture in Jane's head office was a barrier to change. But her comments indicate that the employees were desperate to find a solution to problems that had been inflicted from outside the company. The rumors of a buyout had already led to some questioning of the company's goals. The time was actually quite ripe for a well-managed change program.

John, however, was in a difficult position. Coming in from the outside, he was trying to deal with clashing corporate cultures and at the same time implement a new corporate strategy—a Herculean task.

It seems, however, that John could have done more to improve his situation. He needed a lot more than "lip service" from his superiors and colleagues, since he wouldn't get anywhere without complete support from top management, and he should have spent the time necessary to secure that support. In the branch office he could take support for granted. But at the head office he had to establish his credibility and leadership abilities from scratch. In the Win/Lose Culture, you have to win people over, one at a time if necessary, starting at the top.

Jane was brought in as John's protégé, which was bound to create a certain resentment among the employees already at the head office. Anyone in this position can expect some resistance from colleagues. Under the circumstances, coming into an office where morale was at an all-time low, Jane was viewed with suspicion and hostility. Her association with another newcomer with unpopular ideas made her position doubly difficult.

John and Jane needed to be assertive as well as supportive in promoting and selling their approach to turning the company around. Their ideas were good, but good ideas must be sold to colleagues and employees, not once but constantly. We see this over and over again in change-management programs. It is easy to assume that everyone will instantly see the wisdom of your ideas and sign on. In practice, it is a hard slog to get people to recognize good ideas for what they are, let alone to get their commitment to putting those ideas into practice. In Win/Lose Cultures, the battle starts all over again every morning.

The approach that had worked for Jane and John in the branch office, teamwork and freewheeling idea experimentation, was not valued in the head office because that wasn't the way things were done. Experimentation is virtually impossible in a Win/Lose Culture. New ideas are dangerous, not just for the culture but for their exponents. If, after the fight to get a new idea through, the idea proves to be less than 100 percent effective, there are plenty of people ready and willing to shoot it down. It's not that they have better ideas, it's simply that they can get ahead if someone else's idea doesn't pay off. David didn't seem to have particularly original or innovative ideas, but he made a lot of mileage out of pouring scorn on John's.

David was clearly a product of a Win/Lose Culture. He entered into competition with John immediately. After all, he had come to the company with a lot to prove. It's one thing to be an outside consultant and tell a company that everything it is doing is wrong; it's quite another to be hired to fix it.

John's idea-driven and entrepreneurial approach clashed with David's leadership style, so David got rid of him. The next step was to get rid of John's protégé, Jane. Regardless of what John could contribute, regardless of what Jane could contribute, David wanted them out. Personal winning came above the needs of the company.

The CEO behaved typically for someone at the head of a Win/Lose Culture. He played the role of protector rather than coach. In the end it was more important for him to protect his selection of David than to protect Jane, the outsider.

People like John and Jane could have been used to help create a competitive edge from within the company. By realizing the full potential of all its employees and being open to new ideas, the company could have changed its focus from one of protectionism to one of adding value to the company and its customers.

In a Win/Lose Culture, good work is a beginning, but it is seldom enough. You have to be smart to get in the game, but you have to get political to stay in it. Conscientious workers often find this state of affairs unendurable. They hate playing political games and they despise schmoozers. However, this is what it takes to survive.

If you are in a Win/Lose Culture, you have to recognize that the quality of your work likely has nothing to do with your public profile. You can either learn to win in order to maneuver yourself into a position where you can effect positive changes, or you can go elsewhere. But don't let the Win/Lose Culture make you doubt your own achievements.

Ultimately, of course, Win/Lose Cultures must be changed, but they have to be changed from within, which means that you have to become an insider. When a mentor leaves, his or her protégé is bound to feel orphaned. Jane was particularly unfortunate because she was an outsider at the head office: an outsider brought in by another outsider who fell out of favor. A company should assess very carefully the benefits of bringing somebody in from the outside versus promotion from within. This company sacrificed two very good people, whom they had groomed to be leaders, to soothe the ego of the "savior apparent" from outside.

The company has lost a lot in the transaction. For example, we've told you what happened to John and Jane in this story, but what about the people they were mentoring? We know for a fact that at least one other promising person left the company. The rest are probably taking stock, realizing that their chances of promotion may be slim if they stay, and polishing up their résumés.

Jane has obviously learned from her experience. Taking time off before starting job hunting was sensible and gave her time to regain her confidence. Choosing a company by its corporate culture was also a smart move. But the real test was Jane's response to the abusive boss. She realized that she had to make alliances. Fortunately, this time she could do so in a culture that was less hostile. She is managing fine on her own, has become stronger, and outlived abusive boss number two.

THE CULTURE OF BLAME

> In the organization I work for the maxim is "If you're not getting the
> results you want, increase the level of pain." Humiliation is thought to
> be one of the best methods of getting what you want.
>
> —*Chief engineer, oil company*

IMAGINE SOMEONE is pointing an accusing finger at
you. Whether you are guilty or not, a icy wave of
emotion crashes over you. In one painful, involun-
tary moment your body and soul flash back to that terrible moment when
you first felt shame. Was it when you wet the bed? Was it being caught
taking the loose change out of Daddy's trousers? Or was it that awful
time when your pal broke the window but everyone said it was you?

The emotion of shame is so powerful that we will do anything to
avoid feeling it. In psychological tests and anxiety research, the fear of
looking foolish, or being shamed, ranked above all other fears and pho-
bias. This is a powerful fear to unleash in a company, and it sets a number of counterproductive behaviors in motion.

The essence of the Culture of Blame is that someone is at fault. The
question that continually arises is not what has happened, but who did
it? In a Culture of Blame the company tends to reward and, more often,
punish individual performance rather than group effort by operating
on an informal "star and demerit" system. A lot of people run around
trying to be seen as the person doing the good work or, conversely, trying not to be seen as the person who has made a mistake.

However, most people just keep their heads down. It reminds us of
an old Japanese adage: The nail that sticks up above the rest gets hammered. No one wants to be singled out, so employees never take any
risks. They are not going to volunteer for anything. In a Culture of Blame

there is an excess of paperwork because everyone knows how important it is to cover their trails with memos and correct procedure.

But you're new to the company and you're eager to perform. You have lots of ideas and the energy to take them to fruition. You create a heroic project that will result in great benefits to the company. You think your colleagues will be as excited about the project as you are, but they seem to be holding back, taking a wait-and-see stance. As time goes by, you realize you're not getting the support you need.

All eyes are on you. You are the nail sticking up above the rest, and you can glimpse the shadow of the hammer above your head. You wonder what you're doing wrong and ask yourself, "Why am I being punished for simply doing my job?" Your emotions range from anger to desperation. Anger for being put in jeopardy and desperation to make everything turn out well.

Whether or not you fail this time around, you now know more about the corporate culture you work in. In a Culture of Blame, the "kill the messenger" mentality is rampant. No one wants to acknowledge the truth in this kind of culture because it may lead to more problems.

If you decide to stay, you'll have to change. You'll find yourself putting on a Teflon coat like the others. You'll keep your head low and keep your big ideas to yourself. You'll feel the other side of shame, fear of being accused. Every day you'll wait vainly for justice. For someone to say, "You've wronged this person!"

If you stay long enough, you'll reach a sustained note. Wendy Burns, a psychotherapist, told us about the sustained note:

> Think of your emotions as the holes on a flute. When you are feeling all of your emotions freely, your fingers dance along the holes of the flute, playing wonderful tunes. However, as you become afraid and start to protect yourself, you cover the hole that represents that emotion.

In the Culture of Blame you might begin by covering enthusiasm, then trust, then anger, and so on, until all of the holes of the flute are stopped. Now when you blow, there is just one dull sustained note: depression. Psychologists say depression is anger turned inward. We could also say depression is the sustained note of a dying soul.

Cultures of Blame are usually very strong cultures. They create a core of insiders who fit the culture and perpetuate it, either because the culture suits them or because their need to belong overrides any other consideration. Newcomers, or anyone with ideas that do not fit, are likely to become scapegoats. The search is never for a new creative idea or a better way of doing things but for somebody to shoulder the blame for anything that goes wrong. Individuals are isolated and change is anathema in this kind of organization.

In a perverse way, Cultures of Blame need scapegoats. Rejecting outsiders reinforces the culture and bonds the insiders together against a perceived threat. This kind of culture is probably the hardest of all to change, since change in any culture can come only from within, and there is no incentive for insiders in blaming cultures to alter their behavior.

Sometimes outsiders can masquerade as insiders long enough to gain acceptance; once they have established reputations as insiders, they can nudge the culture in a different direction. This is a long, slow process, requiring enormous amounts of patience and subtlety. If you are impatient, working at one of these places will feel like beating your head against a brick wall.

The other way in which these cultures change is through violent shake-ups. A takeover or a merger will force a blaming culture to reexamine its way of doing business. A drop in sales or a brush with bankruptcy will concentrate the mind of such a company wonderfully. But for some employees the change may come too late. Let's look at some examples.

THE BIG IDEA

Even in an age when innovation is so critical to success, managers in some companies will go to extraordinary lengths to resist and sometimes sabotage a new idea, particularly when it comes from an outsider or someone new to the company. Great ideas are powerful. They imply change and learning new ways of thinking and operating. That can be frightening for timid people intent on maintaining the status quo, or for those who think new ideas suggest that what existed before was wrong or inferior. In a hierarchical company people with big ideas can seem threatening to those higher up the pyramid. Often they are thwarted, sometimes even punished, for doing the very thing that companies supposedly value the most—coming up with new and bright ideas.

Christine, a creative director for a major branch of an international advertising agency discovered that having a great idea can be dangerous. She had worked in the advertising business for almost twenty years, moving from agency to agency every few years to widen her perspective and develop expertise with new product lines and market areas. She had won several major international awards and was tops in her field as a creative director who was both innovative and focused as well as able to work well with clients and agency people. When she was lured away from a job she loved in the East to work with a regional office of a rival firm, she welcomed the challenge of working with a group of entirely different clients.

> I did very well at the new agency. My group and I continued to improve the creative product of the agency and we pitched and won one of the largest accounts on the West Coast. The account would be worth at least $20 million a year and probably much more over time. But it seemed my success with this client was where my real troubles began.

Christine began to notice that the more successful she became, the less happy Ray, the general manager of the office, and John, the executive creative director, seemed to be.

After winning the new account, the agency had to create an entirely new advertising campaign for the client to launch their business worldwide. Although an enormously successful company, this client had never advertised before in its present form and was virtually unknown to the public. The mandate was to create an image for the client that would instantly position them as global leaders in their product category. The creative department worked day and night, and within ten days they had ideas for several campaigns. Ray and John decided they would look at the ideas and choose which would be presented to the client. Christine was excited about the concept she had developed and was confident the client would see the merit in her idea. The idea positioned the client's business uniquely in the marketplace, and its imagery would create stunning, high-impact advertising. The concept was known in the industry as a "big idea," that is, it was highly competitive and would be relevant year after year. But you can't introduce a fresh, bold perspective without shaking things up a bit. And Christine's idea scared Ray. He chose a safer more mundane treatment to show the client. Luckily for Christine, John insisted, over Ray's objections, that they show her idea to the client as well.

In the meeting, the client chose Christine's campaign. Unfortunately, the client asked for the television commercial to be finished in six weeks, in time for an international staff meeting, even though the advertising was not scheduled to run for several months. Christine had estimated the commercial, which would involve shooting in ten different cities around the world, would take at least ten weeks to complete. Despite her misgivings, John promised the client a commercial in six weeks.

Christine told John, Ray, and the account director on the business, Henry, that she and the film crew had found a way to produce the commercial on time. However, it would require a lot of coordination and skill on the part of the production company and the agency. At this point she began to sense that Ray and John were distancing themselves from the project. John, who normally would drop by a shoot to see that things were going smoothly, particularly on something as complicated and as important as this, said he wouldn't have time to visit. That night when Christine and a production manager, Carol, went to meet with Henry to discuss the shooting schedule. Henry was very agitated and said to Christine, "You'd better be able to do this or it will be your ass out of here!" Later, when Christine and Carol talked to Ray about the logistics of the shoot and said they may need some flexibility regarding some of the scenes, he said, "Look, I don't care what you do, as long as it's 'knock your dick in the dirt' fantastic and it's delivered on time." They were both outraged at the rudeness of their colleague and stunned by their lack of support. Instead of rallying around to help produce the commercial that was going to bring glory to all of them and more business to the agency, they were erecting barriers and undermining confidence. Nevertheless, Christine and her crew began a grueling schedule that covered ten cities in Europe, Africa, Asia, and North America.

> Normally this kind of assignment would be a creative director's dream, but having to do it in six weeks made it a nightmare. All along the way there were problems to solve and it was physically exhausting. We were traveling and working eighteen hour days.

Henry flew back and forth, from the locations to the agency and client's office, acting as liaison. One day he told Christine that the client, Andrew, wanted to see the locations in Copenhagen. Christine left a series of numbers where she could be reached on the job in Copenhagen.

The next Christine heard was when Henry called the studio where she was doing a wardrobe call. "Where the f—k are you?" he yelled. "Andrew has been hanging around the hotel for two hours and he's really pissed off. It's taken all morning for me to locate you."

Christine returned to the hotel immediately, apologized to Andrew for the wait, and took him to the locations they had scouted that morning. He soon softened and by the end of the day he was smiling and jovial. By the time he returned to the hotel, he was very happy about the progress Christine was making. Later, however, she heard that Henry had blamed her for the delay and had told Andrew that he intended to "kick her ass into shape." Furious, Christine confronted Henry.

> I have to admit that I lost my temper with him. I was stressed and tired and I didn't need the grief he was giving me. He was undermining my credibility with Andrew, and with two-thirds of the shoot to go, I didn't need that kind of tension going on behind the scenes.

Later, Christine called John and asked him to speak to Henry. She also mentioned that Henry had been abusive with the production company and had upset members of the team. John promised he would do what he could and said that her role was not to entertain Andrew but to shoot the film.

Christine and Henry made their peace a few days later in Italy. However, the tension never really disappeared during the rest of the production. Whenever a problem arose, he became angry and defensive.

When the shooting was over, Christine returned to Los Angeles to begin the editing. Henry and John brought Andrew to the production house to approve the edit, after making with a few minor adjustments, Andrew was very happy with the commercial and the three of them went off to dinner.

The next morning John met with Christine and said, "Henry brought up some concerns about the edit and now Andrew is worried and wants to make some changes." Christine was amazed, she took Andrew back to the editing room and together they re-edited some of the film. The music was recorded and once again everyone was happy.

When Christine returned to the agency, her colleagues were impressed with the film. John congratulated her, but Ray and Henry were conspicuously absent. Later, when Christine met Ray in the corridor, he pointedly ignored her. Christine was perplexed and mentioned what had happened to a colleague, who informed her that Henry had told everyone that Christine had screwed up in Copenhagen and that if it hadn't been for him, the whole shoot would have been canceled. Apparently Ray believed him. In fact, when Henry was later transferred, Ray had credited him with the work on the television commercial at his going-away party.

Christine talked about all of this to John. He told her that Ray said the client had found her "too European" in her approach and said that he didn't think she understood the business.

> I was dumbfounded. I had successfully positioned their company to the extent that their competitors were copying their approach. I had given them the international image they wanted. But John said, "Well they've always seen me as the logical one and you as the emotional-arty one."

Christine stated her position in a formal letter to John. He replied in an informal note, trying to minimize her concerns. Within a few months, he shuffled things around and Chris was moved away from the account.

Over the next year Christine watched as the work on the account changed from the original concept and became weaker and more mundane. She felt it was a terrible loss to the client. Even the creative people responsible for the new work were disheartened.

Although she continued to produce good work at the agency, and younger creative people fought to be in her group, Christine felt she was losing ground. Her performance appraisals were always qualified with statements such as, "You produce fine work but you don't have the confidence of upper management." "You should attend more company outings." "You should try to become more American and less European."

Christine pointed out to John that two out of the three comments were on matters that were out of her control. If she didn't have the confidence of upper management after all the good work she had done, then it could only be a matter of personalities. She also told him that although she was originally from Europe, most of her experience and success had been working with American clients. She tried to be universal in her thinking and to create solutions that went beyond national stereotypes. As for the company outings, as a single person she felt that her failure to attend family events wasn't something that would upset anyone else in the company. John agreed with her. Christine added that she felt she was fighting a losing battle at the agency in spite of her good performance record, and asked if he would help her get a transfer.

Shortly afterwards, the agency lost a major account. Ray and John announced that they would have to cut staff by a third. One morning when the staff arrived, many of them had a letter on their desks that told them they would not have a job after the Christmas holiday. Christine received one of these letters. She was very surprised, because her accounts were going strong. Two other executives came to tell her how shocked they were to hear the news. One of them said he had heard that the reason was that she had asked for a transfer and John was known to hold grudges against people who wanted to leave. The other colleague told Christine that Ray once had pulled a list out of a drawer and said, "See this? This is my hit list. Anyone on here is like a deer in my headlights." He thought that Christine's name had been on the list.

> Until going to this agency, I had been very fortunate to have always worked with people who respected one another and enthusiastically shared the joy and the responsibility of the big idea, no matter where it came from. I've seen how ideas flow when no one is afraid to speak up, and I've watched the quality of the work get better and better when the focus has been on the work rather than on internal or external politics. At these agencies, people who behaved disrespectfully would not have been tolerated. I've been profoundly affected and I feel the damage has been greater than I first realized. I haven't lost confidence in my professional ability, but I have lost faith in human nature in avaricious business environments.

Two years later, the agency lost the large account Christine had worked on—plus all of it's major accounts except one, a very traditional account with the "old guard" firmly in place. Ray was eventually fired. John remains with the agency.

ANALYSIS

We saw in the last story how the constant competition of a Win/Lose Culture wore down Jane's resistance until she began to question her abilities and talents. Christine suffered many of the same problems as Jane, but her situation was more complicated.

We mentioned earlier that some organizations have more than one abusive culture operating at the same time. This story has elements of all three cultures—sacrifice, win/lose, and most destructive of all, blaming.

The fact that nobody dared to tell the client that six weeks was too little time to prep, shoot, and edit a major television commercial set in multiple locations, suggests a Culture of Sacrifice; the fierce, antagonistic competition among the players is a characteristic of the Win/Lose Culture; and finally, the scapegoating of Christine turned this corporate environment into a Culture of Blame.

A lot of companies pay lip service to developing bold, cutting-edge strategies either for their clients or themselves, but when it comes to making the presentation, they choose the familiar and the safe. Sometimes they don't feel capable of carrying off a bold, challenging campaign, sometimes they're too lazy, most often they are afraid that a highly visible campaign might backfire and create negative publicity.

Yet great ideas are like gold in today's economy. In a nonabusive company everybody shares ideas, and in the process good ideas become even better as they are refined and enlarged. That's not what happened to Christine. Her idea frightened Ray, the general manager of the advertising agency. For Ray, the Big Idea became the Big Risk, and set off a number of abusive behaviors.

Safe advertising may not hurt the client in the short term, but a steady diet of banal commercials and lackluster images will eventually sell the product short. Inevitably, the client will lose business and the advertising agency will lose the client. We read all the time about clients switching ad agencies, but it happens in other industries too when companies become so mired in convention that innovation itself becomes a threat.

Even though John supported Christine by insisting her idea be presented to the client, he compromised its potential by agreeing to a production schedule that was ludicrously short. In doing so, he set up Christine for almost certain failure. Then, when Christine told him her reservations, he retreated from the problem he had created.

Ray, John, and Henry all tried to protect themselves by standing back from the project in case it failed, yet maneuvered themselves so that they could reap the glory if it succeeded. In fact, at various points along the way, they even created problems so they could solve them. That is quintessential Win/Lose behavior in which one employee is pitted against another until eventually someone loses.

Although Christine asked both John and Ray for help in coordinating the production of the commercial, Ray did nothing but lay on the pressure to succeed, while John, who would have normally found reasons to get involved, made himself busy elsewhere. By setting Christine up as a scapegoat, they introduced elements of a Culture of Blame, a diabolical combination that can destroy even the most resilient and talented people.

Christine became the scapegoat for a number of people to vent their deep insecurities. The verbal abuse they heaped on her was both personal and deeply offensive. It ranged from gender harassment, intimidation and bullying, to torpedoing her career. Henry, the account director for the project, was the traditional bully. He was at the same level in the organization as Christine, but he treated her like a subordinate. Politically John liked to play it safe, hiding and calculating behind his fear. John's comment, "They've always seen me as the logical one and you as the emotional-arty one" reeks of the grossest stereotyping. When we asked Christine about this sexist remark, she laughed and said:

> John shows so little emotion generally that some of us have thought a bomb could go off and he probably wouldn't blink—next to him anyone might appear emotional. . . . I think he probably leveraged this perception to his advantage behind the scenes with the client.

Initially, all three men increased the risk of failure, not only for Christine, but for the agency. Ray and John abdicated their responsibility by hiding in their offices, and Henry covered his behind by publicly placing the onus for any failure on Christine. As the job progressed, Henry was always in a position to intercept messages and interpret events so that he could cast himself in the best possible light with the client. At various times this meant "whipping Christine into shape," or creating problems for no purpose other than to show he could solve them.

In the end, of course, the agency lost far more than Christine did. She has moved on and continues to help companies create innovative ideas. The agency not only lost business, it lost a creative, risk-taking employee who was eager to inject new ideas and approaches into the operation. Eventually, Ray was replaced by someone within the company, but what was really needed was for someone or several people to come from outside and offer real leadership to the agency. An abusive culture is like a cancer and in this case the head office needed to cut much deeper before the abuse became so widespread it was inoperable.

For the most part, CEOs of large companies are slow to make changes at the top of their organizations, and are *very slow* to make changes at the top in their regional organizations. But often this is exactly what they must do to get the kind of innovative ideas they want. Before bringing in additional talent, CEOs should have a thorough knowledge of what is going on in their regional offices and ask the question, "What are the roadblocks to producing better work from this office?" Obviously, there is a reason why the talent isn't there. Insecurity in leaders will affect moral and hiring decisions as well as tenure—typically the wrong people will stay while the right people will shoot out of the door.

In this situation Christine would have had little to lose by being more confrontational. As she became aware of people playing off one another, Christine could have taken more control by calling a meeting with everyone concerned to present the issues and their ramifications to the task ahead. She could be direct with Ray and John and say, "I see you backing away," or point out to Henry and the others that his defensiveness was leading to a lot of blaming and bullying. A meeting like this, followed by a written account of the discussion, could have protected her from many of the woes she later experienced.

As Christine discovered, Cultures of Blame drive a wedge between people and their work by closing off opportunities for people to make changes. Individuals who try to bring about change are isolated from the herd and often punished.

THE SATELLITE SYNDROME

Don was a senior executive in a large American packaged-goods company. He had been with the company for several years and was considered brilliant by many of his colleagues. The company Don worked for was extremely successful and had saturated the U.S. market with its products. Consequently, Don felt the greatest opportunity for growth lay in opening companies abroad, particularly in Europe.

Don put together a comprehensive presentation outlining his vision to become the biggest brand name in Europe, starting with the United Kingdom. He presented it to the CEO and the president of the company who reacted with enthusiasm—and skepticism. At the end of the meeting, Don was given a challenge: "OK, it's your big idea, you go and do it!" Don picked up the gauntlet and was immediately promoted to president of the European company, which, of course, did not exist at this point.

This was the company's first attempt at doing business overseas. There was nothing in place, nobody to consult, and nowhere to seek guidance.

> When I got off the plane in London and everyone except me was being met by a company representative, it really hit me that I was on my own. I had no idea what to expect. I'd never even set foot in England before.

For the next six months Don lived out of hotels while trying to establish the U.K. subsidiary. The first task he set for himself was to obtain information about international policies from other large international companies, which he then used to develop a strategy for his own company.

Like many executives who go to England, Don was not prepared for the cultural differences he faced. He felt that because the language was the same, everything else would be fairly similar too. But as George Bernard Shaw said when referring to Americans and Britons: "We are two peoples divided by a common language."

> In a way it would have been easier to be in Germany or Italy, even though I didn't speak the language, because at least I would have expected everything to be different.

Soon, however, Don realized that his biggest problem was neither culture shock nor setting up a company abroad; rather, it was dealing with home base. Every time he sent an expense report back to the head office, he would get abusive phone calls from his bosses.

> They couldn't relate to the high cost of living in England. The exchange rate alone meant my expenses were twice what they would have been in the U.S. This did not sit well with the head office.

The company was very parochial and had a strong internal culture with pronounced views on how to succeed and what things should cost. The CEO and other executives at home base thought Don was living high off the hog in England. They questioned every expense and mistrusted his recommendations. They seemed incapable of grasping the high cost of living in London.

The company expected Don to manage with the same budgets he was given in the United States. For example, his car allowance, which was adequate in the States for a quality car, only bought him a compact in England. His wife, Holly, was expected to find a home for the same money as the one they'd had in the States, but when real estate prices and fees were factored in, Holly found she had only half the money she needed to buy an equivalent home.

Don was amazed by the problems that would continually arise regarding budget allocations.

> I desperately wanted to put these issues behind me. I felt the only way to convince home base of the situation in England was to hire an

outside consultant. This seemed like a reasonable solution to me, but my bosses in the States were still unconvinced. When I passed on the information, which I had acquired from an international bank, they still insisted on handling things their way, and in the end it cost the company a lot more money.

Holly was finding it impossible to get even the simplest tasks accomplished at home. She needed plumbers and decorators, but the means of hiring them she used in the States just didn't seem to work in England. This frustration, combined with caring for children in a strange environment and sacrificing her own career to make the move, meant things were constantly at the boiling point.

> We had three small children, one seven months, one two years, and one six years. I tried to arrange health insurance. I talked to everyone and got a good recommendation from another international company, but the head office again said, 'We'll do our own research when we can get to it.' They never got to it!

The frustrations mounted.

> Other expatriates from different companies got a lot of support. Don's company was unwilling to help but wouldn't give us the freedom to do it ourselves, either.

On the business front, Don's budgets were also under scrutiny, and he was repeatedly called back to the United States to justify his plans. Everyone paid lip service to Don's goal of making the company one of the top five in the world, but nobody was prepared to do what was needed to get there.

Typically, Don would be asked to present business plans over and over again, and he would have to pull huge presentations together at the last minute. The CEO, who was a verbally abusive and intimidating leader, humiliated Don in front of his peers regularly. Although Don stood up to the CEO and justified his position, he returned to England feeling alone and mistrusted.

> I would wake up in a cold sweat many nights. I had an almost overwhelming fear of failure. I was on my own. It was sink or swim. I had the stress of putting the business together, I had the stress of putting my personal life together, and I had the stress of not being trusted back in the U.S.

He tried to talk to his immediate boss, Lee, the president of North American operations, but Lee offered no help and had a "just get on with it" attitude. Nor did he support Don to the CEO. Holly believed:

> Everyone back in the U.S. envied Don; they thought we had a dream life. The reality was that 50 percent of his time was spent out of the country. He'd go to North America or Europe twice a month for a week at a time.

Eventually Don's two key assistants, Juan and William, were sent to England to join him. Holly said it was his need to show leadership to these men that helped him hold on.

> Don had a great following of people who worked for him. People trusted and respected him, and he got a lot of support from them, but he was losing support at the head office.

Don's struggles paid off. The product became an overnight success in England, and Don's new task was to do the same in other European countries. But he still didn't get the trust he had earned. Although the CEO included Don more in his strategic thinking, the abusive behavior, penny-pinching, and humiliating tactics continued. Every budget request Don made for the start-up costs in Europe was met with the same mistrust that he had experienced in England. Don was again in the position of having to justify every decision to the executives at home, whose bigoted and dismissive attitudes toward the Europeans appalled him. The head office always felt Don paid too much and just didn't know how to manage properly. According to Holly:

> People outside the company trusted Don more than his bosses did. He would often be in the position of apologizing for head office behavior to people he was trying to negotiate with. No matter how successful Don was, when it came to trust and respect, he was always treated as though it was his first day on the job.

Don said:

> I would go to the U.S. for presentations and come back to England really enthusiastic. Then they would pull the rug out and change plans. I traveled constantly, and the jet lag was catching up with me. I was always being called back to the U.S. to justify my actions, which I could have done over the phone, but they insisted I be there in person.

In spite of all these problems, Don was a success. The company prospered with the new acquisitions. But just as he was negotiating what he felt was the prime acquisition in Europe, he was told, "Forget it!" He had pulled a deal together in Ireland that would have doubled the business, but the head office wouldn't go along with his plan.

In the meantime, Don's boss was promoted to CEO, the CEO became chairman of the board, and Don was told to come home to take his boss's job as president of the North American company. Even though Don's bosses were suspicious of his work in Europe, they couldn't ignore his stellar performance. Still, Don didn't know from one day to the next if they approved of *him*. The only way they acknowledged his capabilities was when they gave him another task.

Don was frustrated and disappointed, but when he got back to the States he put a plan in place to make the American company more profitable. Key to his vision was empowering his employees. Their trust and efforts were essential if he was to succeed, and succeed he did: His company's returns tripled.

This was not the happy ending to Don's story, however. His boss, who by now was the CEO, said the returns had to be better to satisfy the holding company, which needed a continual flow of cash to bail them out from some bad investments. The holding company had diversified and bought several businesses outside the company's area of expertise. These companies were foundering and constantly hemorrhaged money from the core company that Don ran.

> Even though the core business was making large profits, it was always used as "the bank" and always under pressure to make more profit. My boss demanded I close plants and let people go. I tried to save the erosion of the core business by making deals with the employees of the plants that were about to be closed. I told them if they could improve productivity over the next twelve months, we could avert closure. I also promised to re-educate them so that if the plant closed they would be prepared to go on to new functions.

This plan was well received by the employees, and they set records of productivity. But this was not enough. Don's boss wanted the plants closed regardless. This meant Don would have to break his agreement with the employees and in doing so lose their trust. If he lost the trust of the employees of the plants, he would not be able to lead the company. Holly said:

> When Don gave his word he would stick by it, but the company often put Don in the position of having to go back on it.

Not this time. Don informed his boss, the CEO, that if he wanted the plants closed he would have to close them himself. The CEO closed the plants. Soon after, Don was summoned to the CEO's office. He knew what was going to happen that morning, yet for the first time in a very long time, he found himself singing along with the radio on his way into work. In the previous five years Don had felt angry and frustrated over the way he had been treated, and he knew that sooner or later he would be fired. But that morning, the day it happened, he was remarkably cool, calm, and collected. Holly said:

> I was relieved when Don was fired. He was tense all the time and I was afraid for him. I knew he loved his job, in spite of everything, and that he would have continued to try harder and harder to pull everything together.

Don was compensated monetarily, but he suffered a great deal in the year following his dismissal and wondered what he had done wrong. He felt that his dismissal was his own fault. His self-esteem plummeted, and although he was able to make more money as a consultant, he felt damaged by his experience.

> Over the next sixteen months I focused on retooling myself. I experienced greater intimacy with my family and a great period of personal growth.

Don realized that the next position he took would have to be with leaders who shared his commitment and vision. Finding the right company became his quest. He found his new company, and although it isn't as large, he looks forward to doubling their profits and taking them into international markets. His first destination? London, England.

ANALYSIS

We've called this section "The Satellite Syndrome" because Don's company has the same attitude that people often show toward remote technology: I know it's there, and I know that it's working, but dammit, I can't see it! We know that satellites are bringing us television signals and long-distance telephone calls, but we can't see them and don't really understand how they work. And what can't be seen often cannot be appreciated.

An example of this syndrome closer to home can be found with telecommuting. Many companies are reluctant to let employees work from home because they feel that if the employees are out of sight, they are also out of control. Managers want to see who is working for them. They often do not trust people to put in the same amount of hours at home—despite all the studies that show that telecommuters often do more work at home than in the office.

In these days of dispersed workplaces and international operations, satellite offices are on the increase. Making these offices work means doing extensive preparation and planning. Don made a single presentation and got the go-ahead to open a new office, but neither he nor his company had fully explored all the ramifications of the decision. On the one hand, the company set Don up for failure, as a scapegoat who would prove to them that globalization was not for them. On the other hand, Don was so enthusiastic about his idea that he didn't spend enough time thinking about the obstacles he would face.

Don sensed the company's skepticism from the beginning, although there was enthusiasm for the idea of expansion too. He didn't research the problems he would face in England as thoroughly as he researched the opportunities, which meant that the company was unprepared for the differences in the cost of living, the expenses of setting up a brand-new office in a different culture, the start-up costs of becoming known in a well-established and crowded market. Don should have done more homework before he made his presentation. The research that Holly did on house prices and health insurance should also have been completed before they left the United States.

Hiring an outside consultant was a good idea, although perhaps Don should have done so as soon as he arrived. He might have done even better to draw up a list of consultants and let the head office pick one out, making the choice partly their decision. Turning over a decision, any decision, to the head office always makes them feel more involved.

This is a case that shows the worst of acting like a big company and the worst of acting like a small company. Don's employers acted like a big company in the sense that the implicit rule was do not trust any employee. Most large corporations today have built so many checks and balances into their systems that they've become penny-wise and pound-foolish. They assume the employees are out to take advantage of them and treat them accordingly.

The worst of the small-company mentality is the naïveté that comes with international expansion. We can do it on a shoestring. We'll operate just the way we do in our home country. This is a provincial attitude founded on the assumption that business is business the world over. The combination of the two is a formula for failure: the home office believes they know how to get the work done, but they don't trust the ambassador they've sent to do it.

The culture of the company was operating against Don at every turn. The company was conservative and insular and liked to keep its employees on a short rope. This type of culture is diametrically opposed to Don's vision and to the global nature of today's economy. In a global economy the adage "Think globally, act locally" is the rule to live by, but Don's company was not open to learning how to succeed in new markets. Don did everything he could to understand and work within the new culture and at the same time hired a consultant to support his conclusions and to provide the company with as much data as possible.

Perhaps the greatest abuse Don suffered was the lack of trust and acknowledgment of his successes. By its actions the company broke one of the major rules of good management: reward excellent performance. Tangible rewards are promotion, money, and benefits; intangible rewards are trust, support, respect, credit, and acknowledgment. Don was denied the intangible rewards he deserved. Even the tangible rewards he received were not in proportion to the revenue he earned for the company.

There was no support for Don, despite his outstanding performance. The sorry events that occurred after his return to the States reveal the company's scapegoating nature. The holding company, by taking profits from Don's achievements to give to underperforming companies, showed little regard for the welfare of its employees and ultimately made Don a scapegoat to appease the shareholders. Furthermore, because the company did not trust Don to produce results over time, it closed plants. This abused many more people, perhaps unnecessarily, because they had trusted in Don's promise to them. This is where Don broke a rule of good management: Never make promises to employees unless you have the backing of the company's leaders. Allowing people to hope and then dashing those hopes does more damage than telling them the bad news at once.

It is essential to recognize and understand how a Culture of Blame works, if only to try to avoid fiascoes like the plant closures. Don kept hoping against hope that he could change the company's mind, and he made promises to the employees that he couldn't keep, based on this hope. In hindsight, it is obvious that the CEO was never going to reverse his original decision. If there is one thing that CEOs in these cultures hate, it is being proved wrong by a subordinate. It takes courage to admit error and change one's mind; courage does not appear to be part of the CEO's makeup. He did not support Don when he was in England but preferred to toe the company line. It didn't matter that Don's strategy was brilliant and workable; nothing could have saved those plants.

The other significant part of this story is the way the company saw its role. It focused less on what had to be done than on how to do it. In other words, it took a tactical approach when it should have been more strategic in its focus. This meant that Don had to defend his activities to the head office instead of looking there for ideas, problem-solving, and support. This created a hostile environment within the company. Enormous amounts of time were wasted complying with head-office requirements just to make Don's bosses feel comfortable. None of this activity contributed to getting the real job done.

Don's promotion shows that the head office considered him a star performer, despite all the harassment about decision-making and budgets. In a paradoxical way, they trusted him, but they still couldn't give him the autonomy he needed. Companies in Cultures of Blame often depend on star performers and punish them at the same time. It is paradoxical, but they need the talents and skills of people like Don to win new markets, save accounts, and burnish the bottom-line figures, but they also need scapegoats when things go wrong. Don's obvious talent makes him stand out from the other managers, but remember what happens to the nail that sticks up in a Culture of Blame.

The other difficulty with being a star performer is that stars are expected to go it alone; they are not perceived as being part of a team. Don preferred to work with others, but his heroic efforts on his own made him look like a one-man show. The arrival of Juan and William offset this isolation, but by then Don was identified with the role of solitary prospector.

Sometimes when we are given a difficult job, we are inclined to tough it out on our own, without asking for help. We work harder and harder, exhausting ourselves in the process, believing that to do anything less is a better strategy. But consulting colleagues and listening to their advice sends a message that you trust and respect them, whereas working furiously on your own sends the message "I'm the only person capable of doing this work."

As we shall see in section three, the new world of work that is emerging in the 1990s will need team players more than star performers. Old work structures emphasize individual performance and compartmentalization, but the new work regime will need people who know that asking for help is a sign of strength and confidence. Don might have done better to take a colleague with him when he went to England right at the beginning. It would have made an enormous difference to his morale, given another member of the firm valuable experience, and provided backup in his dealings with the head office.

Although we are often seduced by movies and books in which an individual succeeds against overwhelming odds and brings about a change of heart in another person or an organization, in real life this occurs very rarely. People do change, but not overnight, and organizations containing hundreds of people are even slower to see the error of their ways.

Don may have assumed that the decision to expand into the European market indicated a willingness to try new things, but in fact the company seemed almost determined to ensure that the European venture would fail. Don succeeded on his own in spite of the company, not because of it, and this should have told him something. There was no fundamental change at the head office; had he stayed in Europe, the hassles would have continued.

Firing Don was inevitable because this is a culture in which the focus of blame is the individual. If results cannot be delivered in a form that is expected from the head office, there must be someone at fault. Don had to defend himself to the bitter end. No wonder he was relieved when he was fired. He was careful not to make the same mistake again and went looking for a company that would support his ideas, a smaller company that was likely to be more flexible, and a younger company that was still growing.

Ironically, if Don had been less talented, hard-working, and committed, he might have recognized the true nature of his company sooner. A lot of the success that occurs in hostile environments is simply wasted labor. Don's achievements probably did not outlive him at the company. Going international is high risk for any company, but particularly for a small one. This company lowered that risk by using a very successful person who had more than proved his worth over the years, but then it raised the risk again by giving him less, not more, support than he would have received at home.

In the end, by abandoning Don, the company not only lost a leader but jettisoned the key person in its organization who had international experience. What's more, it lost the incremental value of Don's experience because in firing him, it lost somebody who could develop other people in international markets. It simply threw away all the money it had begrudgingly invested in international expansion.

APPLES AND ORANGES

Since the days of Florence Nightingale, the role of a nurse has gone through many changes. Historically, nurses have been in charge of the well-being of the patient. Before World War II, doctors often deferred to a nurse's judgment because nurses often knew more about individual patients.

But when doctors marched home from the battlefield, they brought with them new technological equipment that was outside the nurse's expertise, and a gulf emerged between the two professions. The role of nurse seemed to change from one of power over the well-being of a patient to one of "assistant to the all-powerful physician." In the 1950s some nurses were told that thermometers were something only physicians had the skill to use. This loss of status was further compounded in the 1960s and 1970s when many doctors started to hire physician's assistants from outside the nursing profession.

These assistants had to complete a two-year program to be able to assist doctors with patient procedures. Many nurses felt this system was not in the best interests of the patient, so in 1975 the American Nursing Association created the new designation of nurse practitioner. Nurses with at least two years' experience could increase their nursing and clinical skills by taking a nine-month course that would train them to take over many of the duties and responsibilities traditionally reserved for doctors, such as conducting physical exams, prescribing medicine under the co-signature of a physician, ordering lab tests, and admitting patients to the hospital.

The role of nurse practitioner gave more tools to nurses to fulfill their traditional role of caregiver and patient advocate, as well as their job briefing patients thoroughly on their condition and treatment, a task often too time-consuming for busy physicians. Perhaps most importantly, it gave the nurse practitioner the authority to have an opinion, as opposed to providing information so the doctor could form an opinion.

In 1975 Helen was one of eight persons from veterans hospitals all over the United States selected to take part in the new nurse practitioner program in Arizona. This was both an honor and a challenge for her. She was the first person in her family ever to complete high school, let alone enter a profession, and now she was taking a half step closer to being a doctor.

When she completed her training, Helen was eager to return to her VA hospital in the Northeast and practice what she had learned. However, Helen's chief nurse didn't seem to understand Helen's role as a nurse practitioner, even though she had visited the training hospital to give lectures on the new program and the plans to integrate nurse practitioners into the VA system. She led Helen to a cubbyhole. "This will be your office," she said. "Prepare a document for me that outlines what you can and cannot do."

Helen wrote a proposal for the chief nurse that outlined her skills and defined how the role of nurse practitioner could bridge the gap between patient care and medicine. She also described how she would start a nurse-run diabetic clinic and perform various lab tests. The chief nurse didn't react favorably to the proposal.

> She mostly picked on the language I had used in the proposal and ignored the content. She also said she would not allow me to write prescriptions and would assign me to a physician who would dictate what I could do. When I was introduced to the physician, he just said "Hi" and walked off. In fact, during the whole time I worked for him, he never spoke to me directly again. He used to ask his secretary to call me to come and run his clinic for him.

During this time Helen set up a diabetic clinic that was scheduled to provide care for 10 patients. It eventually grew to provide care for 400 to 450 patients.

> My job was very difficult. I had to bone up on the patients' histories and take their physicals. The physician's attitude made it very difficult for me. I was on my own. I tried to set up a regular monthly meeting, but he was not interested and made it clear I was never to go into his office. He was effectively unavailable.

The chief nurse didn't make it easy for Helen either.

> She saw me as a nurse and wanted total control over me and what I did.
> She wanted me to do things that she needed done in her area in addi-
> tion to my responsibilities at the clinic. She loaded me up with assign-
> ments. She also insisted on putting me on hospital committees. All my
> personal time was taken up with hospital duties. It was very hard on
> me. I was becoming overwhelmed by the workload and felt completely
> on my own.

Helen was frustrated and disappointed by the lack of support for
the nurse practitioner program. She spent a lot of time trying to convince the nurses that the role of a nurse practitioner protects the interest of all nurses, but clearly there was a lot of professional jealousy to
overcome. Then in 1978 Helen left her husband.

> I think in retrospect I probably wanted to run away from my job more
> than my husband. So later that same year I took a position at another
> hospital.

Helen applied for an opening for a nurse practitioner in a VA hospital in Ohio. Although Josephine, the assistant to the chief of nursing,
was familiar with nurse clinicians, Helen had to explain the difference
between a nurse practitioner and other nursing roles. Nevertheless,
Josephine offered Helen a staff nurse job, which was much less than the
position Helen was applying for and qualified to do.

> Apparently the chief nurse at my former hospital had not given me a
> good reference and said that I had difficulty fitting in. So there I was,
> after all my training, basically back to square one. I had never worked
> on a general ward. Prior to becoming a nurse practitioner, I had worked
> in coronary and intensive care and infection control areas. This staff
> position didn't take advantage of any of my skills. I took the job, though,
> because by this time I was a single parent with three children and
> I needed to work.

Helen continued to try to apply for the nurse practitioner job, but
Josephine controlled the applications and Helen was sure no one else
was informed of her skills. One day the head nurse of the ward Helen
was working on said, "Didn't you get that nurse practitioner's job?" Helen
asked which job she meant. The head nurse then told Helen that there
was a nurse practitioner's job available in neurology and offered to write

a memo about Helen to the chief nurse. Later she told Helen, "The chief nurse was shocked that you hadn't been interviewed."

Helen got the job in the neurology department, where she helped to train residents and walked them through their first spinal tap. The young residents were receptive and even grateful to Helen. Initially the other nurses resisted Helen's orders, but eventually they came to see her as an ally.

> I think they began to see that I could teach them things that would make them better nurses and that I was there for the betterment of the patient. The good news was they accepted me; the bad news was sometimes they overrelied on me. So I was working too hard and too long again. And I was still only getting the pay of an intermediate-grade nurse.
>
> By this time I had been with the VA for fifteen years and was up for a promotion to senior-grade nurse with more pay. When I tried for a promotion, I was turned down because I hadn't published a paper or completed a "complex enough assignment." I was determined to qualify, and when the chief nurse was unable to tell me what a "complex assignment" was, I went to the director. He had received excellent recommendations about me from the chief of neurology and said he would support me if I protested the decision.

Helen was beginning to learn the acceptance of her skills as a nurse practitioner was a double-edged sword. The more people understood what she could do, the more demands they made of her.

> I was working from 6 A.M. to 8 or 9 P.M. almost every day. I was burned out. I decided to go to a smaller community.

This was to become Helen's most positive and rewarding position in her career as a nurse practitioner.

> I was able to run a clinic with the support staff I needed, and we were able to give excellent care to forty patients a day instead of only fourteen patients a day. Help was given as I needed it, and the patients really appreciated our efforts.

Outside the hierarchy of the VA hospital culture, there seemed to be greater acceptance of the role of nurse practitioner. But Helen stayed only two years before returning to her original hospital to work with Janice, an old friend who was the chief nurse. Janice was very supportive of the nurse practitioner role, and this looked like a very good move for Helen, with more pay and more opportunity. The chief of medicine

at the hospital wanted Helen to set up a number of clinics, inc
centralized clinic for AIDS patients, which would require more tra
for Helen.

Almost immediately disaster struck. Janice was offered a once-in-a-
lifetime opportunity at another hospital and left. She was replaced by
Doreen, who made it quite clear from the beginning that she did not
approve of the role of nurse practitioner.

> She seemed to come through the door hating me. When we had staff
> meetings, I would speak up on behalf of the nurses about this or that
> and she would say, "You're just a troublemaker." She would cancel my
> vacations and find a number of ways to humiliate me in front of the
> other nurses.

Fortunately, the chief of staff supported Helen in her efforts to get
the vacation she was entitled to. But repeatedly the chief nurse undermined her efforts and gave her only "satisfactory" grades, while the
surgeons she'd worked for gave her "highly satisfactory" evaluations.

> Although the chief nurse was told by the chief of staff to re-evaluate me
> more fairly, she really wasn't reprimanded for her unfairness or ques-
> tioned further. The VA system is similar to the military in that it always
> supports the administration and upholds actions taken by the admin-
> istration, regardless.
>
> It was clear to me that I couldn't succeed as long as I was reporting
> to her. The chief nurse was threatened by me and my role as nurse prac-
> titioner. She never knew what I was there for and really didn't want to
> know. It was her policy to keep all of the nurses at a distance, and I
> think because she was a military woman, she really kept strict rules
> around the hierarchy in the hospital. I always felt I was deliberately kept
> in the dark about things that could impact how I did my job.

By 1990 Helen had taken all she could take from the chief nurse and
transferred to the VA hospital in Los Angeles. Again the request for a nurse
practitioner did not come from the chief nurse but from the chief of
ambulatory care. He wanted a nurse practitioner to set up a nurse-run
clinic and asked Helen to come for two years. But Helen once again knew
she was heading for trouble when she got a call from Loretta, the chief
nurse.

> You're under my control, and I won't pay for your travel expenses down
> here. Staff nurses don't get paid travel and I don't see any difference
> between you and a staff nurse. There will be no favoritism.

Los Angeles, the chief nurse put her at the ierarchy under the chief nurse's assistants, the rs, the head nurse, and the staff nurses. She ·len so far down in the administration that she

managed to set up several clinics, including an a diabetic clinic, and a women's health clinic, which altogether offered care to more than six hundred patients. Helen has not taken a day off in four years. She is so involved with the patients that she doesn't feel she can have a holiday until a replacement nurse practitioner is found. She complains that "no one is prepared to take over my responsibilities."

Helen feels the biggest problem at the hospital is a lack of cohesion.

> Every service does its own thing. Nursing has walled itself off. Physicians' assistants want no part of the work I do. It seems the right hand never knows what the left is doing and often the patient suffers in the process.

The good news for the hospital is that Helen's Women's Wellness Clinic is currently receiving a lot of attention. Traditionally the VA has focused on men, who form the majority of its patients, but it has begun to acknowledge that more and more women are becoming veterans and need all the expertise available to them.

> When someone comes to interview me about the Women's Wellness Clinic, Loretta says, "Put something on my desk by the end of the day to update me." Then she thinks I'm OK. She even shows me off!

When Helen was asked what changes she would like to see in her work environment, her requests seemed reasonable enough:

> I would like to be allowed to continue giving the health care that I am trained to give. I would like recognition for the role of nurse practitioner. I would like more nurses to be trained as nurse practitioners. I would like every VA sent a mandate to set up nurse practitioner–run clinics, and I would like to be able to take a vacation!

ANALYSIS

The Veterans Affairs hospitals where Helen works are hierarchical and bureaucratic. Nevertheless, Helen has found opportunities to move forward, and her persistence is paying off. She hasn't gotten it completely right—she needs to work on her delegating skills and on saying "no" more often—but she has come a long way and is beginning to get some recognition, even if some of it is grudging. Helen's story is a lesson in creating change in a blaming organization. It is a very long-term project: Helen has been at it for thirty years, and she hasn't finished yet.

Helen is an outsider with new ideas in an old-fashioned, often stagnant system. She represents change, and for these organizations, change represents danger. She threatens the status quo. What she experiences as abuse is the outcome of the organization's fear. What many of the hospitals Helen has worked for should have been doing, and weren't, was asking themselves what is the cost to the health care system of not being able to change the environment when change is desperately needed? When a bureaucracy builds a wall against a cheaper, better solution to a problem, the cost is not borne just by one person or one hospital but by an entire system in terms of direct costs and in terms of development by discouraging people from reskilling or retraining. By being so resistant, the system freezes or immobilizes a whole set of aspiring individuals.

The key to this case is changing roles. Helen was a casualty of a hierarchical system not ready for a power shift. Throughout her various jobs, this was the central theme. As in the other cases of abuse, Helen felt out of control. From her perspective, she had gained the training, understood the role, and could demonstrate the benefits to patients; therefore the system was wasting all she had accomplished.

Cultures of Blame destroy people's belief in themselves. Anyone who is different or who wants to work in a new way is labeled "crazy" or "a troublemaker." A person can have a good idea and fight fearlessly for years, but the system may still kill it through sheer inertia. These cultures drive a wedge between people and their work by closing off opportunities to make changes.

Individuals who try to bring about change in Cultures of Blame are isolated, because the system demands and rewards conformity. Many pioneers allow themselves to be convinced that they are wrong and everyone else is right, and they give up at this point. It says a lot for Helen's self-esteem that she didn't give up on her ambition.

Pioneers should keep in touch with other pioneers; not only does this ease the loneliness, but each one can learn from the others. If you are in a new or emerging field, you must reach out to others in your field at every opportunity, particularly if you are under stress in a Culture of Blame.

Helen tried to explain her role to her bosses, but she did not confront the real reason for their resistance and so she was unable to make people change their minds. Her approach did work, however, with people beneath her in the hierarchy. It provided them with a method to improve their own skills. They did not have much power, so they did not perceive a loss of power with Helen's role. With this leap of faith, Helen was able to demonstrate the benefit to patients.

Selling the idea of change is tough. People have to be shown what's in it for them. Helen needed to change the minds of some key decision makers, and this took persistence. If the chief nurse was hostile, the chief nurse had to be won over. What was in it for the chief nurse? Helen outlined what she, Helen, could do, but not how it would make the chief nurse's life easier. Helen needed to look at the role of the nurse practitioner from the chief nurse's point of view and sell it that way.

Helen's relationship with Doreen was a repeat of her relationship with other nurses who had supervised her. Every blaming culture has its Doreens, who have preconceived notions about work and are hostile to new ideas. Like the chief nurse in Helen's first job, she presumably felt threatened. Helen should have spent time finding ways to show Doreen "what was in it for her": how Doreen could use Helen's skills to enhance her own position. Loretta, in the California hospital, has obviously found a way to benefit from Helen's presence, although she isn't lavish with praise.

Helen's experiences in the Ohio hospital show the importance of networking. Josephine was only an assistant, but she acted as a "gatekeeper" because she controlled applications to nursing jobs. Even so, Helen's other contacts helped her get around that block to promotion. Here Helen was acting like a salesperson who never lets a single "no" stand in the way of a sale.

Information gatekeepers are effective only if people rely on official information channels alone. Informal networks bypass these gatekeepers. Helen obviously let everyone know about her interests and experience, so that when the right opportunity came up, she was able to make a move. She could have done even more, such as contributing to the hospital newsletter or giving seminars on aspects of a nurse practitioner's work to raise her profile and sell her skills.

The job in neurology was a step forward because it was designed for someone with Helen's skills, but there were still problems. Helen says that the other nurses "overrelied" on her, but it may have been that Helen "underdelegated" work to them. There was no reason for her not to share the workload.

Helen's inability to get a promotion and a raise is, unfortunately, quite typical of people who have unusual qualifications or are working in new fields. We know a lawyer in the emerging field of intellectual property who specialized in biotechnology patents. He was accepted for partnership long after his peers in more traditional fields like litigation or corporate law because the other partners never understood his work.

Helen was turned down for promotion because she had not published and had not completed a "complex assignment." The only strategy in this situation was for Helen to document her work carefully in a way that would be intelligible to others. Her response should have been to write an article for publication about the role of the nurse practitioner in neurology and to document her work in a way that demonstrated its complexity.

Helen chose instead to change jobs, presumably because she found the requirements unreasonable. However, other pioneers have taken the attitude "If that's what it takes to get recognized, then I might as well just grit my teeth and do what's necessary." After all, every other senior nurse presumably had to meet these requirements. If Helen had been promoted without meeting the same requirements, she might not have been accepted by the other senior nurses. Sometimes you have to jump through a few hoops to show you are a part of a team.

Writing about her work would also have helped Helen achieve greater recognition for nurse practitioners and perhaps helped her to network with other nurse practitioners in other areas. Talking to other nurse practitioners would have given Helen a new perspective and helped prevent her from getting bogged down in the day-to-day concerns of hospital work.

Helen believes that no one is prepared to take over her responsibilities, but this is no reason for working herself to death. There is absolutely no reason why Helen can't book her vacation tomorrow. In fact, she would be well advised to do so. If there are no volunteers, then she should choose a bright nurse and simply tell her she has to take over for a few weeks. Leaders must always train their successors, and there is seldom time to wait around for volunteers.

Helen finds herself overworked wherever she goes, so it looks very much as if she's the type of person who doesn't delegate enough. She is probably the sort of person who has difficulty saying no. Cultures of Blame love these people. They work them to death, give them very little credit, and toss them aside when they burn out. In a Culture of Blame it is essential to learn how to say no and to practice this skill frequently. Put your foot down. Don't do other people's work for them. Delegate.

Part of saying no is being clear about your goals. Helen says that her goal is to get more recognition for nurse practitioners, but her workaholism may be tying her down with unrelated tasks that don't relate to this goal. Be very clear about what is important to you and where you want to go, and don't accept work that won't take you there. By now, certain themes should be familiar: "I felt completely on my own"; "I was overworked"; "Nobody understood what I was trying to do." These are pretty reliable indicators of an individual trying to bring about change in a Culture of Blame. Pioneers don't have time for nonessentials. Cultures of Blame are often bureaucratic, tied up in red tape, and would-be pioneers have been known to strangle in this tape. Cut it any way you can.

Innovation is critical to business success in the information age. Suppressing it is a slow form of corporate suicide. Abusive companies generally fail to innovate, recruit, or reposition effectively because they stifle initiative. In the information age the most valuable asset of a company will be lively minds working together. In the next section we'll look at how—and how not—to cultivate them.

Cultures of Blame are probably the worst when it comes to suffocating innovation and good ideas. In the last chapter we saw that in Win/Lose Cultures, if a person has a good idea and is prepared for a no-holds-barred fight, he or she has a chance, but Cultures of Blame kill ideas through sheer inertia. As if killing ideas were not enough, these cultures also destroy people's belief in themselves. Anyone who is different or who wants to work in a new way is labeled crazy or a troublemaker. Cultures of Blame drive a wedge between people and their work by closing off opportunities for people to make changes. Individuals who try to bring about change are isolated from the herd. Keeping up one's self-esteem under these circumstances is uphill work.

Partnerships, Not Dictatorships

There is a lot of anxiety in the workplace. People are fearful; leaders are bewildered; entire corporations are sending out distress signals. Many corporations are trapped trying to run backward on an escalator that is traveling at an accelerating clip from the industrial age—the known—through the information age to the future—the unknown. They can't slow it down; they can't pull the emergency handle; the best they can do is run on the spot. No wonder they are scared.

Abusive cultures thrive in this fear. In their turn they encourage people to be anxious and dependent and to develop habits that inhibit their ability to flourish in the future. The information age demands not only an entirely new work regime but a new working partnership. Companies need the immediate solutions we have discussed in this section so that people and corporations can recognize abusive cultures and apply remedies. But they must do more than fix what's wrong; they have to move beyond repair jobs to design sustainable and nurturing cultures. That's the long-term, comprehensive solution.

A good way to describe the difference is in terms of that old bugbear—losing weight. Let's say you need to lose three pounds by next Wednesday to squeeze into your old black-tie outfit. That's a short-term solution that you can achieve with a crash diet. But how are you going to get rid of the extra twenty pounds that have crept up on you over the last five years and, more importantly, keep them off? That's the long term. Changing your eating habits and establishing an exercise regimen is the transitional state. A permanently svelte self is the transformed state.

Transformation is every bit as hard as losing weight permanently and keeping it off. Too many companies make the mistake of simply ordering a change from the top and then expecting a miracle to occur. To use a very minor example, after a certain conglomerate bought a company, it wanted its new acquisition to use a particular product. So a memo was sent to all employees saying that from that day on, no one could use anything except this product. One employee read it and reacted by going out into the hall, throwing the memo into the air, and yelling, "Bullshit!" He quickly attracted a group of curious colleagues. Soon they were all chanting, "Bullshit!" The person who sent that memo was being dictatorial about a very minor change. Imagine the effect of being dictatorial when the whole structure of an organization is in question.

The stories presented in the preceding chapters are not tales from Dickensian workshops; they are stories from large, modern organizations and have occurred within the past five years. Many of the same organizations that subscribe to the latest managerial philosophies of empowerment are at the same time fostering abusive behaviors in Cultures of Sacrifice, Win/Lose Cultures, and Cultures of Blame. Needless to say, little real improvement is occurring. People who are being abused at work are quick to see the hypocrisy of "empowering" and "collegial" rhetoric.

It is obvious to many working in today's companies that while business leaders call for loyalty and commitment, they are doing little to take the pain out of working in today's business climate. Where they could give respect and acknowledgment, they give ultimatums. Where they could share problem-solving, they maintain secrecy. Where they could focus on long-term business solutions, they make ruthless short-term organizational decisions.

The irony is that while experts and business leaders are promoting the importance of individual contributions and creativity within corporations, few people, if any, are looking beyond organizational systems for the emotional and—dare we say it—spiritual road blocks to initiative and creativity.

Often what is binding corporations together is a partnership of fear and insecurity. Being afraid of failure and having to fend for oneself are common denominators in the preceding stories of abuse. In one destructive situation after another, people described the experience of being stranded with no help from the company: "I was on my own," "left alone," "abandoned." Add to this countless examples of unfair treatment, and instead of loyalty, hard work, and inspiration, corporations breed resentment and may even set the stage for sabotage.

Corporate abuse drives away good people. They can't flourish in an abusive culture. Nothing creative can for long. Corporate abuse generates a workplace populated with ruthless self-maximizers, complacent rule followers, frightened automatons, or a combination of the three.

Abuse doesn't make a company competitive over the long haul; it doesn't help employees produce better-quality work; and it doesn't foster an idea-generating environment. And in the future world of work, ideas are the new currency. In the next section we'll take a closer look at how we can strip away the layers of abusive behavior and reveal the creativity that we all have locked inside us.

CIVILIZING THE WORKPLACE

CIVILIZING THE WORKPLACE

AS CREATIVE CONSULTANTS, we visit hundreds of North American organizations that are trying to cope with the challenge of change. Some are struggling just to survive; others are trying to prosper in a global economy. In our separate ways we've both found many highly committed organizations that are floundering. They want to embrace new strategies and technologies, but their values, attitudes, and management practices are more in keeping with the industrial age than the information age. They've bought progressive technologies; they've spent hundreds of thousands of dollars on change-management experts and consultants. They have delayered, restructured, re-engineered, downsized, right-sized, mentored, managed total quality, learned continuously, and replaced managers with team leaders. None of this has helped to create a more motivated workforce or a more sustainable company.

Why not? Because CEOs and presidents have been too preoccupied with theory and jargon to look inside the heart and soul of their corporations at how they treat their own employees. They fail to go beyond the flow charts and organizational diagrams to see the people who must work within them. Oh sure, they talk about empowerment and generating ideas, but they don't know how to let go of authoritarian habits and abusive management styles to promote democratic organizations of shared power, shared purpose, and decision-making freedom. Yet that is what is needed if organizations are to survive, let alone prosper, in the information economy. Nowadays it's not enough to work harder or faster or more efficiently. We have to work smarter.

What's the Big Idea?

If there's one question on the minds of business leaders around the world, this is it. In the past one good idea could take you a long way down the road of success, but today businesses must rely on constant innovation just to stay in the picture. Look at the development of the air bag in automobiles. One day it was the hottest innovation of the automotive industry; the next day it became the industry standard and cars with an air bag on the driver's side only fell far behind those that offered dual air bags.

But before many of us even had a chance to test drive the new vehicles, let alone trade in our old cars, there was yet another innovation—the side impact air bag. What's next?

That is the question, not only for those in the automotive and high-technology industries, but for everyone trying to survive in business today. What can we offer our customers in new products or better service that will ensure sales and loyalty? How can we maintain the highest quality and fastest production possible? How can we make sure our ideas hit the street first?

Asking the right questions and finding the right answers are the keys to innovation and to success. If everything else has changed in our global economy, that is the one constant. Asking questions is the essence of creativity.

The question that business leaders must ask now is "What can we do to encourage ideas and innovation in our company at all levels?"

New ideas have always made the world go round, but technological innovation has accelerated change in the marketplace to a degree impossible for most of us to imagine. The speed at which products are developed and introduced to the global market is staggering. Information technology has created a much more competitive business world by making information itself a commodity to be sold and traded by anybody who can hook up to a network.

The more turbulent the business environment, the more corporations need innovation and flexibility to stay ahead of the competition. We can't do that unless we have working environments and company cultures that encourage creative responses.

We have seen how abusive cultures kill spontaneity, hobble risk-taking, burn people out, and eventually damage the bottom line. In this section we're going to learn how to identify and destroy abusive cultures and to replace them with idea-generating cultures.

In one sense it has taken advanced technology to bring us back to basics, to our origins, to our human capacities and souls. Companies are now back to relying once again on the contribution of people rather than machines for business success. This involves giving people the power to contribute their ideas freely and without fear. To harvest the ideas of all workers, we must be open to new ways of working and managing people. We must be willing to give up traditional controlling behaviors, embrace the idea-generation process, and find new ways to induce people to contribute ideas to their fullest capacity.

Workers are facing the hard reality that there is little, if any, employment security. As the workforce realizes that "golden handcuffs" and "golden handshakes" are as rare as golden eggs and corporations rely more on contract and temporary workers, the entire power dynamic between employer and employee will shift. In the transformed state, corporations won't distinguish between the way they treat internal, permanent workers—the ones who get a paycheck every week—and external suppliers, consultants, and contract workers—the ones who do a job and then move on. Both short-term and core workforces will be equally important to the organization, and all workers will be valued for the skills and experience they bring to the task.

The concept of an employee attached to a particular organization will give way to workers who have ownership of their own careers and who have varying degrees of employability. The distinction between staff and contract workers will not be as clear as it is today. Workers will be in control of their own careers, and they will negotiate their services with corporations on short- or long-term contracts, moving in and out of the corporation on a much more fluid and entrepreneurial basis. Leadership will make the difference between workers trying to escape and those wanting to contribute to the organization, either on a project-by-project or a longer-term basis. That is what we mean by partnerships, not dictatorships.

The Internet, in the way it makes global links and has countless access points, suggests the corporate structure of the future—with one major difference. The Internet has no center. Organizations that thrive in the future will be corporations built around a vibrant core.

Imagine that the organization looks like a web in which leadership radiates from the center and all communications flow along interconnecting strands. At the center there is a source of energy and a focus for common interests. The new psychological contract will run like a current along the strands of the web, bridging the gap between individual needs and corporate expectations in the altered work environment. Psychological contracts will be individual and personal. They'll take the high-minded talk from corporate mission statements and put them into the context of day-to-day work. After all, this is how corporate change should occur: with leadership and commitment radiating from the center and spread throughout every strand of the organization by individual participation and cooperation. But that is not what happens in so many corporations.

We have seen it over and over again. Instead of welcoming ideas and working together to embrace progressive change, people sink into fear and resentment because the work has changed. Those who resort to intimidation, power struggles, bullying, and defending their turf will not succeed in the long run, and their businesses will suffer. The first stage toward the idea-generating culture of tomorrow is getting rid of corporate abuse today. So let's get down to basics.

In this section we'll give you some tools to help you pinpoint the sources and effects of abuse in the corporation. These, along with some of the coping strategies discussed in section two, should provide some short-term relief from corporate abuse. But although a tourniquet may stop the bleeding, it won't heal the wound, so in this section we want to move toward long-term strategies for change. We'll look at some of the forces counteracting the tendency toward corporate abuse and at some of the ways in which corporations are changing their cultures. We'll talk about the need for innovation and creativity, the demands of informational technology, and the generational clash that is helping to clear a space for the new civilized workplace. Above all, we will suggest ways to construct sustainable corporate structures and give you tools that may help you draw your own road map for getting the corporation from here (industrial, hierarchical, rigid) to there (idea-generating, weblike, flexible).

As part of this journey, we'll take a look at the new psychological contract between corporations and individuals and describe the idea-generating culture of the future. This is the goal, the transformed company, which may not look like a company at all and which may not have employees as we define the term now, but which will bring people together for tasks in ever-changing groupings. Yet even though the structures are fluid, there will still be a need for commitment and connection, for teamwork and a sense of shared purpose in a corporation.

We must not delude ourselves that downsizing and streamlining are temporary measures and that bloated workforces will roll back in with prosperity, along with all the trappings of the big, old-fashioned corporations. Those days are gone. We are moving toward a completely different corporate world in which the concept of employee as we know it today won't exist. Welcome to the future.

Dancing with the Devil: Identifying Abusive Cultures

MANY CORPORATIONS seem to be in a midlife crisis. The systems and solutions that worked for them in the past are working against them in today's business environment. Business has evolved and we must evolve with it in order to survive.

We know that without innovation, companies will have difficulty staying competitive. And we know that abusive cultures kill innovation. So why are there still abusive cultures around? Why haven't they all died off or been swallowed up by more innovative and less abusive competitors?

One reason is that abusive companies sometimes find short-term substitutes for innovation, like cost-cutting or producing copycat products using other people's good ideas. Another is that certain companies, particularly institutions, survive because they function in less competitive sectors. For example, if you are the only hospital in the county or the only supplier of Finnish-language books in Florida, there is less incentive to innovate. How do you know if you are spending more than you should or losing sales or missing new opportunities? There are fewer external pressures to make you face up to your mistakes.

Many companies react impulsively to change instead of examining their systems and policies. Troubled by a downturn in sales, many CEOs grab for the panaceas offered by the latest management guru. Management consulting is a multibillion-dollar industry. Ironclad strategies are taken into boardrooms, and CEOs cling to them as if they were life preservers. The CEO is the advocate and the protector of the strategy—

rallying the troops around *the* answer and silencing dissidents. This approach to strategy development probably sounds very familiar. If you're an executive, you know how hard it is to adapt the reality of the workplace to a rigid theory that doesn't allow for supplier delays or labor problems. And if you are a production manager, you know how frustrating it is to try to innovate in an inflexible system. It's like Cinderella's stepsisters trying to squeeze their feet into the glass slipper. It won't work.

Yet desperate companies keep on clutching at external solutions without realizing that they are sabotaging themselves by tolerating and even encouraging corporate abuse. The only logical explanation for this erratic corporate behavior is that they don't recognize the harm they are doing.

In section one we look at three different kinds of abuse: systemic, structural, and deliberate abuse by individuals.

Systemic abuse occurs in companies that have outdated systems and structures yet enlightened policies and visionary mission statements. The dislocation between expectations and reality creates abusive situations. On the surface, the company may say that it values initiative and innovation, but these claims are contradicted by everything in the policies and procedures manual. The abuse is embedded in the systems, procedures, policies, and hiring practices. Employees often find it confusing working for companies that spout slogans like "People Are Our Number-One Resource" or "We Believe in Empowerment" while the employees still feel like cogs in a wheel. The companies say they invest in people, but they never get around to sending workers to professional development courses. Or they hang suggestion boxes on the walls and then smother new ideas in red tape and approval hierarchies. In this demoralizing climate people begin to doubt themselves and think it is their fault that they can't sell their ideas or move up in the ranks.

Another type of systemic abuse occurs when a company promotes two or more contradictory goals. For example, a telecommunications company created a number of special-purpose teams to discuss process re-engineering. At the same time, however, the facilities management group was told to reduce the amount of office space the company used. Their solution was to turn meeting rooms into offices. This meant that the teams couldn't get together quickly and informally because the few remaining meeting rooms were always booked weeks in advance.

After trying to convene meetings in the cramped cubicles in which people worked or in the noisy cafeteria, which was like holding a private meeting in the middle of a marketplace, the teams gave up trying to brainstorm. There was literally no space for creativity or innovation in this company because one stated goal—teamwork—was in conflict with another goal—reduction of office space.

Structural abuse occurs when an entire corporation is under the gun because of downsizing, mergers, buyouts, technological change, or globalization. The pressure usually comes from outside the company, and it can put everybody on the inside—from the CEO to the receptionist—in shock. Managers are thrown into budget-busting mode, and employees live in fear of losing their jobs. People work harder and harder, but nothing changes. All the available creativity is absorbed by people trying to justify their existence or protect their turf. When everybody is stressed and worried, change is too risky to contemplate. Here's an example.

A manufacturing company was restructuring. In fact, no radical downsizing had been planned, but because the company did not communicate its plans to its employees, they worked themselves into a lather worrying about job security. As the planning dragged on with no announcement and no reassurances from top management, the staff became demoralized and productivity declined. As for innovation, everybody was terrified to start new projects or push new ideas. They were all keeping their heads down, hoping they wouldn't be noticed when the big chop came. By the time the employees learned that most of them would keep their jobs in the new order, it was too late to make up for months of lost productivity and creativity.

Deliberate abuse is just that, a premeditated policy or strategy developed and executed on the wrong-headed assumption that it will get results by forcing workers to toe the line. Deliberate abuse can promote a Culture of Blame, or it can lead to a Win/Lose Culture with workers fighting each other. Many managers who worked their way up through an abusive corporation believe that deliberate abuse works because they not only survived it but succeeded. They have noticed that people snap to attention when they are yelled at. Abuse does not provide long-term dividends, but it does produce quick results.

At one retail company the president was called Godzilla behind his back. He specialized in humiliating his staff in public and was universally feared and hated for his blistering criticism. His administrative assistant had a nervous breakdown, and one of the buyers had a car accident when he was driving home in shock after a particularly bad attack of Godzilla's wrath. Godzilla kept close tabs on all of his staff, who were so afraid of spies in their midst that it was very difficult for co-workers to trust one another. When one employee commented that the pressures of her job had contributed to the breakdown of her marriage, Godzilla remarked, "Well, that means you can spend more time at work." Although Godzilla was grudgingly admired for his financial success and his ability to spot retail trends, all the ideas in the company had to come from him because staff members were too terrified to make suggestions that might be seen as a criticism of his way of doing things.

Deliberate abuse can emanate from a single individual in a corporation, as in the case of Godzilla, or it can be the management style throughout a company. The best that can be said about it is that it is easy to spot and to trace to its source. The abused employee knows that he or she is being abused and knows who is doing it, whereas in situations involving systemic and structural abuse, the source of the stress may be harder to pinpoint.

It's easy enough for us to spot and classify abuse. But how do *you* recognize it within your organization? It is always so much easier to identify the problems in other people's lives than in your own. Here's a rule of thumb: if employees are not coming forward with suggestions and new ideas, suspect abuse. We've had plenty of CEOs come to us in despair, saying, "I don't know what's wrong. I've paid hundreds of thousands of dollars to consultants, and yet people are fighting, nothing is working, and we are way behind in sales."

Unfortunately, the change-management report card for many businesses shows a solid "A" for good intentions but a borderline grade for execution. Despite great expectations, incisive strategic plans, bright minds to master the process, and impressive levels of activity, many major initiatives neither live up to their advance billings nor deliver promised payoffs. Change objectives seem to dissolve, leading to lost strategic vision, lackluster results, high blood pressure in the executive suite, and despair and burnout in the workforce.

As more and more companies operate on a global scale, they are less able to control circumstances that affect their businesses. Constant change—in the form of new technology, global trade, currency shifts, environmental disasters, or the phenomenon of countries reinventing themselves—has thrown businesses into unpredictable situations that require answers to questions that, frankly, have never been asked before. The answers will have to come from people, not from technology or statistics based on past experience.

The most significant barrier to changing from an abusive to a nurturing culture is the determination to find the complete and correct answer to all problems. If you insist on textbook responses and concrete strategies, you will breed a stultifying culture that will discourage innovation and foster abuse. The wheel cannot reinvent itself. Individuals must produce a constant stream of innovative ideas to meet local and global business demands. As Alvin Toffler points out in his book *Powershift:*

> *The need for innovation encourages worker autonomy and this implies a totally different power relationship between employer and employee. It means that intelligent error needs to be tolerated. Multitudes of bad ideas need to be floated and freely discussed in order to harvest a single good one, and this implies a new liberating freedom from fear.*

Tolerating error takes a lot of trust. Giving people power means giving up control. To many managers and leaders, this is a terrifying prospect. They would rather manage their own fears—of the future, of the unknown, of change—by producing fear in other people. This takes work, but the alternative is, to them, unthinkable. Meanwhile, one by one, like little candles going out, ideas are snuffed.

Nothing disturbs the peace of creative minds as much as fear. Fear of ridicule from abusive bosses or fear of losing face or losing jobs must be eliminated from day-to-day life in the workplace. People who have to protect themselves in abusive corporate cultures have little time or mental energy for inspiration. Fearful employees play it safe, and playing it safe is the complete opposite of innovation. In a book called *Driving Fear Out of the Workplace*, Kathleen D. Ryan and Daniel K. Oestreich quote a manager in a West Coast service firm:

> *Where there is a lot of fear of screwing up, people don't change behaviors or work systems. Creativity is inhibited. People work one day at a time, rather than looking to the future. High fear environments just create "knee jerking." You spend all your time putting out fires.*

This is especially true of Win/Lose Cultures, where the fear of losing kills innovation, but it can happen in any abusive culture or in the immediate vicinity of a single abusive manager. The stories in this book indicate that many companies have abusive cultures that work against creativity.

The more turbulent the business environment, the more corporations need innovation and the more we need to create working environments and company cultures that encourage creative responses. Although the particular kind of creative solutions will differ from industry to industry, all companies will have to create cultures that encourage their employees to challenge conventional wisdom and to experiment.

This involves giving people at all levels the power to contribute their ideas freely and without fear. In her work with several of the world's largest corporations, Rosabeth Moss Kanter discovered that

> *the degree to which the opportunity to use power effectively is granted to or withheld from individuals is one operative difference between those companies which stagnate and those which innovate.*

Sharing power, particularly in time of crisis, does not come easily to traditional executives in typical hierarchical corporations. Giving others power is often seen as giving up control, and the more out of control we feel, the more we feel we must batten down the hatches and rely on old formulas to help us survive the storm.

The desire to control one's way out of a situation is very human. Just glance at the self-help section in any bookstore and see the volumes offering us the answers to such perennial questions as "How can I gain control of my life?" and "How can I survive any obstacle life throws in my path?" The plea "Just give me the formula and I'll follow it to the letter" follows us into the workplace.

Leaders who follow old methods of hierarchical problem-solving rely on two methods to gain control:

- they compartmentalize the problem; and

- they use workers at the top of the hierarchy to find the solution.

A typical hierarchical structure has a number of departments that, for the most part, act independently of one another. Within the departments there are further vertical and horizontal separations. By compartmentalizing a problem, leaders give ownership of the problem to specific individuals within a particular section of a particular department.

This process reduces problem-solving to a small unit regardless of how many other departments may be affected by it. Even though the problem involves many workers and many departments, the answer is expected to come from as few people as possible, all working in isolation. Keeping problem-solving within the domain of those at the top of the pyramid and involving as few workers as possible gives the leaders a sense of direct control, as well as the delusion that the problem is "managed," "addressed," and "under control."

One advertising executive who witnessed the effects of compartmentalized thinking provides the following story.

> I was working as a senior executive at a large international advertising agency in the U.S. We were faced with the very big problem that one of our largest clients was not convinced the work we were doing for them was as effective as it could be. They decided to invite competing agencies to present advertising concepts. Our agency was invited to make a presentation to defend our position and prove we were capable of finding new solutions to their problems. This business represented about $70 million worldwide for our company. It was important to keep it. For my regional agency it was crucial. We knew that if we lost this business, at least one-third of our office would be laid off. Our agency leaders chose a team of twelve people from the top of the company's worldwide pyramid to work on the presentation.
>
> The director and four of the creative directors on the team had not worked on the client's business before. We didn't think this would be a problem because they had lots of experience and we thought they would bring fresh ideas and so break old patterns of thinking. Besides, the two account directors from the London office and the creative director from the Paris office knew the client well, and we had a freelance creative director who had worked on advertising for the client's competition.
>
> We all gathered at headquarters in New York City, where Jonathan, the team leader, told us we had three weeks to pull together a presentation on all aspects of the client's marketing and communications problems.
>
> Jonathan broke the group down into three smaller groups—the account executives, the creative people, and the general support people. Then he sent each group into a separate area.
>
> The business leaders shut themselves away in a meeting room to work on the strategy of the presentation; the creative people holed up

in another boardroom on a separate floor to work on theme lines for the client's advertising; and the support staff gathered information about the client's business and the current industry environment affecting it.

I was in the creative group. We were all clever, capable people, but our talents and abilities were not used in an effective way. Many of us felt the way we worked was a prime example of what not to do. Normally we would work closely with all the groups in the agency to develop concepts based on the client's business as a whole. This would lead to a number of ideas, out of which would come theme lines.

After two days the entire group met to discuss the hundreds of theme lines we had written, none of which, standing on its own, amounted to much. The creative people were all very frustrated. Collectively, we felt we needed to go through the process of developing an advertising idea before we tried to come up with the all-encompassing theme line. Wordsmithing theme lines was like trying to find a tail to wag the dog. Jonathan insisted we continue to focus our time on theme lines. His attitude was "This approach worked before and it will work now."

Days passed and still the big theme line was nowhere in sight. Jonathan and his team had been hard to talk to before, but now they literally locked themselves into their boardroom. I felt we had a good shot at saving our creative lives, but nobody was listening. The creative teams tried to arrange meetings, but no one seemed to be available. It was clear they wanted to be left alone to do their work. Our impression was that the focus had shifted from what we were doing to something they were doing, but what was it? No one was communicating.

For the next week we were all going in different directions. I spent three days editing a film that was canceled just before completion. The creative group was frantic. We were drowning and somebody was tying our hands. The deadline was looming and we were stuck in a process that wasn't working.

The evening before the presentation was due to be completed, we assembled to see how all of the pieces fit together. They didn't. There was no clear point of view. There was no wonderful theme line. There was no strong business idea. There were only isolated bits of information. At the eleventh hour we tried to pull all of these disconnected ideas together, but it wasn't enough. We lost the business. I lost my job, but Jonathan kept his.

Is this corporate abuse? Of course it is. A hand-picked team of highly qualified and experienced people are brought together only to be kept apart, isolated, frustrated, and denied the opportunity to do what they do well. Jonathan didn't use the brainpower in the room because that would have meant loosening his control. An enormous potential for creativity was utterly wasted. Why?

There is nothing in the story to suggest that Jonathan was an ogre as managers go, and he certainly didn't intend to stifle creativity. On the contrary, he desperately needed the team to be creative. Jonathan wanted to keep the client's business, but he was so anxious that he resorted to a method that had worked in some previous situation. He was trying to follow an analytical method of problem-solving when he needed a creative method. Analysis usually involves breaking a problem down into its component parts and looking at them separately, rather like taking a clock apart to find out which piece needs fixing. Creative problem-solving, on the other hand, means putting things together, trial and error, brainstorming, throwing things at the wall to see what sticks.

Alas, Jonathan is not alone. It is quite a common error to try to use an analytical approach to achieve a creative outcome. It is more rare (but it does occur) that people apply a creative approach to an analytical problem. A lot of good ideas founder at the implementation stage because people are still freewheeling rather than focusing.

The main point to remember, however, is that compartmentalization is deadly to creativity. At 3M, a company that is so creative that more than a quarter of its sales come from products that are less than four years old, leaders discourage what they call "turfiness." As the CEO, Livio (Desi) DeSimone, puts it, "We should always have people from as many disciplines as possible talking to each other." Marshall Loeb, who interviewed DeSimone for *Fortune* magazine, agrees: "If you put fences around people, you get sheep."

Another point worth noting about the Jonathan story is the enormous amount of effort that went into the approach he imposed. Killing creativity is hard work. We never said that corporate abuse was easy. No one sums it up better than Alison, who runs a company that provides training programs for manufacturing industries and is universally acknowledged by her employees to be a terrific leader:

> Actually, I'm terribly lazy in certain ways. For example, the idea of micromanagement makes me feel exhausted, it takes so much energy. Honestly, I don't know how bad managers make it through the day, doing everyone else's work as well as their own. I prefer to listen rather

than talk, it's a lot less tiring. And I can't be bothered enforcing stupid, picky little rules. For one thing, I'd have to obey them myself. For another, people are quite capable of figuring out the necessary rules for themselves without me hassling them. I also love delegating and getting other people to do things. After all, I'm not getting any younger and they are all so keen. I need every scrap of energy I've got for the really useful part of my work: solving problems, dealing with conflicts, promoting ideas.

Alison isn't really lazy; she works as hard as anyone, but she knows when to step in and when not to breathe down her employees' necks. Why is it so hard for people to be "lazy" in this way? Why do people put themselves to such trouble to abuse their employees and strangle innovation? The bottom line is the issues of trust and control. The difference between Alison and many other managers is that once she has hired people (and she is very careful about whom she hires), she trusts them to get on with the job in their own way. She trusts them to bring problems to her attention and she gives them her full support when they run into difficulties. Because she trusts her employees, she doesn't need to control everything they do, and she knows it would be counterproductive to do so. This isn't the same thing as abdication, which can be another form of abuse; it is a vote of confidence for her staff.

Now that automation has replaced assembly-line production, the need for predictable, controllable bodies (or hands, as in "factory hands") is waning, but many companies still haven't figured out what to do with the other parts of their workers. By that we don't mean just their brains and intelligence. We also mean their creativity, their commitment, and their loyalty—the qualities that we have been referring to as soul. Remember, technology doesn't have ideas; people do.

Although the particular kind of creative solutions needed will differ from industry to industry, all companies must encourage their employees to challenge conventional wisdom. This means giving people at all levels the power to contribute their ideas freely and without fear. Imagine an environment where if you try something new and it doesn't succeed the first time out, it won't be arbitrarily squashed because you'll have the chance to work out the bugs. The people around you are equally motivated and energized. You can bounce ideas off them and they come to you when they want to brainstorm. And the words "We've never tried that here" can be a reason to do something new instead of an excuse to crush initiative.

When we try to describe really innovative, creative companies, we keep using words like "organic" and terms like "living systems" and "webs." In a sense, these organizations are like biological ecosystems. They grow, they mature, they adapt to changes in the weather, they organize themselves in a way that is sometimes hard for outsiders to appreciate. Ecosystems are a creative regenerative force. If you mess with them, they can die.

Corporate abuse has the same effect on an organization that pollution has on an ecosystem. It interferes with natural processes. It gums up the works until processes that used to occur spontaneously begin to wither. Restoring life to an ecosystem like a river or a wetland means taking away the source of environmental stress and letting the ecosystem heal itself. Restoring life to a company means getting rid of psychological stress and letting people's natural creativity surge.

The key to knowing whether your company is fostering an abusive culture is to look around and listen. If the suggestion box is empty, if challenges are greeted with stolid silence instead of debate and enthusiasm, suspect abuse. The next step is to ask *why* people are not coming forward with good ideas. Dr. Göran Ekvall, a Swedish organizational psychologist, has developed a checklist of symptoms for negative cultures:

1. The company has a negative atmosphere in which every new suggestion is criticized and obstacles are raised to ensure that new ideas are destroyed.

2. Harried employees must meet unrealistic expectations for productivity, leaving them not enough time to think.

3. The company is characterized by a high level of suspicion and mistrust in which people fear being exploited and robbed of their good ideas.

4. Rules are strictly imposed and people are monitored to stay within closely defined boundaries.

5. There is an atmosphere of destructive internal competition, politics, and interpersonal conflict, characterized by plots, traps, gossip, and backbiting.

If you recognize any of these symptoms, then your company is probably harboring an abusive culture or perhaps even a combination of abusive cultures. If so, you are not alone. We have listened to so many horror stories and seen so many abusive cultures up close that we have developed a diagnostic tool to help companies uncover specific areas of abuse.

THE DIAGNOSTIC TRIANGLE

We have based our diagnostic tool on the fourth letter of the Greek alphabet, delta, which is triangular in shape and is the scientific symbol for "change." Inside the diagnostic triangle are three smaller triangles representing the three key components of any corporation: organizational context, group interaction, and individual behaviors.

Corporate abuse can find a breeding ground in any of these triangles and quickly spread throughout the organization. Often it is nurtured unwittingly by CEOs who believe that if they find the right system, the right technology, or the right design, their strategic objectives will fall into place. Unfortunately, the only power that drives systems, technology, and design is in the minds and hands of the people who use them.

No business is all machinery or systems. It is run by human beings. How workers feel about each other and how they work together within the organization makes the difference between an abusive culture and a

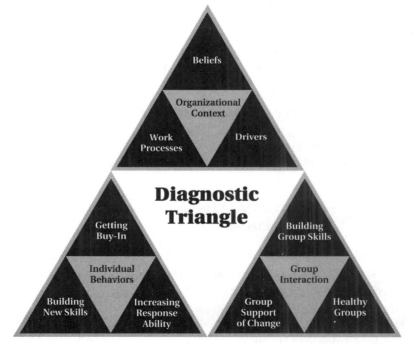

© PeopleTech Consulting Inc.

sustaining one. If a corporation is to survive and thrive, all three internal components in the change triangle must be aligned as tightly as though they were pieces in a puzzle. Weaknesses in any one area will stall or even sabotage the entire organization.

ORGANIZATIONAL CONTEXT

Let's begin at the top of the triangle, with the organizational context. There are three components that make up this part of the triangle: beliefs, work processes, and drivers.

Beliefs

Organizations hold beliefs, just as people do. Often they are described in the company's vision statement, its corporate values, and its business strategies. Those are the company's explicit beliefs, but there are also a lot of unwritten rules and shared understandings about how people should behave, who matters and how much, or how systems should operate. These implicit beliefs are unstated but agreed-upon ideas such as "We believe we should make a profit" or "The customer comes first" or "Stay late and get the job done before you leave the office" or "If I yell at people, they will achieve the results I want." Explicit and implicit beliefs combine to make up the corporate culture and dictate the way people in the organization behave.

Problems arise when the explicit, stated belief system is at odds with the implicit, unstated one. A leader who says, "Give me input," and then ignores what the employees say is cultivating an abusive culture. If you are following the explicit rules and getting nowhere, you may be working in an abusive culture. Idea-generating cultures express their commitment to creativity and empowerment in an explicit way and then follow through on their stated (and unstated) beliefs, mission statements, and strategies.

Work Processes

"Work processes" simply means how work gets done. Re-engineering is about work processes, finding better and more efficient ways to do the job. The reason that re-engineering fell into disfavor was that companies jumped onto it as an end in itself rather than using it as part of a integrated change strategy. The effect was like putting one snow tire on a car—the changed work processes were pulled out of alignment with all the aspects of the company.

There is nothing wrong with asking whether there is a different, more efficient, less labor-intensive way of doing work. After all, we would never have had laptop computers if we had been content to write everything in longhand. Technology gives us tools, and people give us ideas about doing work differently to satisfy the customer's needs. How we organize work and how we use technology, however, are decisions that are open to abuse.

Abuse can happen in two ways in work processes. The processes themselves may be abusive. People may be asked to do too much or to work in uncomfortable or unsafe conditions or to function without adequate tools or support. The work may be compartmentalized to make each person's job so circumscribed that it is boring, repetitive, and meaningless, like the work on an old-fashioned assembly line. Workers may be excessively monitored, which erodes privacy and causes stress. This kind of abuse is fairly easy to spot.

The other way that abuse may occur in work processes is during the transition from an old way of working to a new way. This kind of abuse can be seen when human jobs are replaced by machines or when companies undergo radical change from the top down, in a way that ignores the needs and concerns of the workers who have to carry out the changes. Although most companies recognize the need to alter work processes to fit the information economy, the way in which the transition is carried out can be a source of stress and abuse. For example, when companies replaced typewriters with word processors, some of them failed to provide support workers with adequate training. Quite a few secretaries and clerks were terrified of the machines, using them incorrectly if they used them at all, and productivity nose-dived. Word processors changed the work processes of support staff, and those affected should have been supported and eased into place. Now that CEOs are expected to use laptops, a similar stress can be found in corner offices, and top executives are discovering for themselves how difficult it is to change work processes.

Drivers

Performance drivers reinforce people's actions and support the organization's belief system. For example, organizations in the industrial age believed that managers should closely supervise workers, so they set up elaborate checking systems. They asked for monthly, weekly, or even daily reports. These reports were supposed to tell managers everything that was going on and became a work process in themselves. Of course, many of the reports were not read. There was too much information for any manager to cope with, but producing the reports supported the theory that workers didn't work unless they were supervised and that bosses needed to know everything.

Drivers also include compensation systems. If you believe that workers need a commission to make sales targets, then you build one into the pay packet. The problem with this system is that in the information age, many people have to work in teams, yet companies still compensate according to individual performance. In other words, the drivers are out of sync with the work processes.

Systemic abuse primarily comes in this part of the triangle because managers haven't really seen how changing work processes creates conflicts with beliefs and drivers. If your performance drivers are inconsistent with your belief system, you can't make the organizational changes that are essential to abolish an abusive culture. If you have a new vision or change direction without changing performance drivers, the effect is similar to sending employees the wrong way down a one-way street. You can count on collisions and confusion.

GROUP INTERACTION

Now that we've dealt with organization-wide systems, let's turn to the way the people in the organization work together in groups. How they interact has a tremendous effect on the beliefs, work processes, and drivers of the organization.

People work together in departments or teams that are unique in the same way that families are unique. People who work in research and development are different from those who work in sales. They think differently, work differently, sometimes even look different. The work of these organizations-within-organizations may differ so much that sometimes it is hard to believe that they are part of the same corporation.

Besides the departments or teams, there are cross-functional groups set up by information-age organizations to encourage communication and teamwork. The more committed an organization is to teamwork, the more groups the organization will have.

Then there are all sorts of informal social, community service, and lifestyle groups formed by employees to support activities and causes that they believe in and want to nurture. They range from sports and social committees to support groups for gays or single parents to ad hoc collections like the-twelve-people-who-always-eat-at-Flo's-on-Thursdays. These informal groups can be so extensive that we can take the same corporation and make two completely different organizational maps—one showing the formal group hierarchy and a much broader and flatter one tracing the informal groups.

The existence of many different formal and informal groups can be a sign of a healthy, nonabusive culture, unless, of course, the formal groups are committees whose original function has long since been forgotten and the informal ones are all gripe groups. However, diagnosing abuse requires a closer look at group skills, group systems, and group support of change.

Building Group Skills

Most of us feel that we work best with people who are like us. Working with people outside our circle can create tensions and lead to conflict when we don't speak the same corporate language, don't understand each other's jobs, or have different priorities. An administrator is different from a marketer, and both are different from a production manager. Yet the information economy demands that people work together more and more closely. How can we get our administrators, marketers, and production managers to talk to each other?

Xerox has worked to bring disparate types together by developing a common corporate language. Although Xerox employees from France, Scandinavia, and Spain have different national cultures and different mother tongues, when they come together electronically to solve problems, they can communicate because they all speak the same corporate language. This is just one approach to creating a climate in which teams and groups can thrive.

Working in groups doesn't happen all by itself. It requires a certain set of skills and attitudes. Companies either foster these skills and attitudes or repress them, and therein lies the potential for abuse. If you are trying to diagnose abuse in your company, look for the existence or lack of group skills. How easily can groups form in your organization? Do employees talk regularly to people outside their own area or section? How well do teams function in the corporate environment? Does the company support groups and teams?

Healthy Group Systems

Healthy groups have clarity of purpose, open discourse, and crisp decision-making. They believe in leveling barriers and eliminating stereotypes. Mutual respect and understanding allow room for growth and create an environment where it just might be possible to achieve the impossible.

Whereas healthy groups move in a definite direction, unhealthy groups tend to go around in circles. The members jockey for position as star performers; they do not listen to each other; they may even undermine each other's efforts. Their stated purpose is usually fuzzy, and their unstated purpose may be negative: protecting the status quo or promoting a political interest that is contrary to the corporate vision.

Potentially healthy groups may be the object of abuse if they fail to get the support they need, but unhealthy groups can be the source of abuse in the corporation. Before adopting the current enthusiasm for teams, it is a good idea to check out just how well teams actually function. You might be creating a monster without realizing it when a team set up to, say, solve a production hitch gets derailed and spends its time plotting strategies for removing the production manager.

If you can build even one healthy group in an otherwise abusive culture, it can foster another healthy group and eventually spread across the organization. Healthy groups are so different from unhealthy ones that simply by existing and getting on with the job, they can help expose abusive behaviors in other groups. They can also be mentors for teams struggling with the transition from abusive to nurturing cultures.

When you look at the groups in your company, look at what is happening among and around them. How many are healthy? How far does their influence extend? How many are dysfunctional? What damage are they capable of wreaking?

Group Support of Change

The group is an important medium for individual change. People find change easier when they are part of a group that is moving in a common direction, as anybody knows who has signed up for an exercise class after trying and failing to do solitary sit-ups. Groups provide a powerful forum for dealing with the emotional challenges of change. When you are working in an abusive culture, feelings of fear, anomie, and confusion are common.

When you look at the groups in your company, look inside at what they are doing for their own members. Are they shoring up individual insecurities and neuroses, or are they helping people come to terms with new work processes, new beliefs, and new directions?

INDIVIDUAL BEHAVIORS

Individual behavior is the litmus test for abusive cultures. This is probably the easiest way to diagnose abuse in any company.

Getting Buy-In

People respond negatively if they are pressured to commit to change before they are ready. Getting buy-in is a process that happens in stages. You can't have buy-in unless you first have communication. Understanding change means letting people know what is supposed to happen; getting buy-in means they believe it needs to happen.

The opposite of buy-in is cynicism, and that is what you will find in an abusive corporation. If you hear things like "Here we go again: the suits have a new pet theory" or "Don't worry about that—it's just window dressing" or "Same old story: do what I say not what I do," you are not hearing the sound of buy-in. You are hearing the sound of abused employees who are fed up with being jerked around.

Real buy-in sounds very different. It may be tentative or hesitant, but it implies commitment: "I'm not absolutely sure about this, but if we don't try it, we'll never find out if it works" or "Let's give it our best shot before we make a final decision" or "You know, I think this just might work." You will also hear a lot of questions. "Do you think I should start collecting data on that?" "What if I tried it this way?" "How can I learn more about all this?" Buy-in seldom starts as energetic enthusiasm, although we hope it leads to it. People take time to change and need a lot of support through the process. Failure to provide time and support is a form of abuse, and you will be able to hear the difference.

Response-Ability

To translate buy-in into action, people need to be able to respond. We call this giving them increasing response-ability. Other people call it "empowerment," but we are not very fond of that term because it implies that someone is bestowing power on someone else and that the same someone can also withhold power if he or she feels like it. Response-ability is what employees already have, although they are not always given sufficient opportunity to exercise this ability. Increasing response-ability is the opposite of micromanagement. It means backing off, giving people room, letting them follow up their ideas, ensuring that they have an appropriate work environment and resources for what they do without demanding that they account for every minute of their time or nickel of their pay.

Diagnosing abuse means looking for the things that kill response-ability. How much initiative do employees take? Can they make decisions in their area of competence, or do they have to run to someone else to get minor decisions rubber-stamped? How many people have to "sign off" on any deviation from protocol? When a small problem occurs, how long does it take for employees to solve it? How often do you hear employees say to a client or customer, "It's not up to me; I'm just following company policy"?

Building New Skills

You can't build new skills without training. This requires coaching and counseling from managers and courage and the ability to take risks and innovate on the part of workers. Anyone who has broken an arm or a wrist and has had to use the other hand even temporarily knows how difficult it is to learn a new skill. The same thing happens in organizations when we don't help people move past the awkwardness of trying and perhaps failing at new skills. But it is worth making the effort, for the more skills people have, the more valuable they are to the corporation and to themselves as employable workers.

If you are examining your company for abuse, look at whether or not employees have the opportunity to build new skills. Healthy corporations encourage people to tackle new challenges and give them the support and training they need. Abusive corporations tend to reinforce dependent behavior by keeping people's skills narrow and work-related. They assume that helping people to broaden their knowledge and skills means that they will get too ambitious and want more power or another job, probably in a less abusive environment. In some cases stingy companies hate to pay for training and justify their stinginess by stating that people will "pick up" needed skills. Remember the companies that gave their support staff word processors but did not provide training on how to use them?

Detecting abuse in this area sometimes means looking for what is not happening as well as what is happening. Are certain kinds of equipment not being used because no one understands them? Are opportunities being lost because no one knows how to follow them up? Does the company hire from outside and fail to promote insiders because employees have not been able to learn the skills they need to move up?

Abuse affects every organization differently, and there is no set formula that will work to eradicate it in every instance. There are no easy answers and no single right answer. If you identify one source of abuse, look for its effects on other parts of the diagnostic triangle because all the parts are interdependent and interconnected.

For example, if you discover that in the area of groups there are a couple of dysfunctional groups that are spending more time rumor-mongering than problem-solving, look at the effects of those rumors on individual buy-in and implicit organizational beliefs. Or if, say, you find that the transition to new work processes is being handled in an arbitrary and clumsy way, make sure you consider the likely fallout in the area of group support of change or response-ability.

The diagnostic triangle is an integrated tool. One source will lead to another source. It has been designed to help you examine your organization and analyze it systematically to uncover corporate abuse. Every time you lift up the corner of a triangle, imagine that it is a rock. If a snake slithers out, watch where it goes, because chances are, it will lead you to another rock and another snake.

Don't forget that the diagnostic triangle can be applied to all parts of the web around an organization, and that includes contract workers, partners, and suppliers. How are you training the people you used to call suppliers? What are you doing for them in terms of self-esteem? Do you have a common language for the people in your web? These are the questions we must ask about our corporations to make the changes necessary for us to thrive in the future.

The diagnostic triangle is also intended for repeated use. Diagnosing abuse is not a one-time event. Don't just ask the questions once and then put the diagnostic triangle back on the shelf. It is a tool for continuous analysis and evaluation. Keep turning up those rocks every so often and see if something new slithers out.

Once you've spent some time gazing unflinchingly at the snakes and other assorted fauna you've found, it's time to think about how you are going to turn an abusive culture into an idea-generating culture. That is what this book is all about. There's not much point in wringing your hands about how awful it is out there and what a shame it is that good people are being treated badly. The idea behind diagnosis is to start appropriate treatment—preferably before the patient is beyond hope of recovery.

Let's start by looking at where the workforce is going and who's going to be in it in the next twenty or thirty years. We said that the people who will best suit idea-generating organizations are workers who can manage their own careers, who are confident about their abilities and willing to upgrade their skills and market their talents. The task for corporations heading into the next century is to attract these highly skilled and entrepreneurial workers. The dedicated foot soldiers and middle managers of the baby boom who signed away their lives in the hope of one day occupying a corner office and a seat at the boardroom table are being followed by a generation of workers who are not going to sign away anything they don't have to and who know that the corner office and the boardroom chair are not all they are cracked up to be. What they want is work that is challenging and environments that are stimulating and innovative. They will vote with their feet and walk out the door when they sense abuse. Attracting and keeping these employees is both a reason to get rid of abuse and a way of doing so—if you pay attention to them.

THE BOOMERS AND
THE BUSTERS

My first job was a culture shock. They put me in a tiny cubicle in a huge room full of little cubicles. I felt like a lab rat. I kept expecting somebody to time how long it took me to find my way through the maze to the washroom. The computer they gave me was older than the stuff I'd been using in college. And the work itself seemed to involve all these preprinted forms that had been copyrighted in about the 1950s. Everything had been thought out in advance, and if there wasn't a preprinted form for it, it wasn't part of the job. I lasted six weeks, then I found a job designed for humans, not lab rats.

—Bryan, age 27

HERE ARE LOTS of Bryans out there. They were born between 1960 and 1975, and they belong to that slice of demography called Generation X or the Baby Busters. Vancouver writer Douglas Coupland, who baptized them Generation X in his best-selling novel of the same name, portrayed them as a disappointed, alienated generation of overeducated and underemployed hamburger flippers.

The baby busters are the younger siblings of the baby boomers, that huge generational surge of more than 75 million babies born between 1946 and 1960. Boomers grew up in crowded families in a society of expectation and excess; busters have fewer siblings and are more likely to have working mothers and divorced parents. The boomers barged their way into the workforce, grabbing jobs and holding on tight until the leveraged buyouts and mergers of the 1980s and the recession of the early 1990s led to massive layoffs and downsizing.

That economic downturn marked a critical watershed: On one side there was a society of excess, and on the other a society of scarcity. Many

boomers who invested their careers in old-style hierarchies are now finding themselves out on the streets. Those who worked their way up and
scrambled to hang onto their positions are having trouble managing a
dispirited and decimated workforce. They find the attitudes of Generation X, the skinnier, less materialistic, less extravagant cohort on the other
side of the prosperity divide, difficult to understand.

> I know this makes me sound old, and I'm not old, but I keep wanting to
> start sentences with "When I was your age . . ." to some of the younger
> employees around here. I want to tell them that I started work in a re-
> cession too, in the early 1980s, and it took months after my graduation
> before I found a job that really used my education and qualifications.
> It's not like they are the first people ever to suffer disappointment get-
> ting started in their careers and to have to put up with a few boring jobs
> before they find something that suits them. We've been there before,
> but they won't listen to us.
>
> —*Val, age 40*

When these two generational cultures meet in the corporate world,
the potential for misunderstanding and conflict is great. Typically,
boomers came to corporate life with high expectations and groomed
themselves to survive in hierarchical structures. But the kind of worker
who will fit the new corporation best is one who is entrepreneurial, and
that's more likely to be a baby buster. To understand the clash of values
that is at the heart of the conflict between the boomers and the busters,
we have to look more closely at the economic and social conditions that
shaped these generations.

The boomers—both men and, increasingly, women—learned the
ways of the workplace from those who were tied into the old psychological contract that promised rewards for hard work and loyalty. When
they were children, they watched their fathers (less often their mothers)
devote their lives to work, whether that meant climbing the corporate
ladder or working split shifts at the plant. They benefited from the
material rewards that were the fulfillment of postwar prosperity.

When the boomers left school, they made a dramatic entrance into
the workforce not only in numbers but also in terms of their ambitions.
Many of them were the first in their families to have the sense of entitlement and expectation that accompanies a university education. They
were welcomed by organizations, and following the example set for

them, they worked hard. Recruitment and training programs gave many boomers a leg up onto the corporate ladder.

They played by the rules and took it for granted they would one day reap the rewards of their sacrifices. And because they were used to material comforts, they spent their money freely, acquiring the trappings that were held out as rewards.

Then everything changed. With the 1980s came the frenzy of leveraged buyouts and mergers. New technologies began reshaping the marketplace, and a more competitive, global economy was emerging. The impact on business was tremendous. In the 1990s downsizing has eliminated millions of jobs, and restructuring has flattened the old pyramid structure and reduced the number of management levels.

Caught in the changing dynamics of today's economy, boomers feel cheated out of what they believe they rightfully earned: power, respect, and security. Those who are in middle management feel the ground shaking beneath their feet as more and more middle management slots are being eliminated. As they see opportunities dry up, they cling to their positions, often becoming autocratic and rigid, fighting for ownership of ideas and engaging in politicking and power plays.

Just as the Great Depression and World War II shaped the lives of those who came of age in the 1930s and 1940s, and the prosperous postwar years influenced the outlook of the baby boomers, the globalized information economy and the recession of the early 1990s have affected the prospects for Generation X. The busters entered the workforce feeling cynical about their prospects in the corporate world and about their bosses—the ubiquitous boomers. Not only are there fewer jobs out there, but once busters do make it into entry-level positions, they may be blocked by the boomers who dominate the upper levels of management and who are years away from retirement.

Corporate cost-cutting means busters cannot always expect high starting salaries if they work for established corporations. Nor can they count on substantial raises and bonuses as rewards for outstanding performance, as the boomers did in the past (unless, of course, they are one of those high-tech wizards who become millionaires before the age of twenty-three). The trend toward downsizing means they cannot even count on keeping their jobs. With the incentives of job security, rapid advancement, and financial rewards removed, the busters have a very different relationship with the corporate structure. Their stake in it is minimal, and so are their expectations. They will not tolerate Cultures of Sacrifice, Win/Lose Cultures, or Cultures of Blame. They will shut down their computers and walk out the door when they feel the effects of corporate abuse.

Robert Barnard, a consultant who specializes in helping companies recruit from the generation that is now eighteen to thirty-two years old, points out:

> Boomers paid their dues at the bottom of the corporate hierarchy; they expect Generation X employees to do the same. But the younger employees have already had a lot of education, often more education than entry-level Boomers twenty years ago, and they don't want to spend years paying dues. Some expect to move up immediately, which is unrealistic, but most of them feel that they've already done a lot of preparation and they want more challenging work.

According to recent studies, the busters define success differently from boomers. They seem more interested in a balanced life in which the quality and enjoyment of living are at least as important as material gains, perhaps more so. They still want monetary rewards and material comforts, but other concerns, such as balance, flexibility, and challenge, influence their career decisions. They see boomers as workaholics who don't know how to enjoy life.

> I graduated second out of a class of sixty-three, and I got three job offers within two months. The one that paid the most money was with a huge firm, a real industry leader, offices around the world. At first I was really excited. I had visions of European travel and buying a Jeep with my first year's earnings. Then I took a closer look at the job description and backed off. I realized that if I did travel, I would see the inside of hotel rooms and offices only and that I'd never have a chance to drive the Jeep except to work and back. In the end I went with a job in a much smaller firm that offered less money but more flexible hours and more generous vacation arrangements. I've been there for a year and a half now, and I don't regret my decision at all. I'm prepared to work hard, but I can't do that if there's no time to recharge my batteries.
> —*Matthew, age 25*

Busters come into the scene as nonbelievers in the hierarchy and view the boomers' behavior as paranoid, controlling, and counterproductive. A twenty-nine-year-old programmer for a southern California software company described how a power struggle among boomer managers overseeing the development of a new product delayed a project for a year. The chief villain was a vice president who insisted on making every decision, even if the staff had to wait weeks to fit in with her schedule.

Boomers expect their Generation X employees to show the same kind of loyalty that was required under the old psychological contract. Busters know the payoffs are just not there so they have become more independent and pragmatic in their attitudes toward employers. Busters as a group are more technically skilled than their predecessors, and studies have found that they tend to take more personal responsibility for their own careers. To a middle-aged manager who has dedicated a career to learning the management skills suited to a pyramid-type organization, the busters' independence and technical literacy can seem very threatening in the new business environment. But in order to maintain productivity demands, corporations will have to attract new workers by keeping pace technically and reflecting Generation X values in their corporate cultures

Since busters do not depend on the corporation for advancement and security, they are more willing and likely to walk away if the pressure gets too intense or if they feel as though they are spinning their wheels. In an abusive culture their response is usually "What do I need this aggravation for? I can always work for myself." Boomers interpret this reaction as arrogance and impatience; they see their younger workers as upstarts who want instant success and recognition without paying their dues.

> I left one job after less than five months. It had seemed like a good fit: it tied in with my degree and they said they wanted fresh ideas. But after about a month I was going out of my mind. The pace was incredible, and they kept changing direction. I'd knock myself out working on a project, and then they'd say, "We've decided we need a new approach on this," so I'd have to drop what I'd been doing and come up with something new in half the time I'd taken to develop the original idea. After I left, I had to take a vacation just to get my pulse back to normal. Then I waited tables for another couple of months before I found a place that didn't function in a state of constant crisis.
>
> —*Lauren, age 29*

Although there are obvious generational conflicts at work here, too many managers miss the bigger issue: the basis of the economy has changed and both generations will have to make adjustments. While many busters are well suited to the entrepreneurial system, many boomers possess the necessary experience to lead workers capably. Each side must understand and accept the need for change. Then each group must recognize and identify what assets the other is bringing to the new workplace. Finally they must find ways to develop and use those assets in partnership.

What do Generation X employees want? Robert Barnard sums it up: "More than anything else, what the Generation X employees want is challenge, freedom, responsibility, credit for their ideas, and some respect for their education, which is often at the level of a graduate degree." He adds: "Keeping Generation X employees is sometimes a matter of small changes, like allowing for flexible hours or relaxing the dress code. If they are happier and more productive in jeans and T-shirts, why not let them wear jeans and T-shirts?"

Generation X has grown up surrounded by electronic technology. To them, networking via computer makes more sense than going to an office every day. It is faster and more efficient and allows them more control over their time. "Networking," in the sense of creating a system of corporate allies and building a personal power base, is a concept that is alien and old-fashioned to them.

Since most companies will probably continue the trend toward smaller staffs, they will have to rely to some extent on outside sources of brainpower. Workers who are looking for a permanent employer will find fewer and fewer options. As we move toward the idea-generating culture, those people with their own resources and a base of operations away from the traditional office will be a valuable source of supply in the new marketplace.

When we look at the needs of today's corporations, the baby buster profile should be a comfortable fit—if the culture is flexible and innovative enough to accommodate *their* needs and to offer them the kind of environment in which they can thrive. Lots of busters are high-tech wizards and energetic entrepreneurs. Many of them have founded businesses of their own, often in innovative fields that didn't exist a generation ago. *Forbes* magazine calls them "the most entrepreneurial generation in American history." The magazine ran a cover story on seven Xers, each of whom owns a $1 million plus (revenues) company. Writer Randall Lane, himself an Xer at age twenty-seven, says that even those in traditional jobs don't think "working for some big company and climbing the corporate ladder is the way to go." According to Lane:

> We go out for a few beers and the talk always shifts to starting software companies or real estate ventures or opening a place that makes a real Philadelphia cheesesteak. My peers have a kind of practical cynicism: Nobody is going to take care of me except me, so I'd better get hustling.

Boomer bosses must realize that they are facing extinction if they do not recognize what their young workers can contribute and if they don't make good use of their own best qualities. Business must constantly be injected with new energy; that energy, like it or not, is typically supplied by youth. The busters offer the creativity, independence, and perspective that business needs to stay fresh and competitive. The boomers, who have found a defining voice for every wave of change since their youth, have to meet that challenge once more, at a time in life when change always comes harder and much more is at stake.

Boomers are well suited to the task. They belong to the generation that forged the modern meaning of change. At a time in their youth when humanist values had been forgotten, they revived the belief in the transforming power of the individual. These attitudes may seem naive and idealistic to those approaching middle age, but they are exactly the ideas that boomers must revive, however strange it may seem to apply those ideas in a corporate context. Managers must understand the need for true partnerships with their workers. True empowerment—not empty "sensitivity" sessions—must be developed as an integral part of the corporate structure.

> I remember the 1960s when my friends and I were going to change the world. I think I was going to teach organic farming techniques to inner-city dropouts or something like that. I used to laugh at my old ambitions, but then when my kids get after me about recycling and the environment, I begin to think maybe it wasn't such a dumb idea after all. I can't go back, but I try to be sympathetic to people who believe that we've got to put back more than we take out of this world.
>
> Some of our younger employees are an odd mixture of pseudo-sophisticated cynicism and high ideals. I try to find a way to break through the cynicism and capitalize on those ideals. I don't always succeed, but I try to let them know that it's their job to put meaning back into the workplace. Nobody else can do it for them.
>
> *—Sandy, age 45*

Busters may have a technological edge on the older generation, but they must learn the value of experience. They must be self-reliant, but they must also learn how to work as part of a team. Boomers, at this point in their professional lives, can provide experience, judgment, leadership, and that essential ingredient, institutional memory. They know what happened in the past—what worked, what didn't, and why. Boomers must learn to impart their wisdom and their knowledge in a way that nurtures and supports all workers.

Success in the future will be a matter of balance and diversity. Creative people need colleagues who are skilled in analysis and implementation to help facilitate their ideas, and people who are good at technical or organizational tasks need creative people to introduce useful innovations. Boomers must learn to appreciate the contribution made by busters and vice versa. The corporation that succeeds in the future will make use of both creative and technical people, boomers and busters. Tomorrow's winners will capitalize on diversity, not smother it.

Although solutions will differ from industry to industry, the idea-generating process is universal. Companies have to create the nurturing and supportive cultures that encourage their employees to challenge conventional wisdom and to experiment with ideas. This will lead to a greater respect for diversity, a new civility in the workplace, and a much more productive company.

The New Work Regime

WE ARE CAUGHT in a hurricane of change as we move from industrial-age to idea-generating organizations. Everything is in flux: technology, the way organizations conduct business, the kinds of people who work in corporations, the workplace itself. Commuting to an office by car or train has been replaced by commuting by modem. We work in cars and airplanes and hotel rooms using cell phones and laptops. Anywhere we happen to be at any hour of the day or night—if we have access to technology, we can work.

Throughout history new technology has served as a catalyst for changing work environments and working relationships between employer and employee. Now, if we survive the transition, the introduction of advanced information technology will force us to develop new corporate structures. Horizontal networks will replace the old hierarchies that once sustained oppressive behavior. Companies that don't adapt will die because connectedness, not compartmentalization, is the only way large corporations can effectively deal with the new business environment.

Change, however, is not just about redrawing organizational charts and learning to use new machines. Remember how we watched the Berlin Wall tumble down on November 9, 1989? The wall had stood for decades as a barrier between people and ideas. It represented totalitarianism and symbolized a rigid, unyielding system. As the wall was taken down piece by piece, many of us felt energized by the thought that the whole world was now on a new tack toward unity, democracy, peace, and prosperity. But today we see that the wall was only a physical representation of the greater barriers that exist between people. The absence of the wall exposed invisible but deadly barriers of ethnic hatred and economic disparity that had successfully separated people over centuries. The real work of breaking down barriers is yet to be done.

In the same way, restructuring a company is the beginning, not the end, of change. Greater barriers exist between human beings than any new system or structure can remedy. Imposing a new system on an old set of attitudes and behaviors won't bring about the desired result. Fear of change and its often brutal repercussions makes people feel dislocated and suspicious. Trying to preach the doctrine of teamwork in an environment of fear and suspicion is a waste of breath.

Unfortunately, we don't have a legacy of corporate trust and goodwill to handle the rigorous test of trying to create flexible, responsive organizations to lead us into the future. Too many corporations are hanging onto the past like grim death—an appropriate simile, because that is where this attitude usually leads them. Jurassic companies are dying out because they can't adapt. The forms that their death throes take are the abusive cultures we have described. And even the people who might be able to help shift Jurassic organizations around are becoming demoralized. That's why organizational failure is such a crisis.

Behavioral changes are painful and hard to achieve. We know that in spite of demands to redefine the organization, most people have stuck to their traditional behaviors. But "most" doesn't mean "all." The good news is that some companies are actually turning themselves around. They are not having an easy time, and it isn't happening overnight, but everywhere you look, great lumbering dinosaurs are slimming down into more agile creatures, and a few may even be sprouting wings.

We've identified five essential steps in transforming corporate cultures from Jurassic to rejuvenated. They all have to be completed if the change is to be sustainable over the long term.

JURASSIC TO DYNAMIC IN FIVE GIANT STEPS

Step One: Adapt to the New Global Realities

- Create borderless organizations that include your suppliers and even competitors. People have been afraid to do this for fear of losing business to their competitors, but money is only one measure of success. Learning is another measure. What we learn by forging strategic alliances may bring us much higher long-term gains. We must draw on the resources of other organizations by bringing them into our networks.

- Improve alliances within organizations by dismantling the walls between departments and divisions. If research and development has a good idea for sales, they should work together to develop it. People don't realize how many walls there are within their own organizations.

- Provide compelling reasons to change by touching people's minds and hearts *simultaneously.* Don't separate ideas from passion. If we are going global, we must define what a company with global vision means in terms that relate to individuals and their jobs. A manager's perspective on the business is very different from the viewpoint of a front-line worker. Corporate communications must take these different perspectives into account.

Starting to talk about the organization of the future requires a new language because the terms we use now imply old relationships and close off new possibilities. For example, we should stop using the word "employees" because that connotes only the people who receive a paycheck and excludes suppliers, clients, consultants, freelancers, and all the other people who must be part of the web. In fact, the whole idea of "inside" and "outside" the corporation needs to be rethought. Perhaps the best word for all the people in the web is "colleagues." And the notion of short-term versus long-term contracts may have to be revised as people sign on for tasks that might take a few weeks to complete or twenty years.

Even the word "leadership" may have to be replaced. What the new business world demands is not one visionary perched on top of a legion of order takers but a legion of entrepreneurial thinkers working in concert to attain a mutual goal.

Some theorists say our organizations are going to operate a lot more like "cat herding." In the industrial age we treated people like cattle, pushing them through the organization from recruitment to retirement. In the future, workers will be as independent and intelligent as cats. They will have control over their own careers, and they will touch base when it suits them. That's why organizations must offer compelling reasons for these "cats" to support new visions. A strategic plan is only the beginning. New goals must touch the heart as well as the mind.

Step Two: Get on Board the Digital World

- Replace multilayers of management with mobile ad hoc teams.

- Put computers, the Internet, interactive television, and visual transmissions to work so you can learn about and react to change faster.

- Reduce the levels of reporting and speed up the flow of information.

Companies have the technology to solve problems by linking up offices anywhere in the world. Soon computer software will automatically translate between languages. But our speed at breaking the language barrier has raced ahead of the human resistance to change.

Jurassic organizations are built around "functional silos." A silo divides people into vertical self-contained units and fosters a mentality of "them" versus "us." There is no need for people in different silos to communicate with each other. The many layers of management filter reporting and decision-making straight up to the top.

Even though an organization tries to restructure its business around technology, the silos block cooperation and slow things down. In effect, the technology outperforms the structures within the organization.

We need to use the advances of technology to replace isolated work groups in functional silos with the dynamic performance of ad hoc teams. Mobile groups of people can use improved information access to solve problems across more than one area of the business. Faxes, modems, computers, e-mail systems, and databases can connect organizational brainpower so that tomorrow's organizations can react to change faster.

As we said earlier in this section, the new working structure will look like a web. All workers are connected to a central source of knowledge, values, and coordinating principles by a multitude of direct lines of communication. We can also delayer the organization by reducing the number of levels of reporting. As technology speeds up the flow of information, we don't need layers of people to slow things down again. We should invest in human resources by training people to use technology in more sophisticated ways.

People tend to use computers to speed up old processes rather than develop new processes. Sometimes we joke about taking Harvard professor Shoshana Zuboff's wonderful slogan, INFOMATE INSTEAD OF

AUTOMATE, and turning it into a bumper sticker. That's the really exciting way to use computer technology. The antidote to fear is knowledge.

Step Three: Remove the Culture of Dependent Employees

- Redefine the meaning of work as being less to do with structure and obedience and more with fluid guidelines and entrepreneurialism.

- Encourage the freedom to take initiatives.

- Help staff members re-establish their own self-esteem so they feel in control of their lives.

We hear a lot about the palace coup by the knowledge workers. And while the shortage of information-age skills is a big problem both for the unemployed and for corporations, we think corporate abuse is an even bigger problem. The rash of mergers, acquisitions, and takeovers has resulted not only in flatter organizations but in large-scale layoffs and the jettisoning of talented leaders.

This abrupt transition has severely damaged our trust in one another—colleagues as well as bosses. The people who are left in our organizations are not always equipped to help the company move ahead because they are too busy licking their wounds and watching their backs. They are also confused and uncertain about their new roles. In the past they were rewarded for obedience; suddenly they are expected to be innovative and take risks. How we help people move from dependence to innovation is perhaps the biggest single challenge facing business today.

The prospect of signing on with a company straight out of school or university and retiring forty-five years later with a gold watch has gone the way of the manual typewriter. Work isn't going to disappear—far from it. What is disappearing, though, is the traditional security and unchanging definition of a job. A job is no longer a predetermined task that you perform according to a strict set of rules and guidelines. Instead, it is a series of activities based on a set of skills and goals.

In the old days we set up apprenticeship schools and programs; in the future, corporations will identify the kinds of skills they need and develop training workshops and pilot programs to attract people who want to be engaged in their particular learning process. That's how the corporation will develop a source of employable people with the skills they want to tap.

People will also learn as they carry out their tasks in the web. Different people can be given the power to experiment within their areas of expertise without affecting the entire structure. Allowing workers to experiment freely in an effort to improve production or add customer value means that the company essentially becomes a living organism that can change and adapt to new situations with greater ease. Most organizational experts agree that flexibility, the power to react quickly, and the ability to mobilize human resources will become the attributes that will translate to success in an increasingly competitive global economy.

We're beginning to see new ways of working already. Vast numbers of professionals who have left traditional employment, either voluntarily or as a result of layoffs, are working in smaller partnerships or independently as contract workers. We predict that this will become more and more the norm. However, this approach demands an entirely different human resources planning and development process. Corporations will have to find new ways to compensate and reward workers, whatever position they take on the web. Because there will be more people hired for specific tasks of shorter duration, the corporate attitude toward hiring will change and so will the attitude of the potential worker. The organization will spend more time making sure that workers understand how the organization's needs fit theirs.

Over the long term people will take greater charge of managing and developing their skills to improve their employability. If the organization cannot demonstrate how their vision matches the individual's, the organization is not going to be able to attract and secure the brightest and the best candidates.

What the new web structure means in human terms is that each worker becomes more autonomous, more expert, and therefore more valuable and harder to replace. The independent worker of the future will be able to make partnerships with many different kinds of organizations. And where now we hear the question "Who's my boss?" in the future the question will increasingly be "What are we doing together?"

To help people understand and adapt to this change in function and mindset, we need two kinds of workers: core people who work within the organization and who are continually upgrading their knowledge and skills and being rewarded for these efforts, and people like the baby busters we talked about earlier, who develop their own skills and provide their expertise and their experience on a contract basis to corporations. When the job is done, they move on. Organizations of the future will need people, whether they are full-time or contract workers, who depend less on the organization and more on their own skills and networks.

This has a further implication. We are not so utopian in our thinking as to suppose that changing corporate structures will somehow change human nature. Bullies are not going to disappear, because there will always be people with the kinds of personal problems that result in bullying personalities. Other people will still try to compete or to resist change or even to steal or sabotage the work of other people in order to make themselves look good. People aren't perfect, and no amount of change in the corporation will make them perfect. What the web means, however, is that the amount of damage that abusive people can do will be limited. No one will be locked into an until-death-do-us-part relationship with an abusive colleague. The fluidity will prevent abusers from embedding their abuse in rigid structures and systems. Just as a telephone call can be routed in any one of hundreds of ways to its final destination, good ideas can be rerouted in the web if a few points in it turn out to be bottlenecks.

Abuse will probably never disappear completely, but its effects can be minimized. And they must be minimized if people are to take risks, because people can only take risks if the organization makes them feel secure enough to make mistakes. Most learning and success come through trial and error. Nobody is going to take a risk while the corporate watchdogs or the bullies are on guard. That's the mistake we made in the industrial age when we robbed people of their independence and their self-esteem. A big challenge in this transitional age is to reestablish self-confidence.

Outplacement is an example of how corporations try to help workers adjust to losing traditional jobs We have heard so often from workers who have been fired that outplacement counseling was a positive process because somebody looked at their career and talked to them about their individual interests, apart from their companies and jobs. What about the people who have to change jobs and who don't get outplacement counseling? We have to develop something to help them.

If this also sounds a little utopian, the following example may help illustrate its practicality. In 1986 British Airways had 350 senior captains ranging in age from 49 to 54. The company could no longer afford such a large contingent of senior pilots. It needed to reduce the number by about a third, or about 80 to 100 pilots. Traditional buyout programs had been in place for several years, but few captains had responded positively and the company expected that only about 15 would leave that year.

Rather than simply chopping people from the top down, British Airways hired the consulting firm of Right Associates to help. Right Associates developed a program called "New Horizons," which offered individual career-planning opportunities as well as money. The consultants met with both working and retired pilots, union officials, flight managers, and flight operators. Then they sent announcements to pilots, telling them about the program and inviting them to attend briefing sessions.

The sessions were open to anyone who wanted to consider leaving, not just those who had accepted the early retirement package. The seminars were augmented with financial planning, pension calculation assistance, career counseling, a flying opportunities registry, and ongoing consultations with the program coordinator and human resources personnel in flight operations.

By the end of 1986, 94 people had resigned, and more were expected to do so before the end of the program. This represented a six-fold increase in the acceptance rate for the early retirement package. British Airways had met its goals, the retiring pilots were happy, and a successful outplacement model had been created that could be adapted to other areas of the industry.

This example shows that it is actually possible to be Lean and *Humane,* not Lean and Mean. All it took was a little consideration for the individuals and a program that helped them think creatively and constructively about their careers and their futures. Cost-cutting is a fact of life these days, but by allowing employees to make informed decisions, it can end up as a win/win situation.

Step Four: Bury Old-School Leadership

- Build new leadership skills around coordinating and brokering rather than commanding and controlling.

- Ensure that leaders are accessible, open to change, and able to tolerate ambiguity and uncertainty.

- Find leaders with enough self-esteem to model cooperative, nurturing behavior.

When leadership moves from the top of a pyramid to the center of a web, not only the role but also the qualities of the individual in that role must change. In the old days, great corporate leaders were like matinee idols. Everyone knew the glamorous and revered patriarch of the old-style organization—let's call him Mr. Fairbanks. People respected Mr. Fairbanks because he was remote and inaccessible.

Today's organizations don't need movie stars; they need ensemble performers. Mr. or Ms. Smith, a.k.a. John or Judith, must be seen, heard, and most of all accessible. The job of the leader is to radiate common values, goals, attitudes, and expectations out along the strands of the web and to act as the receptacle for knowledge, information, experience, and a sense of purpose and continuity at the center.

The kind of person who can fulfill this role is not the leader of old, who was respected because he or she was always right and always in charge. The new leadership qualities will be a tolerance for open-ended questions and ongoing change rather than a desire for closure; a healthy sense of self-esteem rather than an ego that feeds on other people's insecurities; and an ability to broker and bring people together rather than a penchant for ordering people around.

Some management writers have even compared the new role of the leader to that of a parent who imparts a set of values, expectations, and attitudes that family members come to share but allows for a diversity of interests and activities within the family. This should not be the same thing as paternalism but an adult-to-adult relationship based on openness and trust. The metaphor may not be appropriate in all situations (and may conjure up memories of dysfunctional families for some people), but it shows how people are struggling to redefine leadership in the future.

Step Five: Develop the New Psychological Contract

- Avoid the two extremes of paternalism and dissociation and strive for a middle ground in which corporations offer challenges and the chance to contribute in exchange for participation and ideas.

- Create meaning for people to work beyond the paycheck.

- Think of the corporation in terms of membership and fellowship, not just in terms of economic and legalistic contracts; people's jobs will change and nothing can be carved in stone.

All of the changes we have called for should enable workers to gain more power and demand more respect. The new web structures promise to be more effective in reinforcing egalitarian work. More information will be shared; less information hidden. More of the real purpose of the organization will be made clear and matched with the real objectives of the worker.

However, replacing old structures and systems with new ones does not always guarantee better human relationships. It is obvious to many working in today's companies that although business leaders call for loyalty and commitment from their people, they are doing little to reduce the pain of working in the current business climate. Charles Handy, in his book *The Age of Paradox,* suggests that the future of business lies in "membership organizations":

> *Membership is a way of thinking about the psychological contract between an individual and the organization. If the individual is seen as an instrument, even an "empowered instrument," he or she is there to be used by others for their purposes. Such an instrumental contract no matter how well intentioned or how benevolently interpreted, is a denial of democracy. Our economic well-being and the continued success of capitalism depend on efficient and effective organizations of all types. One way, perhaps the only way, to match our need for efficiency is to think of our organizations as membership businesses.*

How will corporations lure the brightest and the best to be members of their organizations? More important, how will corporations sustain new forms of loyalty and commitment? The answer lies in the creation of a new psychological contract. Leaders need to have a really good understanding—from the strategic to the tactical—of the reasons behind change. They have to be humble enough to admit when they make mistakes and willing to have frank and open discussions right down the line.

We know a CEO from a Fortune 500 company who stood up in front of one hundred of his people and said: "It's tough to be sixty years old and to realize that I'm half of the problem." He was sincere. His goal was to liberate the company so that employees would never have to suffer the bureaucracy, politics, or opposition that he'd had to experience to make his way to the top. He wanted to liberate people's minds so the company could survive.

In the community outside work, the goal is for each individual to function as an equal member of society with certain rights, responsibilities, and obligations. This give-and-take relationship is our source of identity and civic pride. It gives us a sense of belonging to a larger group, offers us a purpose, and fosters feelings of well-being and self-esteem.

The paternalistic psychological contract changed the dynamic of our sense of community. The contract we negotiated with the leaders of the company meant giving up control of our contribution in exchange for security. As our responsibilities and obligations were compartmentalized within the company, we lost sight of our contribution and felt alienated from the larger community of work.

Similarly, the current psychological contract of independent, just-in-time workers alienates us from the organization and denies us a secure place in the work community "Virtual organizations" and web structures, in which people come together for specific projects, make economic sense, but they must be accompanied by new psychological commitments that enhance our sense of community and create feelings of fellowship and connection. If our goal is to integrate work into our lives, then the work community must foster a sense of belonging to the group as a whole and allow us some control over the contributions we make and the rewards we receive.

That's not to say that leaders can abdicate their responsibilities. They are still accountable for profit and results, of course, but they have new responsibilities in sustaining and nurturing workers.

The new psychological contract should be the emotional equivalent of profit sharing. It should be one of shared purpose, shared responsibility, and shared power. Our need to be part of the work community goes beyond doing good work. By meeting our need to belong, the company will enhance our commitment, stimulate our respect, foster our loyalty, and spark our creativity. Put another way, the new psychological contract must nurture the soul by acknowledging its need to belong as part of an idea-generating culture.

THE GOOD NEWS

W E'VE TALKED a great deal about corporate change and the company of the future, but before you feel as if you were born twenty years too soon and that the corporate structure that would bring out the best in you doesn't yet exist, we want to remind you that even in these difficult times it is possible to have a sane work life and a life of the soul.

Where to start? Start with yourself, with your own hopes and desires and fears, with a little soul-searching and a lot of replenishment. Put the five giant steps into practice. The three stories that follow are examples of people and organizations who have done just that—and succeeded.

WORKING WITH MISTAKES

A company called Trendmaker Homes (a division of Weyerhauser Corporation), a developer and home building company, has earned an almost evangelical following among many of its employees. The employees we talked to—entrepreneurial sales executives, builders, and tradesmen—are convinced they have found the very best place to work in the home building sector in the region and that the Trendmaker culture is better than any other they have experienced.

What is Trendmaker doing right? Will Holder, the general manger of the region, believes he can point to specific areas of cultural change that he has initiated that have created much happier and loyal workers and substantial business gains as a result. The first was changing his own management style.

> By the time I took this job, I had gone through some personal growth and changed my management style from one of management by intimidation to a kinder, gentler approach.

Will said that his predecessor at the company was a highly intelligent, creative individual, but someone he recognized as never having endured what he calls humbling experiences.

> Without humbling experiences, I think, people see themselves as very powerful, and they come across to other people in an overpowering and intimidating way.

At one time Will had been the same way. Having achieved success at a young age—starting college at seventeen, getting his M.B.A. at twenty-three, and being offered great jobs right out of college—made him over-confident and often overbearing. Initially these traits, among others, served him well in the Win/Lose Culture and Cultures of Blame he found himself in.

> Inside the firms where I worked, if everyone else looked stupid . . . if everyone was seen making mistakes—then your value increased to the owner. You wouldn't take steps to cause someone to make a mistake but when they did, you saw it as an opportunity.
>
> If you made mistakes you could get fired, so you were very busy covering your tracks. Certainly if implementing the solution meant admitting you made the mistake, it wasn't worth it. You would keep the mistake and the solution to yourself, cover your tracks, and hope it would happen again to somebody else—when it did, you'd be sure to get the owner to observe the mistake, then reveal the solution and be seen as the solution finder and the hero. That's how careers were made. You wouldn't just help your fellow worker fix the mistake for the good of the company.
>
> In the 1980s I had worked for three companies where I had spread my mismanagement skills around.

Will learned to survive by taking on the values of the companies he worked in, but eventually he become both a purveyor and a victim of their cultures. Owing to his early success, he often found himself in positions above his capabilities and as a result had some failures.

> I saw my income over various positions rise to the mid-$100 thousands when I was still only in my thirties. Then I was demoted and saw my income crash to a third of that. My marriage of fifteen years failed, and I'm sure my wife would tell you that was partly because I brought the aggressiveness of my working culture into our home. Those were my humbling experiences—they gave me a different outlook on life. I went

through a growing process that made me realize I wanted a calmer, less threatening existence in and out of the office.

Will was able to evolve in the job he had before taking the position at Trendmaker. The culture in that building company was not one of intimidation, but neither was it a creative environment. It was a highly bureaucratic, large corporate environment that had an "ostrich-with-its-head-in-the-sand approach to problems."

> In that environment you could make a mistake, admit it, and not implement a solution, and that would still be OK. It was important not to rock the boat or talk about problems. They didn't want you to make any changes; they wanted you to just get on with it—just proceed.

Between the two extremes of his experiences, Will was able to come up with a balanced approach for his new company. When he took on the role of general manager of Trendmaker, he was confident that the company could be successful if it created an environment where people were not afraid to make mistakes.

> A big theme for me was to fix every problem we had in the company and to do it by talking openly about our mistakes. I told everyone that if they made a mistake, we were going to put that mistake on the board-room table and talk about it and come up with a solution. In the beginning people were really uncomfortable having their dirty laundry out for everyone to see, but as I put my problems on the table and as more and more people did so, and everyone saw there were no horrible consequences, people began feel safe. In about a year and a half people really started to trust the process.

As a result of this process, the people at Trendmaker came up with solutions that substantially improved their operations and the value they could give to their customers. This open process also enabled them to break down barriers that had existed between sectors of the company.

> We discovered that the most important way to ensure our success as a building company was to get our buyers to refer and recommend us to other people, so we put a system in place whereby meeting buyer expectations was key to high referral scores. It was not that buyer expectations were too high for us to meet, but rather that once we had promised something or raised expectations, we had to make sure we kept our promise. Research told us that one of our biggest obstacles

to getting referrals was that our on-time delivery of the completed home was really low.

This raised a contentious issue between the salespeople and the builders—each blamed the other for the problem and each felt the other was holding the control stick. Sales was always put in the position of promising an expected move-in date for the buyer, but the builders would be noncommittal. In defense of the builders, they were building homes within ninety-five days, which is the industry standard, but the problem was there was no way to tell buyers accurately when their home would be ready. To the buyer, the perception was that the completion date was always late.

To solve this problem, Will asked the builders to come up with a point during the construction process when they would be able to tell the buyer what week they could move into their home and then at what point they could commit to the day the owner could move in. The builders came back saying they could commit five weeks in advance to the week of completion and one week in advance to the day of completion. When the salespeople heard this they were ecstatic. Immediately a rolling closing-report program on the computer was created to monitor the construction process.

When the house hit the five-week line—and only the builders could say when it hit that line—the salespeople could go to the customer and promise the house five weeks from that day. Both construction and sales feel they have control of their jobs, and our customer "willingness to refer" results reflected the change dramatically.

This solution as well as others that came out of "the mistakes on the table" process is reflected in the fact that between April 1991 and March 1995, on-time delivery increased from about 60 percent to 95 percent. In the same time period, the willingness of customers to refer new customers to Trendmaker went from 68 percent to almost 98 percent.

Employees are very happy about the changes:

"Other companies pay lip service to wanting you to have a personal life—this company helps you do it."

"Most other home builders make salespeople work six days a week and over holiday weekends; they burn everyone out—at Trendmaker we have two days off a week and we're refreshed."

"This company is the fairest; they treat us democratically."

"It's the only builder I've worked for where salespeople are asked what buyers want and they actually listen to us."

"I think it's the best company in the industry. No salesperson makes less than six figures . . . they work to protect our income . . . so we're not at each others' throats for the sales."

"There isn't a huge disparity between the income of people at the top and the rest of us."

SETTING LIMITS

Earlier in the book we talked about time abuse. This is becoming such a common form of abuse that it is almost taken for granted in the lean and mean 1990s, but the following story comes from someone who has found a personal solution to the problem in one of the most demanding of all professions: the law.

Margaret told us how she learned how to protect her time during her career without sacrificing the caliber of her work or her chances for promotion. She is now a managing partner in a very successful firm. Her approach can only be called *setting limits.* And now that the have-it-all 1980s are over, it's an approach that may be coming back into style. Margaret explains:

> I think I started with an advantage over many of my contemporaries who went into the legal profession. I set my priorities very early from two perspectives. I decided I would not give my entire life over to my job, and secondly, I would have a modest lifestyle. Many people who become lawyers want the big houses, the fancy cars, the cottages in the country, and all the luxuries they associate with being a successful lawyer. All too often I've watched my fellow professionals overextend themselves financially from entry-level positions throughout their careers. They create enormous external pressures for themselves to achieve more and earn more at work in order to support their lifestyles. They can't afford not to do well. They paint themselves into a corner, leaving no escape routes, should work life become too demanding. I came from a modest background. As a result I think I learned to be a more conservative spender.

That isn't to say Margaret has gone without. She owns two houses and lives comfortably. But she acquired what she has over time and always kept her tastes modest.

Now, as a corporate leader, I see another side of overextended lawyers. Their income needs become their income expectations, which in turn puts pressure on our corporate budget. I also see the stress and the fear that they bring to their jobs.

When Margaret started in law, she worked in a firm of six people. She liked the intellectual challenge of litigation, but she wasn't sure she liked the business. She never held back her uncertainty about her career when she talked to her colleagues.

> There may have been some comments from the others, such as "Is Margaret committed to the profession?" but most were tolerant of my approach. I also made it clear that I cannot do law seven days a week. I need my weekends to clear my head and relax. I think what made them tolerant of my needs was that they knew they could depend on me. As an associate I worked ten- to twelve-hour days, and they knew when they handed a case to me that I would get it done and do it right and keep our clients happy.

The culture at the small firm was collegial. Although the lawyers came from different backgrounds, they respected and trusted each other. They often socialized together, and they still do. It was an open, friendly work culture.

After a few years, however, the small firm went through its first merger. Suddenly Margaret was working with eighty other lawyers.

> This was the most uncomfortable time for me. The firm we merged with was a banking corporate firm and was very conservative. It was a real culture shock.
>
> I wanted to make partner, and the pressure was on me to perform. They gave me a lot of files to test me. I experienced a lot of stress and insecurity. Before the merger I was internally motivated to perform, I wanted to learn everything I could about litigation and be a better lawyer to achieve my own inward goals. This was the first time I felt an extrinsic need to please others at work.

At the same time, Margaret was dealing with emotional conflicts. She had just met the love of her life—who lived a thousand miles away. She needed to maintain the long-distance relationship on weekends and felt torn between her work and her private life.

> Although the pressure was on at work, I still insisted on my weekends off. To compensate, I worked super efficiently. I would work from

8:00 A.M. to 7:00 P.M. solidly, without taking lunch. I had the added advantage of being a good decision maker. I've seen smarter lawyers than I am practice inefficiently because they didn't have enough confidence in their ability to make decisions.

It took Margaret's colleagues longer to understand how she worked. Many of them were driven by their own pressures to work seven days a week, but she was getting excellent results and was considered a good lawyer. The more conservative members of her firm realized that even though she didn't spend her weekends getting new clients, she had a strong and loyal client base because she was thorough. They knew they could trust her with any work they gave her, and she was made a partner two years after the merger. She also began to take on more administrative duties, particularly working with associate lawyers and articling students.

A second merger brought a new round of culture shock. This time the firm grew to more than three hundred people. Today the firm expects 1,800 billable hours a year, which means six to seven docketed hours a day, five days a week. Professional development time and client relations are also expected outside those hours.

It's definitely tougher now for entry-level lawyers. The standard needed to make partner is much higher, and new technology necessitates much faster processing. There is no longer any downtime when one can catch a breather.

I have a very good lawyer on staff who is married to another professional and has young children. I spend a lot of time talking to her, helping her coordinate and manage her family life so that she can handle the time she has to spend at work. But as managers, we have to set some limits on our demands too. We have regular meetings to devise ways to keep our people happy at work and at home. We have even told people, "You are working too hard"!

We've set up a mentoring system whereby one lawyer will review another's work and ensure standards are maintained. In one case an excellent lawyer was docketing 2,300 hours a year, but when his mentor investigated his work, he found it lacked organization. Apparently this fellow couldn't say no and took on more and more cases so that he could be seen as a better performer. We took swift action and forced him to put the brakes on for a year. He was given a lighter workload. The mentoring system has worked well to discover where limits need to be set.

Margaret says her firm is consensus-oriented and democratic. She feels this is the right approach, particularly when she considers some of the new lawyers coming into the firm.

> Compared to the competition, we are a very young firm. Our leaders are in their mid-forties. We are seen as the up-and-comers in our field. We don't have a lot of rigid systems in place, unlike some of the older, more established firms.
>
> I think our style is more suited to the new entry-level lawyers. They are Generation Xers and are wary of the profession. They question whether or not this is really what they want to do. It helps that we are seen as a less structured place that lets them be themselves.
>
> Some partners discourage feelings of doubt and are not receptive to questioning. They take it as an insult, but I think it is an important part of learning who you are and how you can fit into the company. Sometimes I'll ask them, "Are you sure this is what you want to do?"
>
> I am also pleased that because of our diversity we offer something for everyone. Our mix of work fires up idealistic young lawyers. They love it and work hard because they are excited about it. They know they've chosen the right firm.

Margaret's firm also stands out from the competition for its earnings policy. None of the senior partners makes more than four times the salary of the other partners.

> Every year we have profit-split discussions and review this policy. Every year we vote to maintain it.
>
> One very successful lawyer came over to join us and took a cut in earnings because of the policy. He brought a large client and five other lawyers with him. His reasoning was that it was more important to work with a happier group.
>
> We also have a very generous vacation allowance.

This story is significant for what it says about individuals and their relationship to corporate cultures. Margaret learned to set limits at the beginning of her career, and now she is at the top of a firm that also sets limits, surrounded by like-minded people who share her attitudes. That is not sheer coincidence.

Often people feel powerless, as if the decisions they make will have no effect on their immediate surroundings, let alone the wider world of work. Yet we have seen time and again that people who have the courage to stick to their principles do find that, over time, their environment begins to reflect those principles. Ending abuse has to start somewhere, and it can only start with individuals. With you.

UNLEASHING THE IMAGINATION

Many of us have said to ourselves, "If I were the CEO of this company, I'd know exactly what I'd do to make it work better," but few of us actually work our way from the lower ranks to the top job in one company. Ron Compton of Aetna is one of our exceptions. He is now attempting to make the changes he'd dreamed of come to fruition.

Aetna was a typical huge corporation with 50,000 U.S. employees, a solid pyramid structure, and a cradle-to-grave paternalistic culture. It had become a household name as one of the nation's largest and most comprehensive insurance providers. The headquarters was a massive building in Hartford, Connecticut, the sort that is so formidable that one instantly wonders about the task of organizing the vast population within.

Compton began at the bottom of the managerial ranks. From this worm's-eye view, he could see the need for change, but he knew that the conventional approaches wouldn't work. So he had to "go undercover" to change the system.

This was a functional organization. To get anything done, agreement was needed from leaders of six to ten functional areas. Well, you know how difficult it is to get ten people to agree on something. Consequently, nothing would get done, particularly if it was something that wasn't their idea. However, the flip side of that kind of bureaucracy was that it also took forever to stop a project once it had started. My tactic was to start projects and seize opportunities that came up without telling anyone. I had to cheat the system to get things done. This was very risky. I made myself very visible by my undercover initiatives and on a number of occasions I was passed over for bonuses and almost fired. If anyone on the outside world asked me what it was like to work at Aetna, I'd say, 'It was a terrible place. Don't work here!'

A lot of people shut my ideas out. I started to believe that if I wanted to get anything done, I had to do it myself. That's fine if you're managing one or two people, but it's not going to work when you manage 500 people.

But I was lucky. My boss was a natural-born leader who understood and practiced twenty years ago what very sophisticated organizational experts are subscribing to today. It was because of his genius that, in my division, I was able to head a fully matrixed organization within the company.

When Ron was appointed CEO of the company, it was clear to him that Aetna had created a lot of its own problems, and he was facing the fallout from errors made fifteen or twenty years earlier. The decisions that had created short-term profits in the past were now having a devastating effect on the company, and he had to stop the hemorrhaging of funds to support those mistakes. He streamlined the company by selling off divisions and reinvesting and focusing on fewer, more profitable insurance sectors.

Barriers to change were apparent at all levels. The leaders were not innovative; middle managers spent most of their time protecting their turf; and many of the remaining employees were not performing as well as they could because the low pay structure of the company did not attract ambitious people. The company trained managers to believe that their value was based on the number of people who reported to them. Division managers resisted attempts to shed staff or break divisions into smaller units. Compton had to re-educate the managers to understand that their value had nothing to do with the number who reported to them. He explained that their job security and salary would in the future depend on their contribution to the company.

Despite these barriers, Ron knew from experience that the solutions for the future lie within people. His goal was to "unleash the imagination of the people who work at Aetna." But he also realized that he would have make radical changes to the way the company operated. He had to make sure that no one else had to go undercover to get his or her ideas through. "Mistakes are made that way. Costly mistakes. We have learned that by far, most mistakes are made by those who are loners . . . and who don't use an open process." He wanted to find out what the roadblocks to creativity were and remove them.

Like a lot of leaders, Ron thought at first that simply directing managers to unleash the power of people in their departments would be enough. But nothing happened. Senior management either took credit for good ideas or rejected any ideas that weren't their own. They also felt uncomfortable with the challenges and inevitable friction caused by change and empowerment. Compton hadn't anticipated this reaction:

> I came from a lower-middle-class family. Every meal was a conceptual war. Lines were drawn, battles fought—we argued everything with a

passion and were influenced by ideas and concepts both generational and philosophical. The intellectual exchange of ideas was the norm. There was a lot of grabbing and yelling. This was an acceptable way to behave at my house. So I have a real tolerance for discord and friction at work. I tell people that it takes friction to make heat and light, and ask them to welcome diversity, but not everyone came from my background and not everyone feels comfortable being challenged by others.

He had to show his managers how to create open systems for problem-solving. He told them to go out and pick ten terrific people with diverse backgrounds and skills, put them in a room with a problem and as much information as possible, and then walk away.

This is not the same thing as sharing power. That means that no one is held accountable or in charge of final decision-making, and that can lead to an abdication of responsibility. It's more about sharing the opportunity to contribute. I know so many people at Aetna are desperate to contribute and do whatever they can to make the company better.

Compton soon found that this method of problem-solving did more than generate new ideas; it became a litmus test for managers.

The best managers would be hot on the idea and use the open process throughout their divisions. Other managers would involve only close associates and trusted people. This allowed me to find out who the road-blocks were.

The best managers are open. They are not afraid to be vulnerable, not too concerned with how they look to other people, not afraid to look like a fool and say, "Hey, I just did a really dumb thing." The best managers focus on the job and the results, no matter who has the solution or the ideas.

Compton is also trying to replace the old psychological contract, which promised security in exchange for blind obedience, with a new kind of contract.

We owe you job security by creating a strong, competitive company and giving you the opportunity to contribute to what we need to do that. You owe us your productivity, ideas, and imagination.

We're not there yet. I think a lot of people would tell you that the contract is "We'll pay you as long as we need you." My job is to make people believe that they are safe to challenge authority and that they won't be punished for having a bad or stupid idea.

Compton feels that it will be a long time before the old culture of Aetna is replaced with a new idea-generating culture. Like a large locomotive, it takes time to stop a company in its tracks and turn it around. But he feels they have made a start.

THE IDEA-GENERATING CULTURE

Everyone keeps talking about the Information Economy and Knowledge Workers and so forth these days, but to me this misses the point. We live in an Idea Economy. Sure, information and knowledge are important, but they are not the same thing as ideas or creativity. Look at some of the dried-up old academics in their ivory towers. They've got knowledge coming out their ears, and they haven't had a new idea in several decades. For me, information is what you go out and collect after you've got a good idea, to make sure it hasn't been done before, to find out if it will fly, to use as a reality check. Information without ideas is like food that doesn't get eaten; after a while the stuff gets moldy and you have to throw it out.

—Roger, industrial designer

DAME EDITH SITWELL used to lie in an open coffin with her hands clasped on her breast before she began her day's writing. The poet Schiller used to keep rotten apples under the lid of his desk and inhale their pungent bouquet when he needed to find the right word. George Sand smoked cigars while writing. In 1915 she went so far as to buy 10,000 of her favorite Manila stogies to make sure she could keep her creative fires kindled. Colette used to begin her day's writing by first picking fleas from her cat. Poe wrote with his cat sitting on his shoulder. Kipling demanded the blackest ink he could find. Hemingway sharpened pencils obsessively, waiting for the right moment to begin work. Robert Louis Stevenson, Mark Twain, and Truman Capote all used to lie down when they wrote, but Virginia Woolf stood. Benjamin Franklin wrote while soaking in a bathtub, whereas the painter J. M. W. Turner thought being lashed to the mast of a ship in a violent storm helped his perspective.

These accounts from Diane Ackerman's *A Natural History of the Senses* describe the rituals that creative people use to invite inspiration. Clearly, the creative process is a strange and mysterious thing. And what people do to prime the creative pump and start the juices flowing is equally strange and mysterious.

Although we still know very little about the creative process and why some people are more creative than others, we have come to believe that creativity requires certain conditions that differ from noncreative work. In the 1980s, Swedish organizational psychologist Dr. Göran Ekvall developed the Creative Climate Questionnaire. By "climate" he meant the attitudes, feelings, and behaviors that characterize life in an organization. The climate exists apart from the feelings and perceptions of the people who work in the organization, but it affects the quality of their work and the way they do it.

The climate of an organization affects us just like the weather. Just as we are agitated by high winds or depressed by fog, exhilarated or frightened by storms or cheered up by sunshine, so the climate of the workplace can make an enormous difference in the way we approach our work, especially problem-solving, decision-making, and communications.

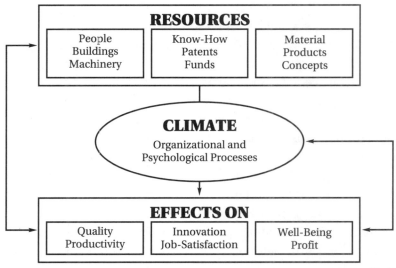

© Göran Ekvall

Dr. Ekvall used the idea of climate to develop his Creative Climate Questionnaire. It contains fifty questions in ten areas, such as challenge, freedom, trust, playfulness, conflicts risk-taking, and idea time. The kinds of things Ekvall is looking for in his CCQ reminds us of the climate in an advertising agency. It is a good example of how a company will allow its creative department certain conditions and freedoms that are not given to other departments simply because certain people have been designated as idea people.

Although by no means free of abusive cultures, advertising agencies are among the most successful industries in fostering creative environments. To understand the creative process and what is needed to create an idea-generating environment, we can look to these companies for examples of what works and what does not work to encourage creative thinking.

An ad agency's survival depends on a steady flow of new and innovative ideas. A typical advertising agency is made up of four main areas of expertise: marketing and account services, where employees discuss the advertising and marketing needs of the client relative to the competition; media buying, where employees think of the most effective ways and places to put the client's message; print production, where employees explore the latest techniques to enhance the production of advertising materials; and the creative department, where employees decide how to communicate the client's message in the most compelling and interesting way. Work in all of these departments requires creative problem-solving, but only one department is given the title "creative," and its working conditions are designed to foster creativity.

A typical tour of an agency might go like this. You are greeted in the main reception area by an account executive dressed in a fairly conservative business suit with perhaps a little less than conservative tie. He shows you around the floor of the client service department, where you see men and women working in individual offices. All are well dressed and singularly involved with their work. At this point you see little difference between these executives and the executives in other companies. They could be lawyers, accountants, or government officials. Continuing on your tour, you are taken to the media and print production departments, where you see more of the same—individuals working in individual offices with little evidence of group activity.

But when you get to the creative department, you step into another world. This feels like an entirely different company. The first impression is usually one of dramatic visual stimulation. The walls are covered with posters, pictures and words that may or may not have anything to do with advertising. Color is everywhere. The individual offices are similar to the ones you have seen but some are occupied by two or more people. In these offices people are working together. Large pieces of paper covered in scribbles (presumably ideas) are everywhere—on the desk, on the floor, pinned to walls. Outside the individual offices are common areas with couches and more open space than you've seen in the other departments. One area is big enough to house a Ping-Pong table. You notice the way people are dressed: blue jeans, T-shirts, and minimalist chic seem to be the uniform on this floor. Comfort is obviously a priority not only in clothing but in posture. These people are relaxed. Many of them even have games and toys in their offices to aid in the relaxation process. People who are working alone are reading books or simply staring off into space. You ask yourself, "What is going on here? Are these people really working or just hanging about having fun?"

The answer is both. What you're seeing is the result of what has evolved over time to represent a creative environment in an idea industry. This is what idea generation looks like from the outside. It reflects some of the freedom that people feel is necessary to reach a creative state of mind. The environment is free from many of the confines of the normal business workplace. But if you stayed longer in this environment, you would also see a variety of working adjustments that have been made to enhance the creative process.

This is what creativity looks like in one particular industry, and in advertising it is appropriate and functional, but it is not the only way to achieve creativity. If we stopped here, we would be saying people can only be creative in a colorful, informal setting. People can only be creative when they are wearing jeans and a T-shirt. People can only be creative if they have studied at an art college and work in a department labeled "creative." If they are in a department labeled "client relations," creativity is not their job. In fact, if they work in a department labeled "accounting," creativity is another word for cooking the books.

Although all of the people in the ad agency need to be innovative, only the people with the sole task of having ideas are given the circumstances necessary to enhance creative thinking. This "pigeonholing" of idea generation in the agency works against innovation from people in other areas. Ideas are less likely to be generated on an ongoing basis from the other departments. If you tell someone she is a numbers person, she will be a numbers person. If you don't tell her you have creative expectations of her, she will feel that creativity is not part of her job.

The agency structure is a microcosm of what is happening in corporations everywhere. If we believe that continual innovation is critical in today's business world, we need to make everyone a part of the process, and this calls for creating a company-wide idea-generating culture.

Where did we get this notion that creativity is OK only for certain people and not for everyone? Perhaps because few of us are capable of producing something that resembles a work by Monet, Mozart, or Milton, we assume that we are not creative. Nothing could be further from the truth.

The arts are one outlet for creativity, but only one. Redesigning a work process, thinking up a new office layout, figuring out a better way to communicate within the company, developing a new purchasing system—these all involve creative problem-solving. Dianne McGarry, the president of Xerox Canada, once took a thousand people to the movies to break the routine and get them thinking about what *is* possible. John Hahn, the president of Tri-Brokerage, a reinsurer in San Francisco, has a model train set running on a platform hanging from the ceiling in his office. We need to celebrate creativity in all its forms and draw examples from all fields.

CREATIVITY NEEDS TIME AND SPACE

Freedom from rigid structures is essential if people are to be able to produce ideas on demand. Flexibility toward working hours and deadlines will increase the chances of good ideas. Although ideas may start with a flash of insight, for the most part they evolve and improve over time. Punching a clock works against the natural evolution of ideas. Of course, we cannot get rid of deadlines altogether, but feeling that someone is standing over us with a watch in one hand and a revolver in the other is not likely to make us creative. Creative energy comes in bursts and requires some periods of downtime to replenish the soul.

Leaders of creative people know they must be flexible about how time is used in the creative process and not panic when they see workers engaging in activities that seem unrelated to the specific task.

Responsible creative people will manage time in ways that add to the process, not take away from it. For example, leaving the office to go for a walk in the park in order to think through a problem can be as much a part of the work as sitting behind a desk. Trust is a big component of idea generation. Leaders must trust their teams; teams must trust each partner; and the individual must trust that he or she will be productive within a fluid arrangement.

Most creative people will tell you the quality of their answer or idea usually reflects the time they have had to think about the question. However, it is not as much the *amount* of time that makes the difference—the luxury of flexible deadlines is the exception to the rule in the advertising business—as it is the *quality* of time that is crucial. The big idea can come fairly quickly—it may even be the first thing that comes to mind—but it always comes out of intense moments of concentration.

Whether we're standing in the shower or sitting in the office, the mind has to be focused on the job in order to find and hit its target. Sharing the mind's space with any other problem is sure to create "shutdown."

> One special technique I aspire to is total seclusion—solitude—a quiet time in complete isolation with zero distractions. It's a form of meditation that allows me to fulfill my potential on any given assignment.
> —*Anthony, musician and songwriter*

The creative mind needs peace. It's through peace that we reach a place of deep concentration, a black hole in the mind's universe where information collides to create a big bang of an idea.

WHAT IS CREATIVITY?

What do we know about creativity? Well, we know that it usually takes one of three forms:

- Making something from scratch (a painting, a poem, a cake, an invention).

- Combining things that haven't been put together before, making unexpected connections (this is how many comedy writers think up jokes, and how many new product lines are developed).

- Improving, modifying, or changing existing objects, structures, and processes, from fine-tuning to major overhauls and breakthroughs.

This last point is crucial. Creativity in the small things is every bit as important as creativity on a large scale. Robert Firestien, a professor at the Center for Studies in Creativity at Buffalo State College, points out:

> *The American view of creativity is the big hit, the home run, the big bang, the instant profit. But creativity is not only the big breakthrough.... Home runs are important, but the game can also be won with a series of singles, too. The industry leaders in quality products and services have progressed through an endless journey of continuous improvement—thousands of singles.*

Creativity can come in very small packages, and these are often the improvements that make all the difference to a company. Adaptation is often as creative and productive as invention. The dual air bag was simply an existing idea that was doubled. Other people have simply combined two good ideas, like the guy who thought of renting out cellular telephones with rental cars. Innovation is constant and incremental, a collective process, not just the product of individual heroes. People build on other people's ideas. This is what happens in brainstorming sessions. People won't be creative if they don't understand what creativity looks like. We need to celebrate innovation wherever it occurs, and that just might include the accounting department.

LETTING CREATIVITY HAPPEN

There are plenty of descriptions of "creative workplaces" in the media. Most of them sound a lot like the creative department of the advertising agency we just described. The headquarters of the Body Shop looks like a pagoda. The offices of the childrens television network Nickelodeon feature a three-story pyramid of conference rooms in the center of the building and chalkboards in the corridors. Creativity is expected and encouraged in a visual way in these unusual environments.

This is one way to foster creativity, but only one way. Creativity is not so much a matter of interesting office layout and colorful surroundings as it is one of attitude. Some companies have quite conventional-looking boardrooms, but brainstorming sessions held there often have creative ideas flowing thick and fast. The key is to eliminate walls in the mind, not just in the office.

Creativity cannot be forced—it can only be invited—but it is possible to set up conditions that make creativity come more easily. The trick is to get people into the right frame of mind. One of the best descriptions of the right frame of mind was written by the British comedian John Cleese, of Monty Python fame, who also runs a company that makes very funny training films:

> *People function at work in terms of two "modes": open and closed. . . . Creativity is not possible in a closed mode. . . . By the closed mode, I mean the mood that we are in most of the time when we're at work. We have inside us a feeling that there's lots to be done, and we have to get on with it if we're going to get through it all. It's an active, probably slightly anxious mood. . . . It has a little tension in it and not much humor. It's a mode in which we're very purposeful. And it's a mode in which we can get very stressed, and even manic. But not creative.*
>
> *By contrast, the open mode is a relaxed, expansive, less purposeful mood in which we are probably more contemplative, more inclined to humor (which always accompanies a wider perspective) and consequently more playful. It is a mood in which curiosity-for-its-own-sake can operate because we're not under pressure to get a specific thing done quickly. And it allows our creativity to surface.*

Psychologists who study creativity talk about divergence and convergence (spreading out to gather ideas, then closing in to focus on potential winners). The philosopher George Santayana said, "Man's progress has a poetic phase in which he imagines the world, then a scientific phase in which he sifts and tests what he has imagined." It's all the same thing, really. Open up, get loose. Do whatever it takes to get your mind off the usual road and out into four-wheel–drive terrain. For the writers described at the beginning of the chapter, getting into the open mode was a matter of small rituals that put them in the right frame of mind. Other people get into the open mode by playing basketball or golf, chatting over lunch, digging in the garden, or taking a walk.

The other point that John Cleese makes is that we need to *stay* in the open mode long enough to generate lots of ideas, not just one or two.

> *I was always intrigued that one of my Monty Python colleagues, who seemed to me more talented than I was, did not produce scripts as original as mine. I watched for some time and then began to see why. If he was faced with a problem and fairly soon saw a solution, he was inclined to take it, even though the solution was not very original. Whereas if I was in the same situation, although I was sorely tempted to take the easy way out and finish by 5 P.M., I just couldn't! I'd sit there with the problem for another hour and a quarter and, by sticking at it,*

*would almost always come up with something more original. It was
that simple. . . .*

*If we have a problem and we need to solve it, until we do we feel
inside us a kind of internal agitation, tension, or uncertainty that makes
us uncomfortable. And we want to get rid of that discomfort. In order to
do so, we take a decision not because we're sure it's the best one, but
because taking it will make us feel better. Well, the most creative people
are prepared to tolerate that discomfort for much longer. And so just
because they put in more pondering time, their solutions are more
creative.*

In a book entitled *Uncommon Genius: How Great Ideas Are Born,*
Denise Shekerjian interviews 40 out of 200 recipients of the MacArthur
fellowship, a no-strings-attached grant that has been given to some of
the most creative and innovative people in the United States in almost
every conceivable field of endeavor. The people she interviewed had
many approaches to creativity, but a number of them emphasized the
need to "stay loose":

*A period of rambling discovery at the start of a creatively minded project
is preferable to premature closure. . . . A loose, uncensored approach
increases the amount of material you have to work with. Volume alone
produces options; options permit the exercise of opinion and taste. . . .
[Staying loose increases] the possibility of being exposed to influences
that at first appear to be completely unrelated to the work at hand. . . .
Don't be afraid of risk. Or even failure, which if seen in its proper light,
brings insight and opportunity. . . . [Avoid] the twin opiates of habit and
cliché.*

Of course, both open and closed modes are needed in the workplace.
It is impossible to work effectively in the open mode alone, the "diver-
gent" or "poetic" phase. Equal time is needed for the "convergent"
or "scientific" phase. Once a decision has been made to follow up on a
certain idea or to solve a problem in a particular way, there is a need for
focus and concentration, for analysis and technical considerations.
As John Cleese puts it, "If you decide to leap a ravine, the moment just
before takeoff is a bad time to start reviewing alternative strategies."
Implementation demands skills that are different from those used in generating ideas but no less necessary. Quite a few small start-up companies come up with great ideas for products, but they never succeed
in getting them to market because they operate in one mode only.

However, the more common problem is that of older companies that operate in the closed mode only.

THE CREATIVE ORGANIZATION

Creativity calls for equality, collegiality, and teamwork. The idea-generating culture fits perfectly with the new web structure and the flattening of the pyramid. The ability to work across boundaries fosters a democratic process and means people hooked onto all strands of the web will be able to contribute to solving problems. Their contributions will be communicated and enhanced by new technology. The rigid control and compartmentalization that limit and dilute ideas in hierarchical structures will be replaced by people using personal computers to send messages and ideas along the strands of the web.

The ultimate idea-generating culture will be organized somewhat like the Internet. There will be some coordinating principles, but they will be very different from the old-style corporation that was based on reporting levels and hierarchies. Work will be organized around the information and data that need to be found, the different assumptions that need to be tested, and the tasks that need to be accomplished. The core values that the culture will espouse will be based on trust, shared dreams, a common language among workers, and a new form of employability that enables workers to move in and out of the corporate web as tasks or jobs begin or are completed.

A model we use when we talk about transforming organizations to unleash ideas and energy is the "shapeshifter." The concept is very simple, once you have thought about it. You can't act unless you focus on rewarding possibilities—goals, in other words. But you can't see these possibilities unless you dream. Our shapeshifter model helps corporate leaders to dream purposefully, to visualize desired results, to clarify strategies and test those strategies with a wealth of research, analysis, and behavioral and communications data.

We've used the shapeshifter model to develop a change program that will help organizations move from abusive to effective cultures. To use the model, corporations must:

- be able to **imagine** new ideas;
- be able to **translate** those ideas into actions;
- be able to **deliver** the actions.

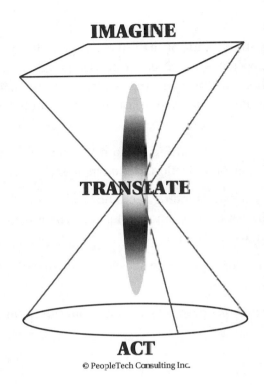

© PeopleTech Consulting Inc.

IMAGINE

Beginning with the hard data, we probe assumptions, raise provocative questions, and bring all the possibilities to the table. We've broken this process into three steps:

- In order to imagine, we must *explore and dream*. This is the stage in which people are opening up their minds and looking at the world in new and even risky ways. What if . . .? is the beginning of the imagining state.

- Once we have imagined the ultimate desires and dreams, we *internalize* that idea by asking what's possible.

- Finally, we *postulate*. By that we mean putting the internalized idea into concrete terms. Have you ever heard the expression "An idea doesn't exist until it's down on paper"? It's very easy to react emotionally to a vague, broad concept. When you look at something concrete, vivid, and quantifiable, then you really do have to acknowledge the potential barriers and rewards.

TRANSLATE

This is where we refine and polish the idea. Armed with a vision, we map out the future, weighing the risks, the consequences, and the different ways of reaching our goals. Our past experience enhances every step from data gathering and analysis to strategy development and decision-making.

- *Visioning* means breathing life into the idea and turning it into something the organization can touch, feel, and absorb.

- *Assessment* means standing back and involving as many people as possible by asking them for their feedback on issues, problems, or implementation wrinkles.

- *Deciding* means making the decision to go ahead or abandon the idea.

- *Planning* means developing a game plan based on the decision to act.

ACT

This is the third and final stage of realizing an idea. With the groundwork laid, we introduce new ideas to the organization, carefully explaining what will happen, when, and why. Throughout, we measure the impact on the organization as we implement the idea from theory to tangible results. Finding the best approach means matching realistic deadlines to far-reaching goals.

- *Launching* means getting it started.

- *Engagement* means getting everyone to go through the process so that they understand it.

- *Evaluation* means reviewing and reassessing so that you can make corrections to your strategies and systems.

These last three steps should look familiar because this is the way all organizations deal with change: by launching a new initiative, engaging people, and evaluating what has been done.

The parts that are most difficult for many managers to consider in this transformation model are the first two: imagine and translate. Their natural drive is to move straight to the bottom of the shapeshifter to action. They are in a rush to see results or to make a profit. And that is one of the fundamental reasons why change is so badly managed and why abusive cultures take root. Organizations have a bias toward action. They feel they must look as though they are doing something all the time. To use John Cleese's terms, organizations prefer to function in the closed mode and find the open mode unnerving.

The role of company leaders in the idea-generating culture will be to provide the open environment conducive to creative thinking and the tools and resources necessary for ongoing idea generation. It must also be the role of company leaders to be sensitive to obstacles or barriers that block free-flowing ideas. But most importantly, the idea-generating leader must guarantee peace and freedom from fear.

A CEO's impatience to see results can destroy the imagine stage and pressure people to skip to the translate stage. The impatience is understandable, but it is counterproductive. When we introduce the shape-shifter model to executives, we say, "Some of this is not going to feel comfortable right away because we will ask you to spend time making sure that you explore the idea and postulate it before you turn it into something concrete." We talk a lot about communicating before they even think about acting because we know that it will pay off in a culture that is creative, not stultifying.

As corporate leaders move from the top of the pyramid to the center of the web, they will need to learn how to tolerate ambiguity, which would have been difficult, if not impossible, for industrial-age leaders. Their goal was to reach closure, make decisions, and get clarity. New leaders have to have enough self-esteem to ensure that their ego doesn't drive their thinking. In the industrial age we built on people's insecurities and made them "prove their worth." We can't afford to do that in the future.

Leaders of the future need to be intimate with colleagues and to bring their personal life into the workplace. We've talked a lot about souls in this book and about how abuse damages people's souls. In the idea-generating culture, leaders will be colleagues who are in touch with their souls and who have a belief in something larger than themselves. The organization can and should never substitute for families or partners, but it can be a community of colleagues where ideas are cultivated and opinions are respected. Another very important quality leaders must develop is the ability to act as brokers and bring people together to work on tasks. They must be masters of coordination and organization who can unite people with a common vision.

The keys are balance and a tolerance for diversity. Time for free-flowing creativity must be balanced with time for analysis and judgment. Too little time spent on either is dangerous. Without time for creativity, a company stagnates and cannot come up with innovations; without carefully planned implementation, a company wastes its good ideas. Balance also means that those who are skilled in logic, analysis, and technical matters must respect and promote the contributions of creative people; the creative types must recognize their dependence on people who are skilled at implementation. The two types of employees need each other and can learn from each other. Analytical employees can learn how to use creativity to improve implementation; creative employees can learn how to handle technical problems and the picky details of making a great idea into a marketable, usable innovation. Because in the innovate-or-die world of the twenty-first century, that is what change will be all about.

THE CREATIVE SOUL

ARLIER WE DEFINED the soul as being the compass point from which all of our actions radiate. It is our center. Our citadel. It houses our courage, our passion, our creativity, our truth, our imagination, and all things sensed but unknown. It is the central source of our power.

In *Care of the Soul,* Thomas Moore talks about the sacred nature of work as it relates to the soul: "Work is an attempt to find an adequate alchemy that both awakens and satisfies the very root of being." In other words, the daily work we do becomes a part of our greater work, to provide that which benefits and thus transforms the soul to something greater. This greater work of caring for the soul is referred to by Jung as *Opus,* from the name used in medieval chemical science to describe the process and aim of bringing together base metals to create gold.

Replenishing deals with the power source of our soul. It is an act of caring for the soul by reinforcing our sense of well-being. For many people replenishing comes from absorbing life in the natural world outside the company and work, by being surrounded by the greater forces of nature, perhaps absorbing the power and consistency in ocean waves, observing the natural order and simplicity of life in the country or the tranquillity of a lake on a still and quiet morning. Others find renewal in intimate time spent with family and friends. Some are recharged through sport; others say introspection and expression through art and hobbies restores their well-being. The ways and means of replenishing the soul seem endlessly varied once we recognize the need.

Many people feel that when they are engaged in activities that replenish them, they are drawing from a great reservoir of energy that fills them with joy. They feel their body, intellect, and soul are orchestrated in readiness to live life to its best. We feel energized, optimistic, and contented. We say that we are replenished when we feel a great sense of harmony with the world around us. We feel everything has its place and we are part of it. We understand our purpose and are comfortable with ourselves. This rediscovery of our sense of belonging is tremendously self-affirming and reassuring. It is an attitude we savor simply by being alive. In our acknowledgment of the coexistence of all things, we are reassured of our own value and our individual importance.

There is a sense in which being replenished is a way of getting back to the truth, a base from which we gain perspective. In the process of replenishing, we have found valuable clues to what drives our inner power. If we listen to what we feel when our soul is replenished, we find several powerful components. One is the power we get from feeling a sense of belonging; another is the power we get from knowing our value; and a third is the power we get from harmony.

The ability to create depends on broadening our world and reaching out in all directions, without fear of consequence and without intellectual and emotional limits. To be as creative as possible, we must be able to call upon the power source of a fully replenished soul.

By caring for our souls, we can better fulfill our commitment to our employers, directors, and shareholders and offer loyalty and the best performance possible. We must get into the habit of caring for our souls as we are in the habit of watering our gardens. Work in itself can feed the soul. Studies on work flow suggest there is five times more opportunity to experience joy in the workplace on a daily basis than in the home environment if it is a workplace that is in tune with the needs of the soul. Shared purpose, shared teamwork, shared achievement, and shared reward can replace the disharmony of abusive cultures with the harmony so important to our sense of well-being.

Clearly it is not easy to describe exactly what the soul is, but we must attempt to bring shape to this amorphous part of our being in order to understand its importance to our existence. If we think of our soul as being the part of us that is capable of generating great personal inner power so long as it is replenished and free from damaging influences, we can turn this power into profit.

In contrast to the destructive and excluding power that comes from abusive corporate cultures and dark motivations, soulful power is constructive and inclusive; it allows us to be assimilated into something bigger, timeless, and more meaningful.

Once we have a community of fully nurtured souls, the possibility for creativity is limitless. Everyone in the workforce will be tapped into his or her own power source as well as being part of a larger community of effort and partnership. This community will nourish our soul's power source and replenish our energy. Going to work will be a joy instead of a drudgery. Maybe then we will go off each day with a spring in our step and a song in our hearts.

NOTES

PART ONE

THE DARK SIDE OF WORK

"One was very gaunt, red-eyed and unshaven": Andrea Adams, *Bullying at Work*, London: Virago Press, 1992, page 37.

"The split between our work life and that part of our soul life": David Whyte, *The Heart Aroused: Poetry and the Preservation of the Soul in Corporate America*, New York: Doubleday, 1994, page 4.

Business costs of abuse: see, for example, Robert Waxler and Thomas Higginson, "Discovering methods to reduce workplace stress," *Industrial Engineering*, vol. 25, no. 6, June 1993, pages 19–21, or Thomas A. Stewart, "Do You Push Your People Too Hard?" *Fortune*, vol. 122, no. 10, 22 October 1990, pages 121–28.

Occupational disease claims: see Evelyn Gilbert, "Stress Common for Working Women," *National Underwriter*, vol. 95, no. 38, 23 September 1991, pages 6, 43.

Study by Commerce Clearing House: Ceel Pasternak, "Unscheduled Absence Costs Up." *HRMagazine*, vol. 38, no. 6, June 1993, page 22.

On average, one million workers are absent daily: Dorothy Schwimer, "Managing Stress to Boost Productivity," "Managing Stress to Boost Productivity," *Employment Relations Today*, vol. 18, no. 1, Spring 1991, pages 23–26.

Twelve percent of all workers' compensation claims: Deborah Shalowitz, "Another Health Care Headache: Job Stress Could Strain Corporate Budgets," *Business Insurance*, vol. 25, no. 20, 20 May 1991, pages 21–22.

In the United Kingdom about 1.5 million working days a year: "Stress-related illness costs U.K. 1.5 million working days," *Personnel Management*, vol. 25, no. 2, February 1993, page 11.

Confederation of British Industry estimates: Andrea Adams, *Bullying at Work*, London: Virago Press, 1992, page 14.

"Corporate America is only very quietly admitting": Monika Bauerlein, "The Luddites are back," *Utne Reader*, no. 74, March/April 1996, page 24.

"Less a code of conduct than a spirit": "The Duty of Civility," *Royal Bank Letter*, vol. 76, no. 3, May/June 1995, page 1.

"We are all aware": David Whyte, *The Heart Aroused: Poetry and the Preservation of the Soul in Corporate America*, New York: Doubleday, 1994, page 29.

ABUSE, JUSTIFICATION, AND ACCEPTANCE

"In their efforts to control workers": Michael Argyle, *The Social Psychology of Work*, London: Penguin Books, 1989, page 24.

"What the time-and-motion folks ignored": Donald A. Norman, *Things That Make Us Smart: Defending Human Attributes in the Age of the Machine*, New York: Addison-Wesley, 1993, pages 13–14.

Eberhard Seminars Training: see Steven Pressman, *Outrageous Betrayal: The Dark Journey of Werner Eberhard from EST to Exile*, New York: St. Martin's Press, 1993.

Employees call this "face time": Sue Shellenbarger, "Eight well-tested methods for saving face," Toronto *Globe and Mail*, 10 January 1995.

ABUSE AND THE CORPORATE LIFECYCLE

"The goals they listed": Anne Wilson Schaef and Diane Fassel, *The Addictive Organization*, New York: Harper & Row, 1988, page 122.

Organizational lifecycles: Ichak Adizes, *Corporate Lifecycles: How and Why Corporations Grow and Die and What to Do About It*, Englewood Cliffs, New Jersey: Prentice-Hall, 1988, page 87–88.

"People won't willingly change": Stephen Covey, *Principle-Centered Leadership*, New York: Simon and Schuster, 1991.

"There is a tendency in this country": Frank K. Sonnenberg, "If a Tree Falls in the Woods . . . " *Industry Week*, 17 June 1991, pages 84–85.

Fad surfers: Eileen C. Shapiro, *Fad Surfing in the Boardroom: Reclaiming the Courage to Manage in the Age of Instant Answers*, New York: Addison-Wesley, 1995.

"Airport Bookstore Theory": Michael E. Gaffney, "The Dark Side of World-Class Manufacturing," *HRMagazine*, December 1991, pages 40–43.

"Just as reading diet books": quoted in Erick Schonfeld, "Clichéd Corporate Conversations from Hell," *Fortune*, vol. 131, no. 3, 20 February 1995, page 22.

Cultural antibodies: see Marti Smye with Anne McKague, *You Don't Change a Company by Memo: The Simple Truths about Managing Change*, Toronto: Key Porter Books, 1994.

LEAN AND MEAN

"How many CEOs of big, downsizing companies": Allan Sloan, "The Hit Men," *Newsweek*, 26 February 1996, page 45.

"Restructuring: a simple plan": Erick Schonfeld, "Clichéd Corporate Conversations from Hell," *Fortune*, vol. 131, no. 3, 20 February 1995, page 22.

"Flattening the organization": Manuel Werner, "The Great Paradox: Responsibility without Empowerment," *Business Horizons*, September/October 1992, pages 55–58.

Effects of downsizing on efficiency and profitability: Kenneth P. De Meuse, Paul A. Vanderheiden, and Thomas J. Bermann, "Announced Layoffs: Their Effect on Corporate Financial Performance," *Human Resource Management*, vol. 33, Winter 1994, pages 509–30.

Study by Wyatt Company: Gilbert Fuchsberg, "Why Shake-Ups Work for Some, Not for Others," *Wall Street Journal* (eastern edition), 1 October 1993, page B1

Airline reservations clerk: Case described in John Hoerr and Michael Pollock, "Management Discovers the Human Side of Automation," *Business Week*, 29 September 1986, pages 70–75.

Robert Thomas: see *What Machines Can't Do: Politics and Technology in the Industrial Enterprise,* Berkeley: University of California Press, 1994.

Donald A. Norman: see *Things That Make Us Smart: Defending Human Attributes in the Age of the Machine,* New York: Addison-Wesley, 1993, page 224.

Research on humanizing automated workplaces: see, for example, Bert Painter, *Good Jobs with New Technology: How Labour and Management Can Achieve Good Jobs in an Era of Technological Change,* Vancouver: B.C. Research, 1991.

SORCERERS AND TYRANTS

"Connors kicked the man's chair": Brian Dumaine, "America's Toughest Bosses," *Fortune,* 18 October 1993, page 39–49.

"Years ago in China": Chin-Ning Chu, *Thick Face, Black Heart: Thriving, Winning and Succeeding in Life's Every Endeavor,* California: AMC Publishers, 1992.

Bullying at Work: Andrea Adams, Bullying at Work, London: Virago Press, 1992.

"Real damage, real distortion": Charles Taylor, "The Politics of Recognition," in *Multiculturalism: A Critical Reader,* ed. David Theo Goldberg, Oxford: Blackwell, 1994, page 75.

WHY DO WE TOLERATE ABUSE?

Toxic parents: Susan Forward: *Toxic Parents: Overcoming Their Hurtful Legacy and Reclaiming Your Life,* New York: Bantam, 1989, page 55.

Experiment at Stanford in the early 1970s: P. Zimbardo, W. C. Banks, C. Haney, and D. Jaffe, "The mind is a formidable jailer: a Pirandellian prison," *New York Times Magazine,* 8 April 1973, pages 38–60.

"Queen bee syndrome": Vincent Bozzi, "Assertiveness breeds contempt," *Psychology Today,* vol. 21, September 1987, page 15.

Theory X and Theory Y: Douglas MacGregor, *The Human Side of Enterprise,* New York: McGraw-Hill, 1960.

PART TWO

WORKING IN AN UNCIVILIZED WORLD

"Humans live in communities": Michael Argyle, *The Social Psychology of Work*, London: Penguin, 1990, page 9.

"A cohesion of values, myths, heroes": Terrence E. Deal and Allan A. Kennedy, *Corporate Cultures: The Rites and Rituals of Corporate Life*, New York: Addison-Wesley, 1982, page 4.

"We have found that the majority': Tom Peters and Nancy Austin, *A Passion for Excellence*, New York: Warner Books, 1985, page 495.

"You've got to keep your mouth shut": The Project on Disney, *Inside the Mouse: Work and Play at Disney World*, Durham: Duke University Press, 1995, pages 122–23.

Nine rules of the addictive family system: Robert Subby, "Inside the Chemically Dependent Marriage: Denial and Manipulation," in *Co-dependence: An Emerging Issue*, Hollywood Beach, Florida: Health Communications, 1983.

"Ideologies cause people": Henry Mintzberg *Mintzberg on Management*, New York: Free Press, 1989, page 275.

"Cultural diversity is dissolved": Hugh Willmott, "Strength is ignorance, slavery is freedom: Managing culture in modern organizations," *Journal of Management Studies*, vol. 30, no. 4, 1933, pages 515–52.

THE CULTURE OF SACRIFICE

Texas Air's "rampant divorce rate": Peter Nulty, "America's Toughest Bosses," *Fortune*, 27 February 1989, page 41.

"The worst examples we ever heard": Brian Dumaine, "Psycho Bosses from Hell," *Fortune*, 18 October 1993, page 44.

"More and better work from fewer people": Charles Handy, *The Age of Paradox*, Boston: Harvard Business School Press, 1994, page 24.

The average employee puts in forty-seven hours: Charles Handy, *The Age of Paradox*, pages 29–30.

"Going to a junk yard": Roger Von Oech, *A Whack on the Side of the Head*, New York: Warner, 1993.

"Organizations are now re-thinking time": Charles Handy, *The Age of Paradox*, Boston: Harvard Business School Press, 1994, page 28.

"A 1976 study asked 434 Americans": Richard A. Kalish and David K. Reynolds, *Death and Ethnicity: A Psychocultural Study*, Los Angeles: Ethel Percy Andrus Gerontology Center, University of Southern California, 1976.

"Second adulthood": Gail Sheehy, *New Passages: Mapping Your Life Across Time*, New York: Random House, 1995.

THE WIN/LOSE CULTURE

Sheetrock Inc.: Hubert D. Glover, "Organizational Change and Development: The Consequences of Misuse," *Leadership and Organization Development Journal*, vol. 13, no. 1, 1992, pages 9–16.

"Throw people in a pit": Richard W. Hallstein, "Forget 'Survival of the Fittest,'" *Across the Board*, January 1994, page 16.

"I'm an adrenaline junkie": Jennifer Hunter, "Rough Trades," *Globe and Mail Report on Business* magazine (Toronto), December 1994, page 67.

PART THREE

DANCING WITH THE DEVIL: IDENTIFYING ABUSIVE CULTURES

"The need for innovation encourages worker autonomy": Alvin Toffler, *Powershift: Knowledge, Wealth and Violence at the Edge of the 21st Century*, New York: Bantam, 1990, page 213.

"Where there is a lot of fear of screwing up": quoted in Kathleen D. Ryan and Daniel K. Oestreich, *Driving Fear out of the Workplace: How to Overcome the Invisible Barriers to Quality, Productivity, and Innovation*, San Francisco: Jossey-Bass, 1991, page 64.

"The degree to which the opportunity to use power effectively": Rosabeth Moss Kanter, *The Change Masters: Corporate Entrepreneurs at Work*, London: Routledge, 1983, page 18.

"We should always have people from as many disciplines": quoted in Marshall Loeb, "Ten Commandments for Managing Creative People," *Fortune*, 16 January 1995, pages 135–36.

"A checklist of symptoms for abusive cultures": Göran Ekvall, "Innovations in Organizations," *European Journal of Work and Organizational Psychology*, vol. 5, no. 1, 1996.

THE BOOMERS AND THE BUSTERS

Generation X: Douglas Coupland, *Generation X*. New York: St. Martin's Press, 1991.

A twenty-nine-year-old programmer for a Southern California software company: "Why Busters Hate Boomers," *Fortune*, 4 October 1993.

They tend to take more personal responsibility for their own careers: Charlene Marmer Solomon, "Managing the Baby Busters," *Personnel Journal*, vol. 71, no. 3, March 1992. page 55.

"The most entrepreneurial generation in American history": Randall Lane, "Computers Are Our Friends," *Forbes*, 8 May 1995, page 102.

"We go out for a few beers": Randall Lane, "To Jim Michaels, editor": *Forbes*, 8 May 1995, page 12.

THE NEW WORK REGIME

Web structures: see Marti Smye with Anne McKague, *You Don't Change a Company by Memo: The Simple Truths about Managing Change*, Toronto: Key Porter Books, 1994.

Infomate instead of automate: Shoshana Zuboff, *In the Age of the Smart Machine: The Future of Work and Power*, New York: Basic Books, 1988.

"Five giant steps": model developed by PeopleTech.

"Membership is a way of thinking": Charles Handy, *The Age of Paradox*, Boston: Harvard Business School Press, 1994, page 192.

THE IDEA-GENERATING CULTURE

"Dame Edith Sitwell": Diane Ackerman, *A Natural History of the Senses*, New York: Random House (Vintage), 1991, pages 293–296.

Creative Climate Questionnaire: Göran Ekvall, "Innovations in Organizations," *European Journal of Work and Organizational Psychology*, vol. 5, no. 1, 1996. Reprinted by permission of Erlbaurn (U.K.), Taylor & Francis, Hove, U.K.

"The American view of creativity is the big hit": Roger L. Firestien and Kenneth J. Kumiega, "Using a Formula for Creativity to Yield Organizational Quality Improvement," *National Productivity Review,* vol. 13, Autumn 1994, page 572.

"People function at work in terms of two 'modes'": John Cleese, "And Now for Something Completely Different," excerpt from a speech to the British-American Chamber of Commerce in New York, *Personnel,* vol. 68, April 1991, page 13.

"Man's progress has a poetic phase": George Santayana, *Reason in Art,* New York: Dover, 1982, first published 1905, page 56.

"A period of rambling discovery": Denise Shekerjian, *Uncommon Genius: How Great Ideas Are Born,* New York: Penguin, 1990, pages 39, 40, 41, 75, 99.

THE CREATIVE SOUL

"Work is an attempt to find an adequate alchemy": Thomas Moore, *Care of the Soul,* New York: HarperCollins, 1992, page 185.

"Five times more opportunity to experience joy in the workplace": Mihaly Csikszentmihalyi, *Flow: The Pyschology of Optimal Experience,* New York: Harper and Row, 1990.

INDEX